ISBN 978-1-332-59849-6
PIBN 10018038

The Dressmaker

A Complete Book
on all matters connected with

Sewing and Dressmaking

from the simplest stitches to the
cutting, making, altering,
mending and caring
for the clothes.

"The Dressmaker" is a standard work, and the different methods of Dressmaking and Tailoring which it presents may be used whenever the current styles call for them.

A New Edition, Revised and Enlarged.

The Butterick Publishing Company
New York London Paris

SECOND EDITION

PUBLISHED BY

THE BUTTERICK PUBLISHING COMPANY

BUTTERICK BUILDING, NEW YORK

PARIS LONDON NEW YORK TORONTO

CONTENTS

THE DRESSMAKER

CHAPTER I

SEWING STITCHES

TO MAKE A KNOT, hold the threaded needle in the right hand. Take the end of the thread between the thumb and first finger of the left hand, stretching the thread tightly. Wind it around the top of the first finger, crossing it over the end held between the finger and thumb. Roll the first finger down the ball of the thumb about half an inch, carrying the thread with it, and with the second finger push the knot thus formed to the end of the thread. If a larger knot is required, wind the thread around the finger twice.

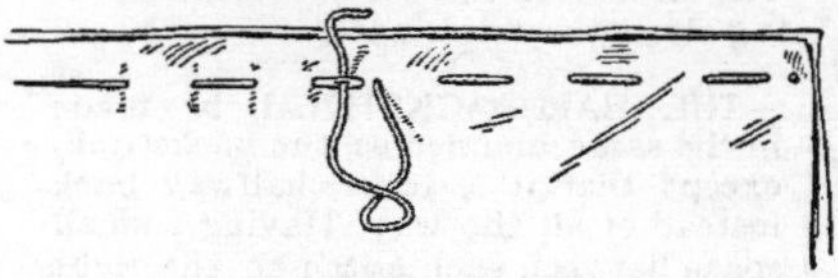

Fig. 1. Even Bastings

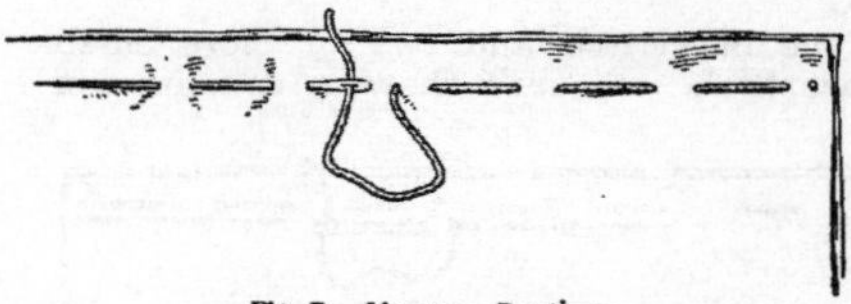

Fig. 2. Uneven Bastings

BASTINGS are temporary stitches used to hold two or more pieces of material together while putting in the permanent stitches. The thread should be smooth and rather fine. Careful basting is essential to successful sewing and dressmaking. There are four kinds of bastings.

Even Bastings start with a knot on the right side so that they may be easily removed. Pass the needle over and through the material, making the stitches and spaces the same length. To fasten the thread, take two stitches over the last one made. (Fig. 1.)

Uneven Bastings are made by the method just described for even bastings, except that the stitches and spaces are of unequal length. The stitches taken upon the needle are about a third shorter than the space covered by the thread. (Fig. 2.)

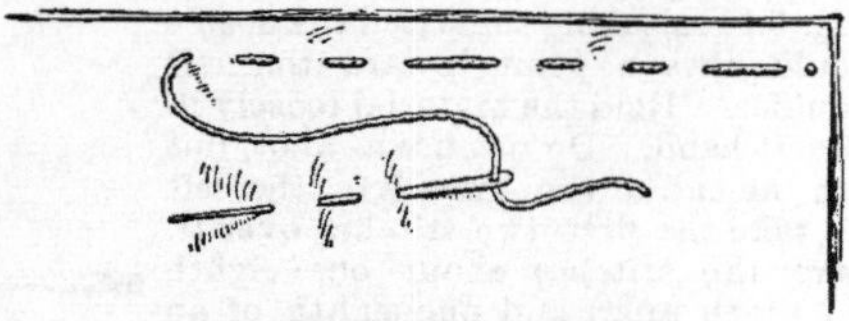

Fig. 3. Combination Bastings

Combination Bastings are used on seams where extra firmness is desired for close fitting. They are made by taking, alternately, one long stitch and two short stitches. (Fig. 3.)

Diagonal Bastings are slanting stitches used in dressmaking to secure the outside material to its lining, particularly where the lining is eased on to the material, as is often the case in waist-making. The method is shown in Fig. 4.

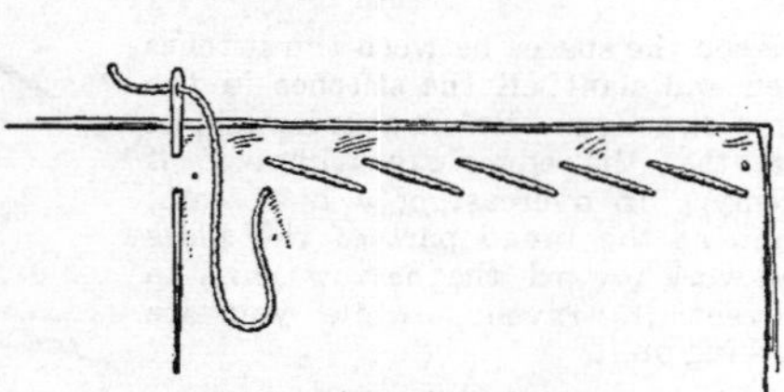

Fig. 4. Diagonal Bastings

RUNNING STITCHES are shorter than bastings. The spaces and stitches are of equal length. They are used on seams that do not require the firmness of machine or back stitching. (Fig. 5.)

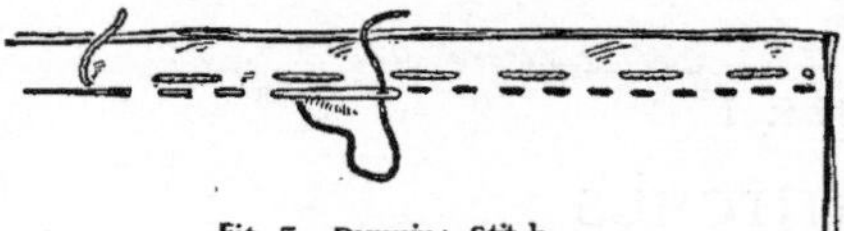

Fig. 5. Running Stitches

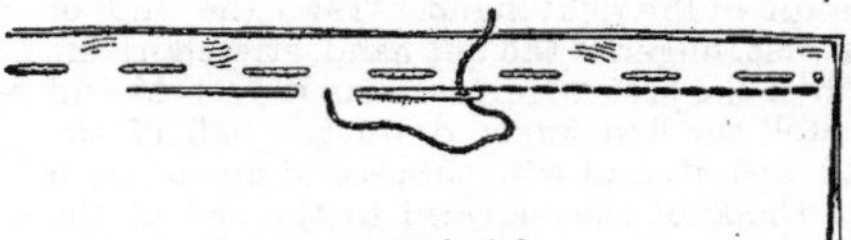

Fig. 6. Backstitch

Fig. 7. Half-Backstitch

THE BACKSTITCH is made by taking up a short stitch back on the upper side and a longer one forward on the underside of the material, bringing the needle out a space in advance. Insert the needle to meet the last stitch, passing it under the material and out again a space in advance of the last stitch taken. (Fig. 6.) Fasten by making two or three stitches over the one last made. The backstitch is used on seams requiring strength and firmness.

THE HALF-BACKSTITCH is made in the same manner as the backstitch, except that it is taken halfway back instead of all the way, leaving a small space between each stitch on the right side. (Fig. 7.)

THE COMBINATION STITCH consists of one backstitch and two or more small running stitches. It is fastened like the backstitch. Figure 8 shows a combination stitch with one backstitch and two running stitches. It is used on seams requiring less strength than the backstitch.

Fig. 8. Combination Stitch

OVERCASTING is a slanting stitch used to keep raw edges from raveling. (Fig. 9.) In taking the stitch the needle should always point toward the left shoulder. Hold the material loosely in the left hand. Do not use a knot, but turn the end of the thread to the left and take the first two stitches over it. Make the stitches about one-eighth of an inch apart and one-eighth of an inch deep.

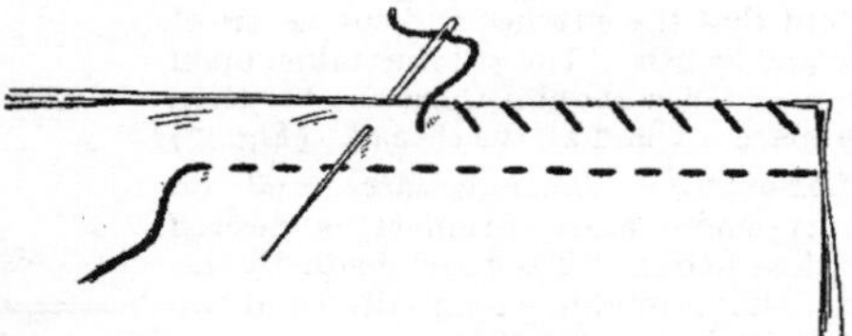

Fig. 9. Overcasting

Keep the spaces between the stitches even and slant all the stitches in the same direction. Before overcasting, be sure that the edges are trimmed off evenly. In overcasting a bias seam, begin at the broad part of the piece and work toward the narrow part, to prevent its raveling while you are working on it.

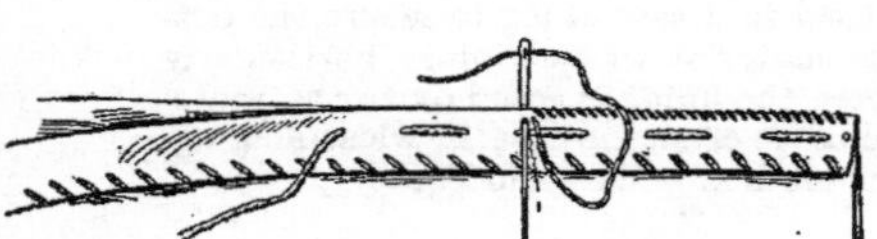

Fig. 10. Overhanding

OVERHANDING, top, or over sewing, as it is sometimes called, is used to join folded edges or selvages. (Fig. 10.) Baste the pieces with the folds or selvages exactly even and sew with close stitches over and over the edges, taking up as few threads as possible, so that when finished the seam will be smooth and flat and not form an awkward ridge or cord on the wrong side of the garment.

CATCH-STITCH, sometimes called *cat stitch*, is a cross stitch used to hold down seam edges. It is the preferred finish for the seams of flannel garments, for it does away with the clumsiness of a French or felled seam, takes the place of overcasting and prevents raveling.

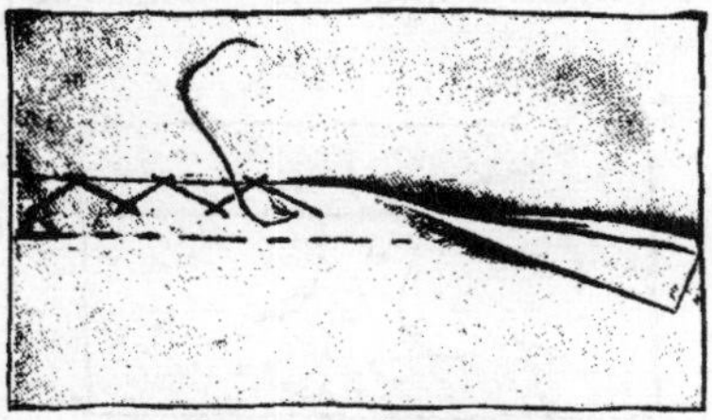

Fig. 11. Catch-Stitch

Place the edges together and run a seam, taking an occasional backstitch. Trim off one edge close to the line of sewing and press the other edge flatly over it, holding the work as shown in Fig. 11.

Make a knot and insert the needle under the edge at the lower left corner, cross the edge and take a small stitch a few threads to the right. Cross back again and insert the needle, taking a similar stitch through all the thicknesses of the material.

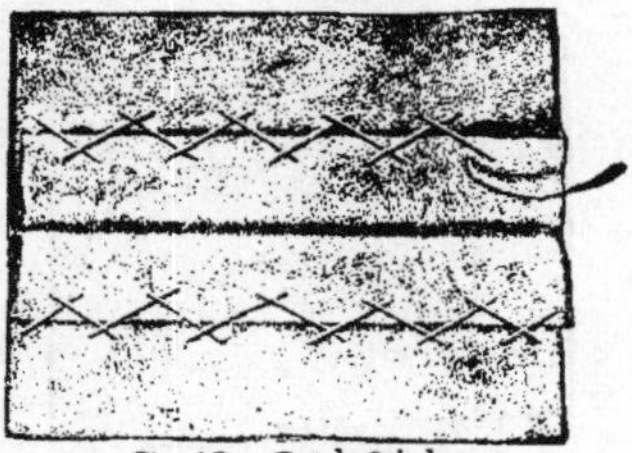

Fig. 12. Catch-Stitch on Open Seam

Always point the needle to the left and make the cross stitches encase the raw edges. The stitch is done from left to right. If preferred, these seams may be pressed open and catch-stitched, working the stitches over the raw edge at each side of the seam, thus holding both down as shown in Fig. 12.

A quicker method of catch-stitching is shown in Fig. 13. This stitch has not the strength of the first method and is only used in millinery and in dressmaking where the work is concealed. This style of catch-stitching is done from right to left.

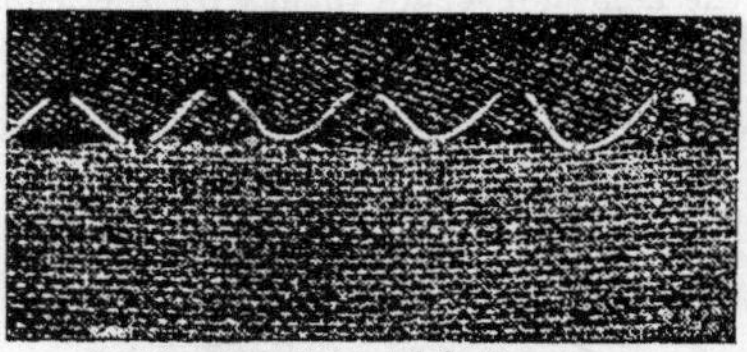

Fig. 13. Catch-Stitch Used in Dressmaking and Millinery

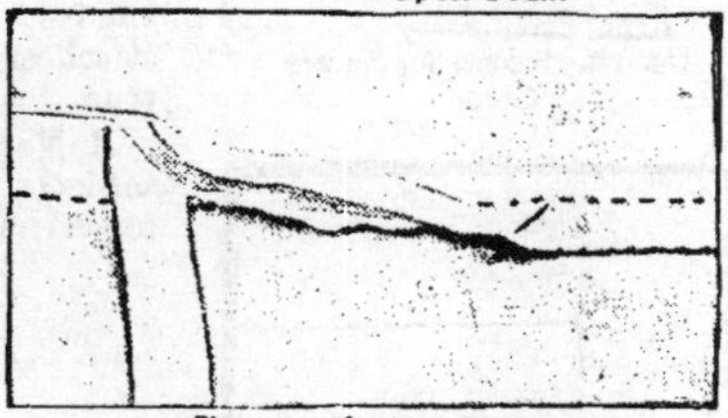

Fig. 14. Flat Fell Seam

A FLAT FELL SEAM has one edge hemmed down to protect the other raw edge. It is used principally for underwear. Baste the edges together, and sew with combination stitch. If the edges are bias, sew from the broad part of the pieces to the narrow, to prevent raveling and stretching.

Remove bastings, trim the edge toward you close to the sewing line, and turn the other edge flatly over it, pressing hard with the thumb nail. Make a narrow turning, baste and hem. (Fig. 14.)

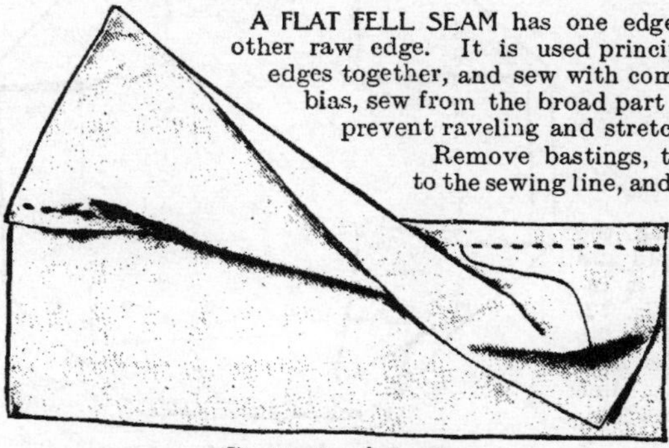

Fig. 15. French Seam

A FRENCH SEAM is a double seam encasing the raw seam edges. (Fig. 15.) Place the edges evenly together and sew close to them on the right side of the garment. Trim off all ravelings from the edges. Turn the wrong side toward you, crease exactly at the seam, and make a second sewing of sufficient depth to entirely cover the raw edges. This seam is generally used in making garments of wash materials.

A HEM is a fold made by twice turning over the edge of the material. (Fig. 16.) Make a narrow, even turning, and mark the depth for the second turning on the material with a coarse pin, chalk or basting, using as a marker a card notched the desired depth of the hem. Fold on the line, and if the hem is wide, baste at top and bottom.

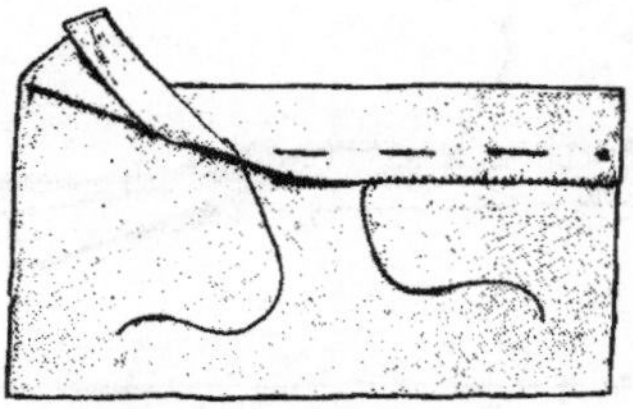

Fig. 16. Hem

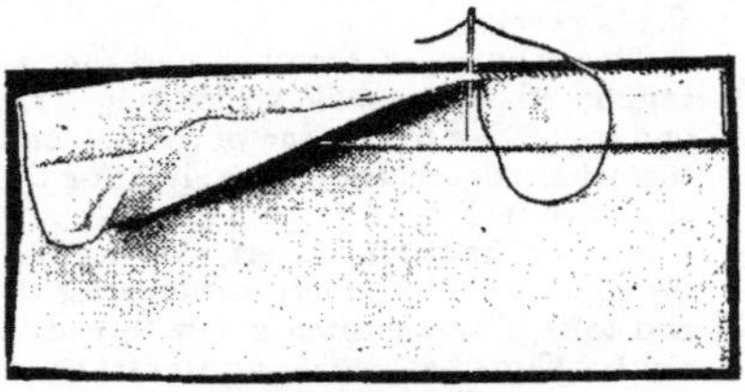

Fig. 17. Napery Hem

Fig. 18. Folding for Square Corners

Hold the edges you are going to sew on, toward you; place the hem over the forefinger and under the middle finger and hold it down with the thumb. Begin at the right end and insert the needle through the fold, leaving a short end of the thread to be caught under the hemming stitches.

Pointing the needle toward the left shoulder, make a slanting stitch by taking up a few threads of the material and the fold of the hem. Fasten the thread by taking two or three stitches on top of each other.

If a new thread is needed, start as in the beginning, tucking both the end of the new and old thread under the fold of the hem and secure them with the hemming stitches. Train the eye to keep the stitches even and true.

A Napery or *Damask Hem* is used on napkins and tablecloths. Turn under the edge of the material twice for a narrow hem. Fold the hem back on the right side, crease the material along the first fold, and overhand the fold and crease together. The needle is inserted straight as shown in Fig. 17. Open and flatten stitches with the thumb nail. If a square is used, turn the opposite side in the same manner. Hem the sides before folding back on the right side. No basting is needed for this hem. Take small stitches so that the work will look well when the hem is turned down. Directions for hemstitching will be found on page 12.

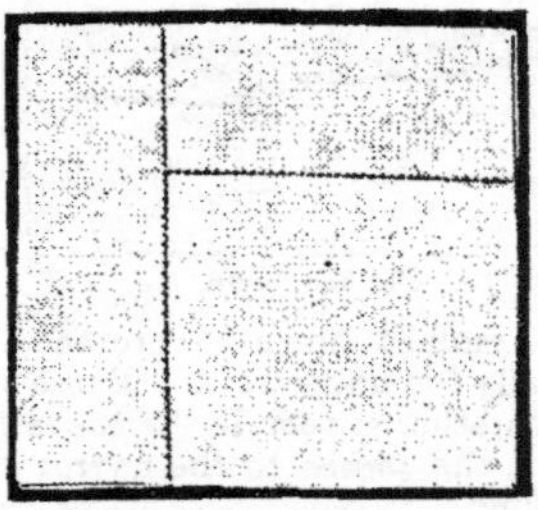

Fig 19. Hemming Square Corners

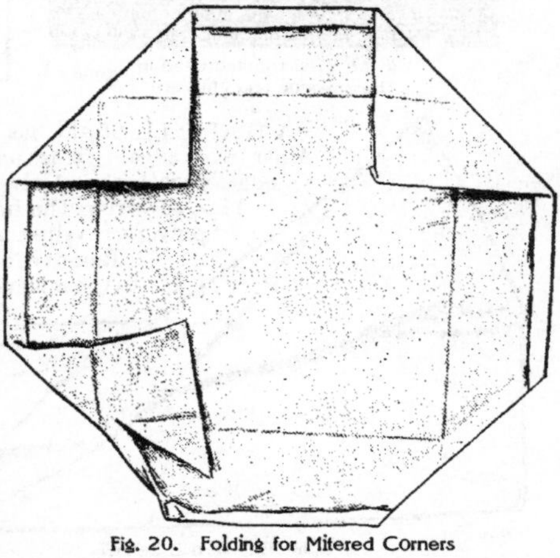

Fig. 20. Folding for Mitered Corners

SQUARE CORNERS are made by turning under the edges as for hems. . Turn the overlapping hem back toward the right side and crease the material along the first fold. Open the hems and cut away the underlapping hem to within a seam of the second turning. (Fig. 18.) Hem the overlapping edges to the hem underneath, but not through to the right side. (Fig. 19.) Overhand the ends of the hems. Finish all the corners in the same manner.

MITERED CORNERS are made by joining two bias edges to form an angle. Turn the edges as for hems. and crease. Open the material, fold the corner toward the center, and crease where the lines cross. Cut the corner off, allowing a narrow turning. (Fig. 20.) Fold the hems down all around, bring the mitered corners together, and hem the side. (Fig. 21.) Hem the corners, but do not catch the stitches through the material underneath.

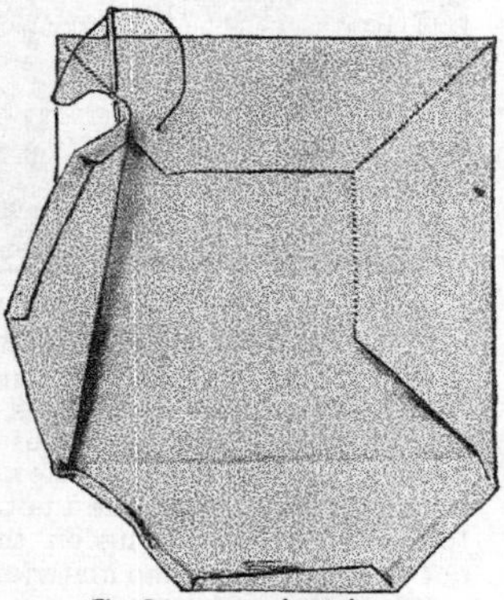

Fig. 21. Hemming Mitered Corners

A GUSSET is a triangular piece of material set into a garment to strengthen an opening. (Figs. 22 and 23.) Fold diagonally a piece of material two and one-quarter inches square and cut it on the fold. Take one of the triangles and fold it down a quarter of an inch all around, folding the straight edges first. Cut away the projecting points at the sides. Hold the wrong side toward you, with the right angle down and fold so that the point at the bottom will meet the fold at the bias edge.

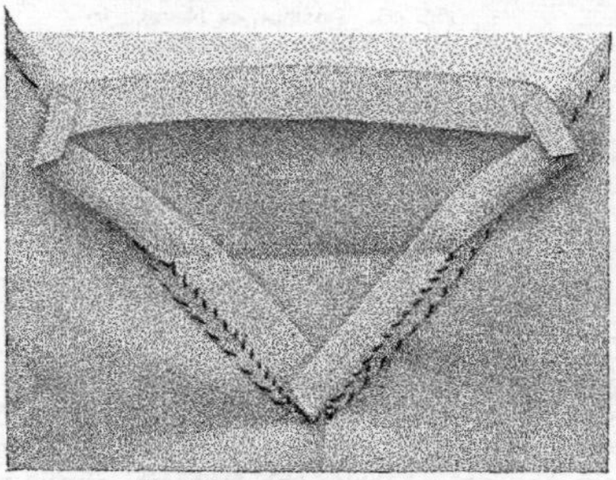

Fig. 22. Inserted Gusset on Wrong Side

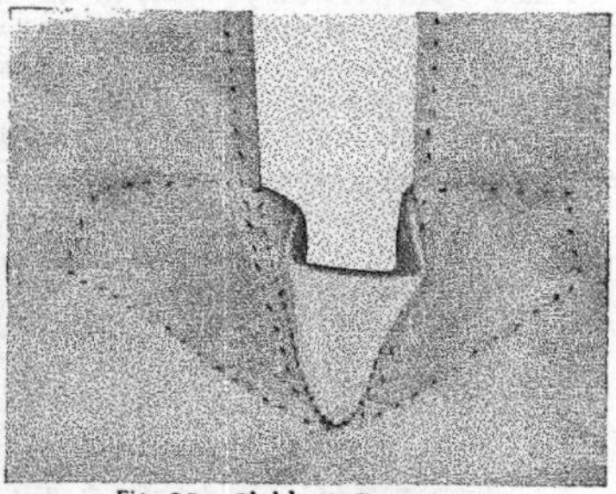

Fig. 23. Finished Gusset on Right Side

Make a narrow hem all around the opening. Pin the corner of the gusset to the end of the opening, right side to right side. (Fig. 22.) Beginning at the center, overhand to the hem as far as the crease in the gusset. Fold the gusset over at the crease and pin at the center and each corner, taking care that the warp and woof threads run parallel with those of the garment. Baste and hem all around. (Fig. 23.) The lower edge of the gusset will have to be stretched to fit the opening.

TUCKS should be marked with a measure so that they will be of even width.

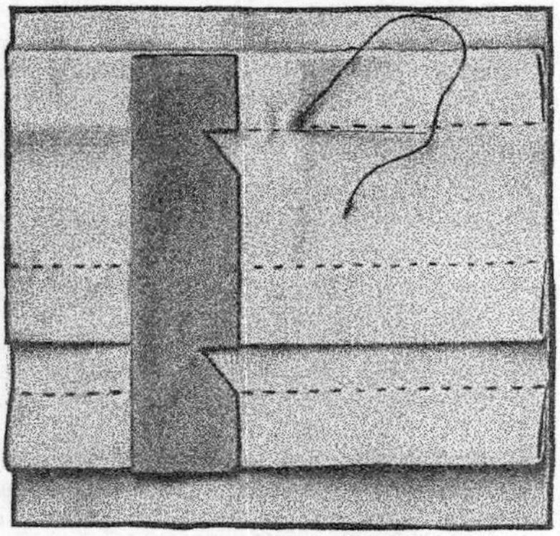

Fig. 24. Tucks

Cut the gage from a piece of cardboard, and from the end measure down the width of first tuck, making a slash and a bias cut to meet the slash. (Fig. 24.) Make a second cut as shown in Fig. 24, allowing for width of space and second tuck.

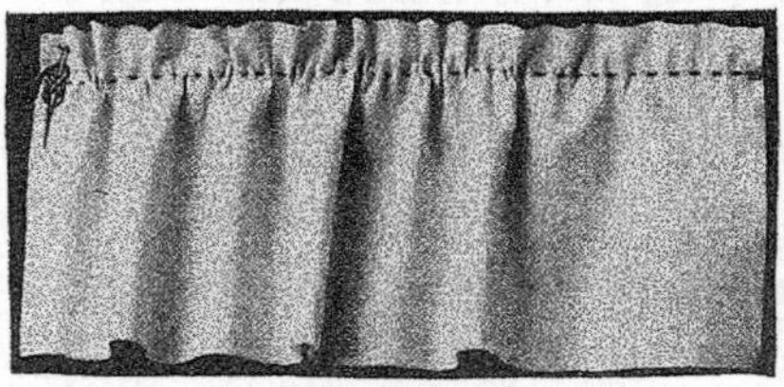

Fig. 25. Gathering

It is quicker and more accurate to make a gage of this sort in measuring short spaces, such as hems, tucks and the spaces between them, than to use the tape measure, as sometimes the eye becomes confused at the small marks on the tape, and mistakes are made that will prove quite serious.

FOR GATHERINGS, make a row of small running stitches. The stitches may be the same length as the spaces, or the spaces may be twice the length of the stitches. Always begin by inserting the needle from the wrong side to conceal the knot. It is better to slip the stitches along on the needle and not remove it from the material.

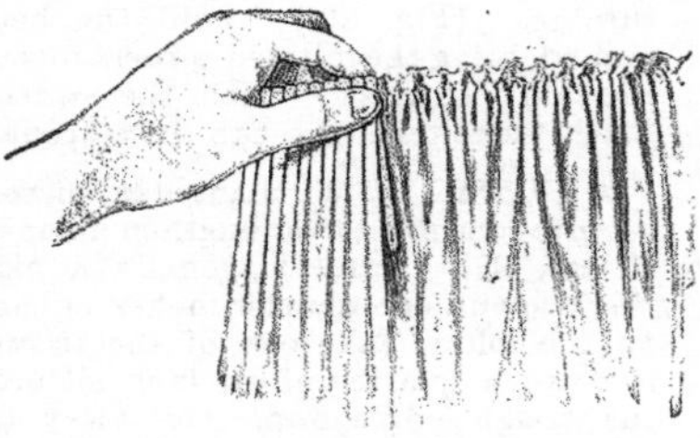

Fig. 26. Position of Needle in Stroking Gathers

When the gathering is completed remove the needle and draw the gatherings up tight. Place a pin vertically, close to the last stitch, and wind the thread several times around the pin in the form of an 8. (Fig. 25.) This holds the gathers firmly together and facilitates the stroking.

In Stroking or *Laying Gathers* the work is held between the thumb and fingers of the left hand, with the thumb below the gathering thread. Put the side of the needle well above the gathering thread and press the little plait under the thumb, drawing the needle down. (Fig. 26.)

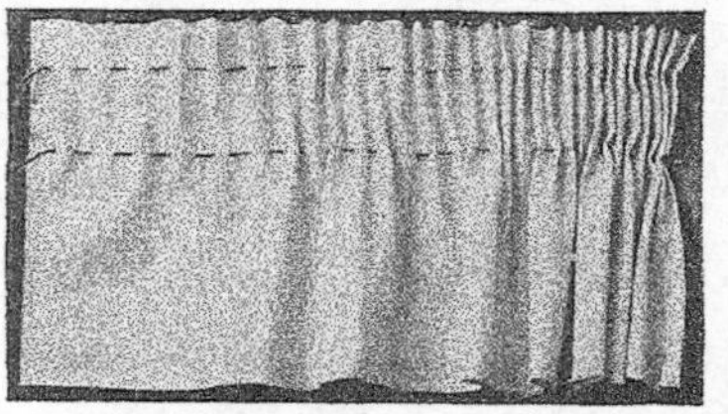

Fig. 27. Two Rows of Gathers

Do not use the point of the needle, as it scratches and weakens the material. Continue entirely across the gathers, putting the needle under each stitch and holding the plait firmly with the thumb. Stroke the material above the gathering thread as well as below it to make the gathers firm and even.

Two Rows of Gathers are often used in dressmaking and do not need stroking. A skirt joined to a band, a sleeve set in a cuff or sewed into the armhole, should be gathered twice so that the gathers will stay in the proper place.

The second row is made with the stitches directly in line with those of the first row and one-quarter or three-eighths of an inch below them. (Fig. 27.) If there is much fulness to be gathered, the spaces between the stitches may be lengthened.

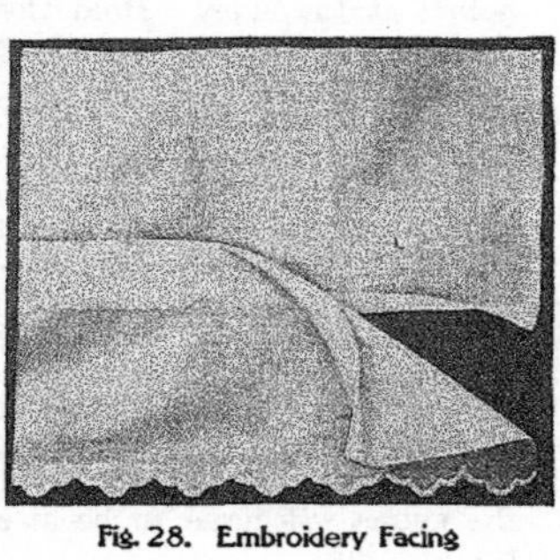

Fig. 28. Embroidery Facing

EMBROIDERY EDGING USED AS A FACING is shown in Fig. 28. The plain material above the embroidery is applied as the facing. Crease the edging off at the depth it is to extend beyond the garment. Baste the material along the crease so that the seam will come toward the inside of the garment. Then stitch the seam. Now turn the edging down, fold in the raw edge at the top, and hem down as a facing. The facing should be no wider than necessary to make a neat joining.

PBSF9695095

DLI-13934827

Sheila Boyd
4411 Springdale Avenue
Apt. 1

Gwynn Oak
MD
21207
UNITED STATES

Shop:	Paperbackshop
Buyer Name:	Sheila Boyd
Order Date:	06/07/2023
Order Number	ALB72073333

	ISBN	TITLE	QTY
=	9781332598496	The Dressmaker A Complete Book on All Matters Connected With Sewing and Dressmaking From the Simplest Stitches to the Cutting, Making, Altering, Mending and Caring for the Clothes Classic Reprint	1

Alibris guarantees the condition of every item as it is described on our Web site. If you are not satisfied that your item is described, please visit the following page for important return instructions:
http://www.alibris.com/returns
All return requests must be submitted via the Alibris Web site. Any item returned without the accompanying paperwork and/or more than 60 days after its shipment date will be discarded and you will not be eligible to receive a refund.

Problems? Questions? Suggestions? Send email to Alibris Customer Service at info@alibris.com

TO JOIN EMBROIDERY IN A TUCK, make several tucks in the plain material above the embroidery if it is wide enough. Then measure carefully the amount for the space between the tucks, the under part of the tucks, and the seam. Cut away the superfluous material and join the edging to the garment. Crease the tuck with the seam directly in the fold so that the raw edges will be encased in the tuck. When the materials of the garment and the embroidery are similar, and there are several tucks above and below the seam, the joining is imperceptible. (Fig. 29.)

Fig. 29. Embroidery Joined in a Tuck

A ROLLED HEM may be used as a dainty finish in joining trimming of any kind to a garment of sheer wash material. Hold the wrong side of the material toward you, and, after trimming off all ravelings, begin at the right end and roll the edge toward you tightly between the thumb and forefinger of the left hand, keeping the edge rolled for about one and a half inches ahead of the sewing. (Fig. 30.)

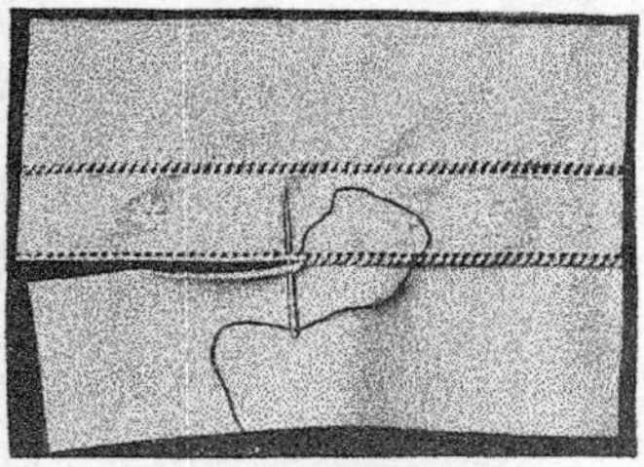

Fig. 30. Insertion Inset with Rolled Hem

EMBROIDERY MAY BE INSERTED by different methods. When a straight-edge insertion is used, the plain cambric may be cut away at each side of the embroidery. The material of the garment is then cut away under the embroidery, leaving a small seam, which is rolled and whipped to the embroidery as shown in Fig. 30. If preferred, a small seam may be left on the insertion as well as on the garment and be put together by a tiny French seam. This is the finish most commonly employed.

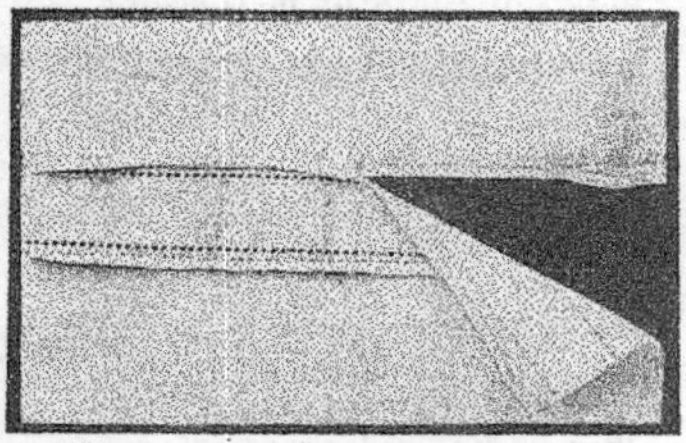

Fig. 31. Insertion Inset by Machine

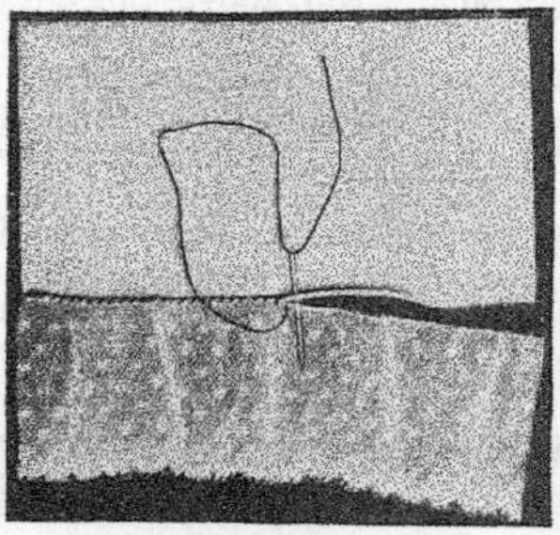

Fig. 32. Whipping on Trimming

Embroidery also may be inserted by a machine fell seam. (Fig. 31.) Baste the insertion to the material with a narrow seam on the wrong side. Trim off all ravelings and insert raw edges in the hemmer of the machine, and stitch as in hemming.

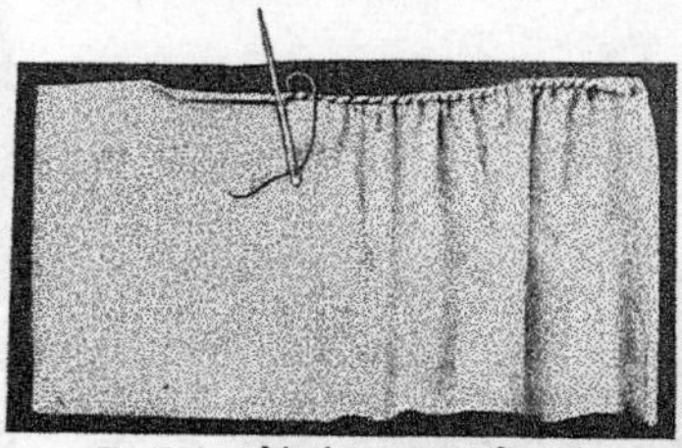

Fig. 33. Whipping and Gathering

WHIPPING ON TRIMMING is generally done on an edge. If lace, it should be either gathered by pulling the heavy thread which is usually found at the top, or whipped and drawn as in a ruffle. Roll an inch or two of the garment material, place the lace with its right side to the right side of the material, and whip both together. (Fig. 32.) Lace may be whipped on plain if preferred, but it must be eased in. Insertion may be inset in the same way.

A Ruffle Used as Trimming may be whipped and gathered. Roll the raw edge and overcast the material as far as it is rolled, taking care to make the stitch below the roll, not through it. (Fig. 33.) Draw up the thread, making the ruffle the desired fulness. Divide the ruffle in quarters and mark them with colored thread. Make corresponding marks on the edge to which the ruffle is to be attached. Roll the edge of the garment

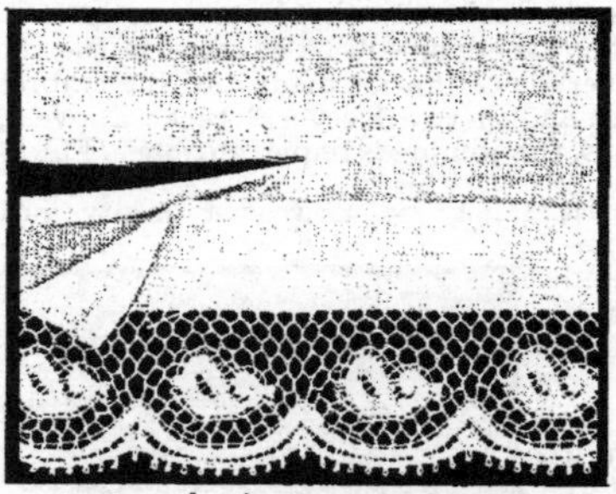

Fig. 34. Showing Cut for Lace Insertion

and overhand the ruffle to it, taking a stitch in every whipped stitch of the ruffle.

Fig. 35. Finished Effect of Inserting Lace

METHODS OF INSERTING LACE and insertion, when the material has a straight edge, are shown in Figs. 34 and 35. Fold the material for a hem, creasing the lower fold hard. Open the hem and baste the lace edge just below the lower fold, and stitch. (Fig. 34.) Turn back the hem and crease the material on a line with the top turning of the hem. Cut to within a small seam above this crease. Fold in the raw edge, insert the edge of the lace insertion, and stitch. Turn a second hem, following the preceding directions, baste the other edge of the insertion just below the lower crease, and stitch as before. As many rows of insertion may be used in this manner as are desired.

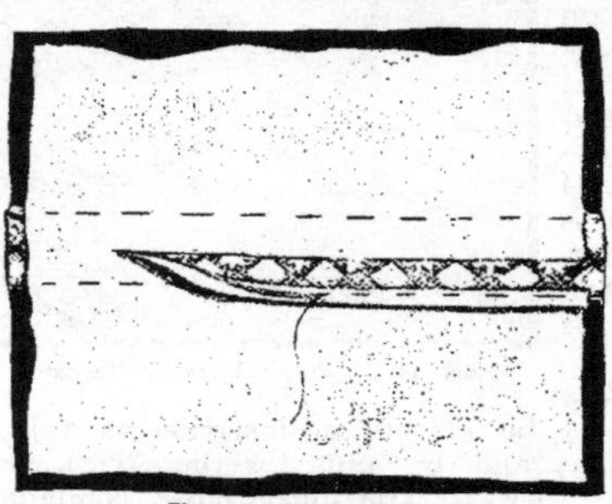

Fig. 36. Lace Insert

To Insert Lace Insertion in a garment, pin the lace in the position desired, and baste down both edges of the insertion.

If the insertion is narrow, the material is cut through the center (Fig. 36); but if the insertion is wide, the material is cut away from underneath, simply allowing a seam on each side. The edge is turned in a narrow hem covering the line of the basting. Stitch the insertion close to the edges from the right side, and at the same time catching through the material hemmed down.

Fig. 37. Lace Insert above Facing

Insertion above a Facing is first basted in position, and the upper edge is finished as shown in Fig. 37. The facing is generally used when the outline of the lower edge is curved or pointed so that it cannot be turned up in a straight hem.

The facing is cut to fit the outline of the lower edge and applied as a false hem, as shown in Fig. 37. When edging is used, it is basted to the bottom before the facing is added and all stitched in a seam together. Turn under the facing at the line of sewing, baste in position and stitch insertion from the right side.

Fig. 38. Ruffle Inserted in a Hem

TO INSERT RUFFLES IN A HEM turn the hem toward the right side of the garment and crease the fold hard. Divide both ruffle and hem in quarters and mark each division with colored thread. Insert the edge of the ruffle in the hem close to the fold (Fig. 38) with the right side of the ruffle to the right side of the garment and the corresponding marks together. Baste and stitch one-quarter of an inch from the fold. Turn the hem back to the wrong side of the garment, fold the second turning, baste and hem. (Fig. 39.)

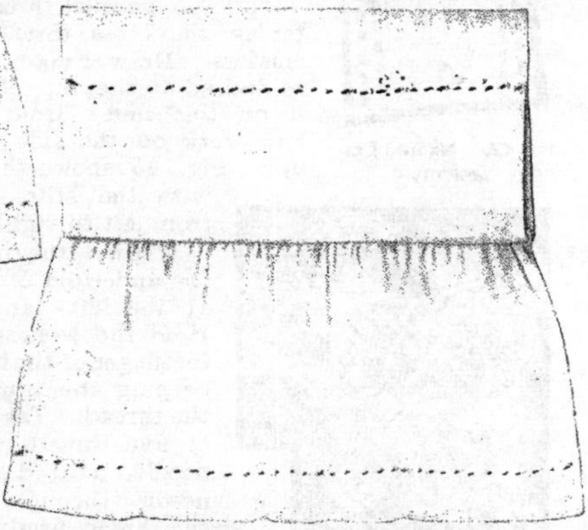

Fig. 39. Finished Ruffle on Right Side

TO COVER THE JOINING OF A RUFFLE, divide both ruffle and garment in quarters and mark with pins or colored thread. Gather the ruffle and baste it to the garment. Turn the raw edges up on the garment and cover with a narrow bias band which can be bought by the piece with the edges turned ready for use. (Fig. 40.) This finish may be used on either the right or wrong side of the garment. Frequently this finish is used on berthas or scalloped edges that are not lined or faced.

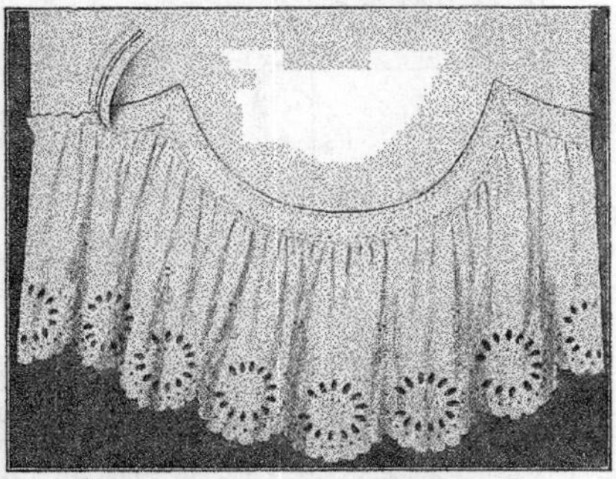

Fig. 40. Band Covering Joining of Ruffle

TRIMMINGS MAY BE MITERED so that the joining will scarcely be seen. If embroidery, fold it over so that the crease comes exactly in the middle of the corner, taking care to match the pattern perfectly. Crease firmly, and cut on the creased line. (Fig. 41.) Place the right sides face to face and buttonhole the raw edges together with short, close stitches. Fig. 42 shows the finished corner. The method of making the buttonhole stitch is shown in Fig. 48.

Fig. 41 Showing Cut for Mitered Corners

Lace may be mitered in the same way, but it should be cut between the cords, not across them. Overhand the edges together, putting the needle back the depth of two cords. (Fig. 43.)

Fig. 44 shows the figures cut around the edge, lapped and hemmed around the figure on each side. If a stronger corner is desired, the lace may be mitered in a very tiny, flat hem.

Fig. 42. Mitered Embroidery

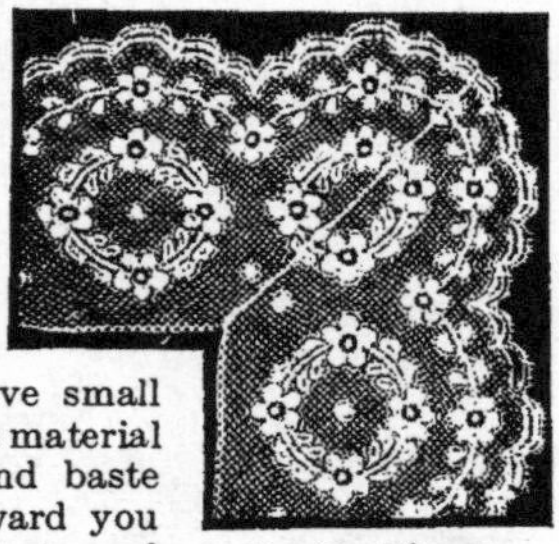

Fig. 43. Mitered Lace

HEMSTITCHING is a line of open-work made by drawing out parallel threads and fastening the cross threads in successive small clusters. Draw as many threads of the material as desired at the top of the hem, and baste it on this line. Hold the hem toward you and work on the side on which it is turned up. Fig. 45 shows the position of the hem with the stitching done from left to right.

Fig. 44. Lapping and Matching Lace

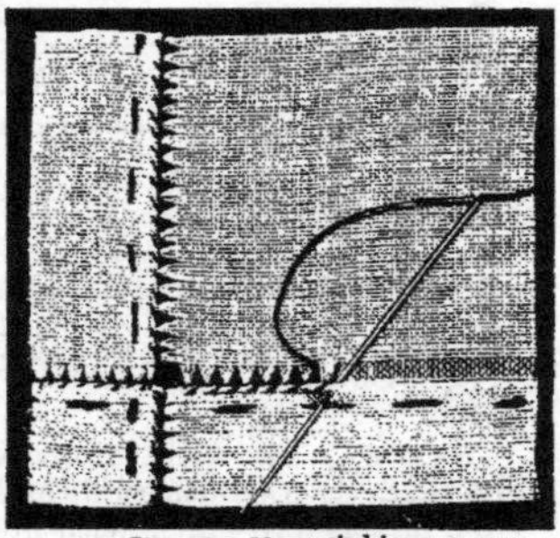

Fig. 45. Hemstitching

Insert the needle in the underfold of the hem at the left-hand edge. Hold the work over the forefinger of the left hand, keeping the thumb over the thread. Take up four or five threads with the needle, and draw the needle through, holding the thread firmly by the left thumb. At the extreme right of these stitches take a short stitch in the fold of the hem, as shown in the illustration. Now take up the same number of threads as before, and repeat. Care must be taken to keep the warp and woof threads exactly parallel, especially in hemstitching a corner where the material has not been cut away.

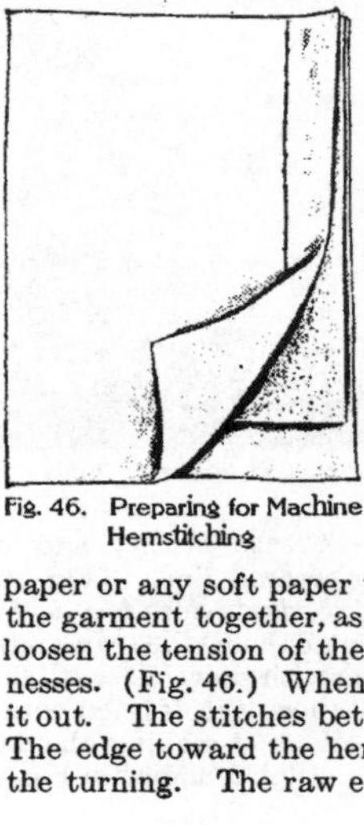

Fig. 46. Preparing for Machine Hemstitching

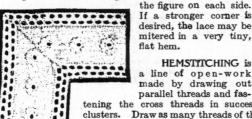

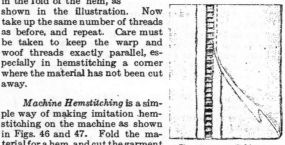

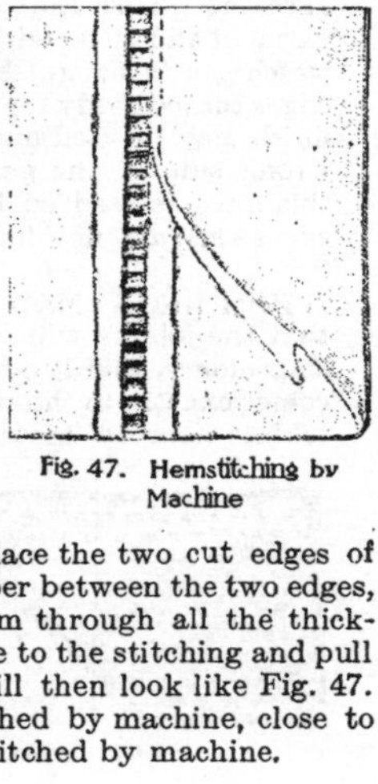

Fig. 47. Hemstitching by Machine

Machine Hemstitching is a simple way of making imitation hemstitching on the machine as shown in Figs. 46 and 47. Fold the material for a hem, and cut the garment off one-quarter of an inch above the sewing line. Fold blotting paper or any soft paper to one-eighth of an inch thickness. Place the two cut edges of the garment together, as if to sew a seam. Slip the blotting paper between the two edges, loosen the tension of the machine and stitch a quarter-inch seam through all the thicknesses. (Fig. 46.) When the seam is stitched, cut the paper close to the stitching and pull it out. The stitches between the two edges of the material will then look like Fig. 47. The edge toward the hem is turned down and the hem is stitched by machine, close to the turning. The raw edge of the garment is turned in and stitched by machine.

CHAPTER II

BUTTONHOLES

A WELL-MADE GARMENT that is otherwise perfect may be greatly injured in appearance by badly made buttonholes. They should always be properly spaced and marked before they are cut. Mark the points for the top and bottom buttonholes, and divide the distance between these two points into the desired number of spaces. The slit must be cut on the thread of the goods, if possible, and must be large enough to allow the button to slip through easily, as a buttonhole becomes tighter after it is worked.

With the buttonhole scissors carefully test the length of the slit and make a clean cut with one movement of the scissors. One of the most noticeable faults in buttonholing results from an uneven or ragged slit. This may be caused by dull scissors or by the slipping of the fabric. To prevent the material from slipping, baste around the cutting line before using the scissors.

There are three kinds of buttonholes, one with the bar at both ends (Fig. 49), another with one round and one barred end (Fig. 50), and a third called the tailor's buttonhole. (Fig. 51.)

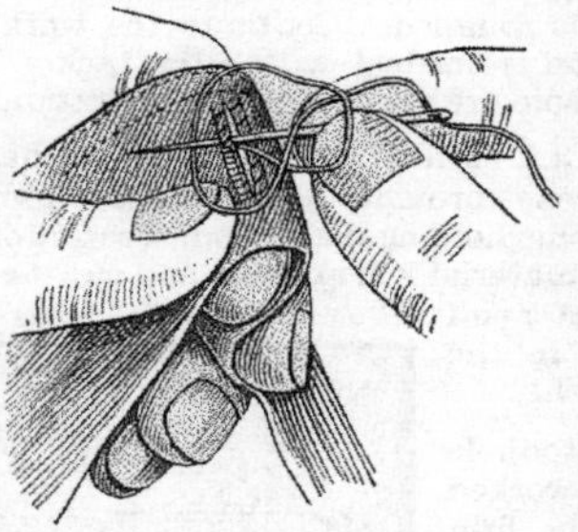

Fig. 48. Correct Position in Making Buttonholes

BARRED BUTTONHOLES as illustrated in Figs. 49 and 50 are used for underwear, waists and shirts. If the buttonhole is in an upright position as in the center of a plait, or if the strain does not come at the ends of the buttonhole, as at the center back of a neck-band, the buttonhole with a bar at both ends (Fig. 49) is used. If the strain on the buttonhole comes at one end so that the button requires a resting-place as in a cuff or belt, use the buttonhole with the round end. (Fig. 50.) Buttonholes are stranded to prevent the edges from stretching. Bring the needle up at one end of the buttonhole, and, allowing the thread to lie along the edge of the cut on the right side of the material, stick down at the opposite end. Do the same on the other side of the cut and stick down opposite the first stitch, with a stitch across the end to fasten the thread. If the material is inclined to fray, the edges may be overcast before working the buttonholes.

To make the stitch, place the buttonhole over the forefinger of the left hand, holding it in position with the thumb and second finger as shown in Fig. 48. Begin to work the buttonhole close to the corner or starting-point. Insert the needle, and while it is pointing toward you, bring the double thread

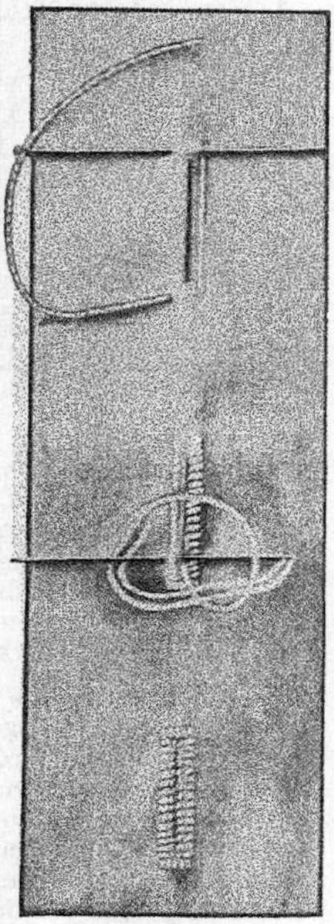

Fig. 49. Buttonhole with Bar at Both Ends

as it hangs from the eye of the needle around to the left under the needle. Draw the needle through the loop, letting the thread form a purl exactly on the edge of the slit. Continue these stitches to the opposite end, being careful to take them the same depth and close together. Now pass the needle up and down through the goods until two or three threads cross the end of the slit quite close to the buttonhole stitches, thus forming a bar tack. (Fig. 72, page 22.) At the end, turn the work around so that the bar end is toward you and make several buttonhole stitches over the bar tack and through the material. (Fig. 49.) Work the other side of the buttonhole and the second bar.

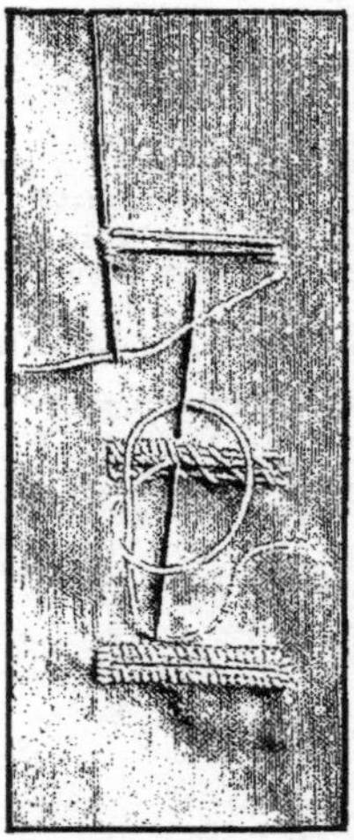

Fig. 50. Buttonhole with Round End

THE ROUND-END BUTTONHOLE is stranded in the same manner as the double-barred buttonhole. Fig. 50 illustrates the steps in the making of this buttonhole with the opening first stranded and then overcast.

Begin the buttonhole stitch as in the first buttonhole, working down one side. When the outer end is reached, the stitches are taken on a slant, inserting the needle each time at a little different angle until the end is rounded. Continue the work on the other side. The inner end is finished with a bar tack. The different steps of this buttonhole are shown in the illustration.

THE TAILOR'S BUTTONHOLE is used for garments of heavy cloth, as the round end or eyelet provides a resting-place for the shank of the button or the stitches holding the button. Baste around the line of cutting so that the material will not slip, and cut the slit the desired length. At the outer end cut a small eyelet as shown in the top figure in the illustration, 51.

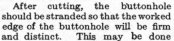

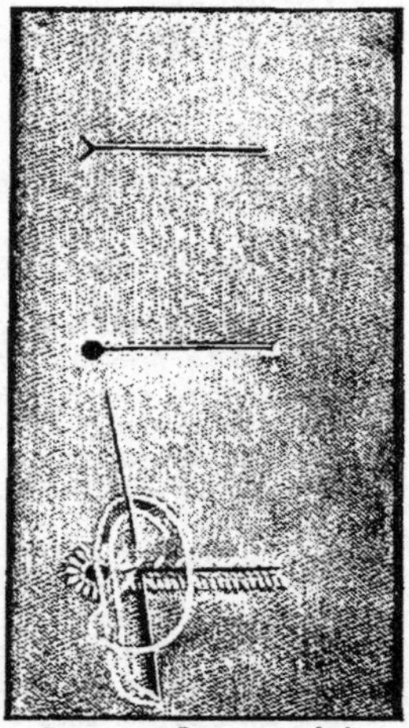

Fig. 51. Tailor's Buttonhole

After cutting, the buttonhole should be stranded so that the worked edge of the buttonhole will be firm and distinct. This may be done with two threads of twist. Tailors follow the plan of using cord formed of several strands of the buttonhole twist, or linen thread twisted together, or a gimp cord. An end of this cord or thread is secured at the inner end of the buttonhole between the fabrics, and the other end is fastened to the knee or some convenient place and kept taut by a slight strain upon the work as it is held in the hand.

By this strain the cord is kept straight and in position just back of the edge of the buttonhole. The stitches are worked over the cord by the usual movements. After each stitch is drawn down, the loose twist should be picked up firmly by the thumb and forefinger quite near the stitch, and two or three circular twisting movements should be made so that the loop formed will settle securely and neatly into its proper position. Be careful to complete each stitch with uniform movements. When the eyelet is reached, the work is adjusted so that the stitches may be made at the proper slant. The stitches should radiate from the eyelet as the spokes do in a wheel.

The inner end of an eyelet buttonhole may be bar-tacked. Sometimes the bars are simply worked with an over-and-over stitch. This is done by passing the needle up through the fabric at one side of the bar and down through it at the other side until the bars are entirely covered with these stitches and the stays look like a fine cord. After the buttonholes are worked, their edges should be closely basted together by an over-and-over stitch made by pushing the needle up and down over the edges just back of the stitches. Then they should be pressed under a dampened cloth. In fact, all buttonholes should be pressed if the goods will permit. Before they are dry, a stiletto should be pushed up vigorously through each eyelet until the opening becomes perfectly round and the stitches around its edges are regular and distinct. When the bastings are removed, the buttonholes will be symmetrical in appearance.

BLIND LOOPS are used on garments fastened with hooks and eyes, to take the place of the eyes. The process of making them is shown in Fig. 52. Mark the position of the loop opposite the hook, knot the thread and bring the needle up through the material. Make a bar-tack the desired length by taking three or more stitches one over the other. Working from left to right, hold the thread down with the left thumb, and insert the needle, eye foremost, under the bar and over the thread. The use of the blunt end of the needle facilitates the work. Draw the thread up, letting the purl come to the lower edge of the loop. Repeat the stitches, covering the entire bar-tack, and fasten on the wrong side. Sometimes the bar-tacks are made in the form of a cross-stitch.

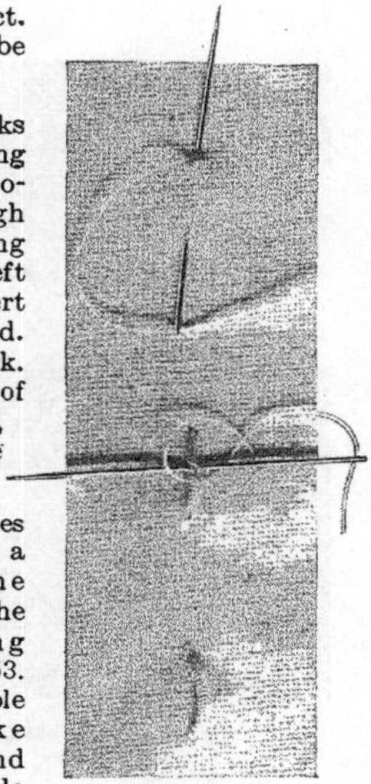

Fig. 52. Blind Loop

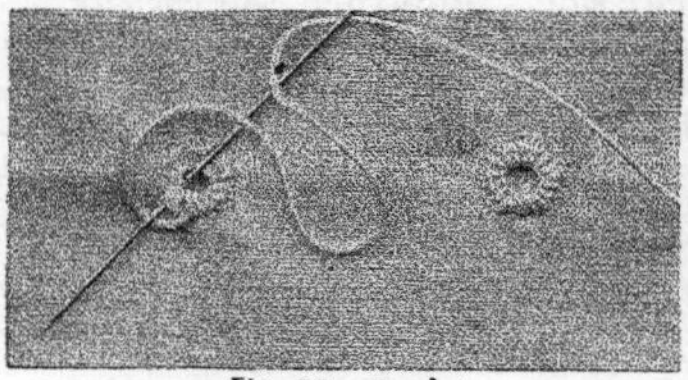

Fig. 53. Eyelet

EYELETS are holes made and worked in a garment to hold the cord or buttons. The method of making is shown in Fig. 53. Pierce the eyelet-hole with a stiletto. Make running stitches around the circle, place the hole over the fore finger of the left hand and buttonhole the edge, covering the running stitches. Work from right to left, as shown in the first figure of the illustration.

METHODS OF SEWING ON BUTTONS are illustrated in Fig. 54. Always use a coarse single thread in preference to a fine double one. In placing buttons in position, lap the edges of the garment, and push a pin through at the outer end of the buttonhole. This will bring the button exactly opposite the buttonhole. Make a knot in the thread, push the needle through from the right side so that the knot will be directly under the button. Place the button in position. Bring the thread up through a hole in the button and down through the hole diagonally opposite as shown in the second figure. Place a pin under the thread on top of the button in order to keep the thread loose, and make a cross-stitch through the remaining holes.

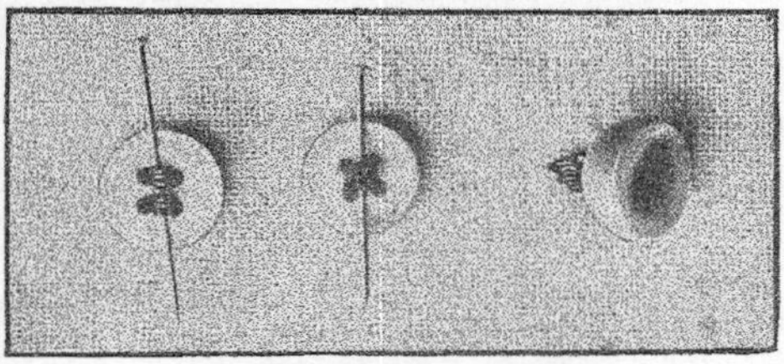

Fig. 54. Sewing on Buttons

Repeat the stitches until the button is securely fastened. Remove the pin, draw the button away from the material as far as possible and wind the working thread tightly several times around the threads between the button and the material, thus forming a thread shank for the button. If a button is too closely sewed to the garment, it will not have room to rest easily in the buttonhole and will crowd the latter out of shape and make the spacing seem irregular. The loose sewing and the winding increase the durability of the work and lessen the strain on the button.

The first figure shows another way of sewing on a button in which the stitches are not crossed. This method is used in dress and coat making, as the stitches are considered more ornamental. The third figure shows the method of sewing on a shank button. Make the stitches parallel with the edge when sewing on this button so that the strain will come on the shank.

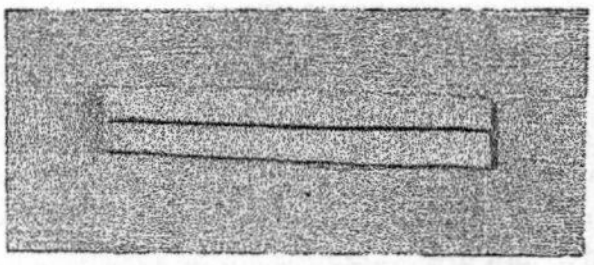

Fig. 54 A. Bound buttonhole

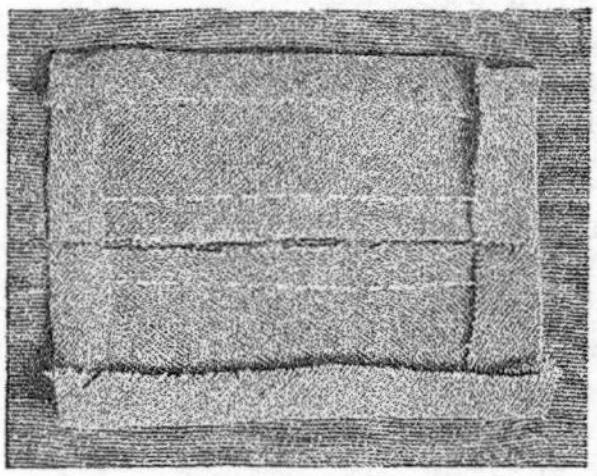

Fig. 54 B. The binding

THE BOUND BUTTONHOLE is shown in Figure 54 A. The length and position of the buttonhole should be marked on the garment with basting cotton. A bias strip of self or contrasting material about seven-eighths of an inch wide is used for binding it. Sew the binding to the right side of the garment with running stitches an eighth of an inch from the buttonhole mark (Figure 54 B). Turn in the other three edges an eighth of an inch and press them flat (Figure 54 B).

The binding should be fully the length of the slash.

When it is sewed on and the edges pressed, cut the buttonhole in the garment. Be sure to cut a clean, straight hole.

Push the binding through to the wrong side of the garment and slip-stitch it to position in the sewing line of the right side. Slip-stitch the corners of the binding so that they will not fray. Figure 54 A shows the finished bound buttonhole.

The bound buttonhole can be used on wool, silk, linen or cotton garments. It gives a finished look to a coat or dress and is particularly effective when the binding itself is in a contrasting color, though the binding is frequently of the same material as the garment.

CHAPTER III

DARNING AND MENDING

NOWHERE is the maxim "A stitch in time saves nine" more applicable than in the household. Here it implies, in a general sense, the immediate repair of any and all household articles. But the proverb is more particularly associated with the thought of mending and darning the household linens and the clothing of the family. Every one will agree that a patch is better than a hole, but it is still better to postpone, and, if possible, to prevent, the hole wherever the case will permit it.

DARNING is a simple remedy for many cases of prevention as well as cure. A few general directions will apply to darning in all its various phases. Neatness and the careful selection of materials most appropriate for the work are the chief requirements for successful darning. Whether the material to be darned is cotton, silk or wool the darning thread should correspond in thickness and color to the thread in the material, and the needle should be neither coarser nor finer than required.

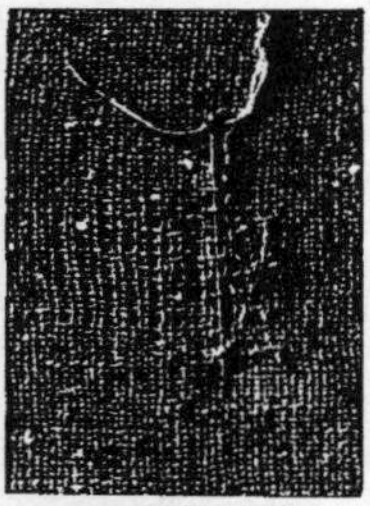

Fig. 55. Reenforcing a Worn Place

For Reenforcing worn places before the hole has come through, particular care should be taken to make the work as inconspicuous as possible. A thread or raveling of the material will do better than one of sewing silk, as the latter, no matter how well matched in color, will be sure to have a luster that will bring the stitches into prominence. The drawn thread need not be long; short ones can be worked in just as well.

Baste the part to be mended over a piece of medium stiff, glazed paper, or table oilcloth. Use a needle as fine as the thread will permit. Darn back and forth with as fine stitches as possible, following the grain of the goods and keeping the threads loose so that they will not draw. (Fig. 55.) The ends of the threads are not fastened, but are clipped off close to the garment when the work is finished.

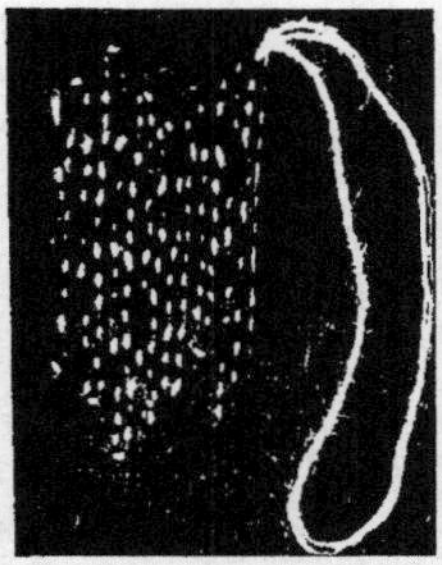

Fig. 56. A Running Darn

A Running Darn is used when the garment is worn too thin to be mended satisfactorily by reenforcing. Insert the needle a short distance from the edge of the worn or thin part, and parallel with the thread of the weave. Run it under a few threads and over a few, to the opposite side of the worn place. Returning, run the needle over the threads that were taken up, and under those over which it passed in the first row. Continue the process until the whole thin surface has been given a new body. In Fig. 56, white thread has been used in order to show the stitches.

When the part to be mended requires still more body than can be given by the running darn, a piece of the material may be laid on the wrong side, and while applying the running darn, this piece is occasionally caught up by the needle to hold it securely in position.

A Woven Darn is necessary when a hole has been worn through the material. The threads in this case are woven both lengthwise and crosswise with the weave of the garment. First baste the part with the hole over a piece of paper or table oilcloth, taking care not to draw it out of shape nor to let it bag. Do not trim the frayed or worn edges off. The unevenness around the edge, which these frayed ends create in the process of darning, helps to make the darned place less conspicuous. The lengthwise threads are run in first. Starting well in from the edge of the hole at one side, take up a few small stitches, cross over to the opposite side and again run a few stitches into the edge. Keep the threads taut, but not tight enough to pull. Returning, leave a tiny loop at the turning-point, to allow for shrinkage of the darning threads. Continue back and forth till the hole has been covered. Now begin the crosswise threads in the same way; darn over and under the lengthwise stitches, alternating with each return thread. The frayed edges are caught in the weave as they happen to come, and are firmly secured between the latticed threads. (Fig. 57.)

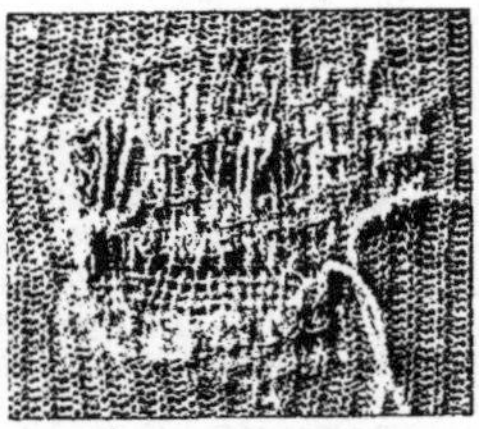
Fig. 57. Woven Darn

STOCKINGS are darned on the right side to keep a smooth surface next the foot. A darning-egg or ball, held in the left hand, is slipped under the hole, with the stocking stretched smoothly, but not tightly, over it. The darning is done with the right hand. In a woven darn the darning threads in a stocking usually run up and down with the rib, and then across, but when the hole is at the knee or heel, where greater elasticity is desired, the threads are run across diagonally.

Fig. 58. Picking up a Dropped Stitch

A Broken Stitch or two in a stocking, sometimes giving the appearance of a large hole, can be very easily remedied if attended to at once. With a silk thread, pick up the broken stitches and draw the edges together, and by a web-like weaving close the hole.

A Dropped Stitch is an ugly imperfection in a stocking that is more easily remedied by the use of a crochet-hook than by darning. Slip a fine crochet-hook through the little loop at the lower end of the hole; catch up the first thread, and pull it through the loop. Continue until every dropped thread has been caught, then securely fasten the last loop at the end with a few sewing stitches. Fig. 58 shows the position of the crochet-hook in the process of picking up dropped stitches.

To Set in a Piece is a very satisfactory way of extending the term of usefulness of the stocking when the hole is too large to be neatly darned. For this purpose it is always well to keep on hand the leg portions of a number of stockings of which the feet have been worn out and discarded.

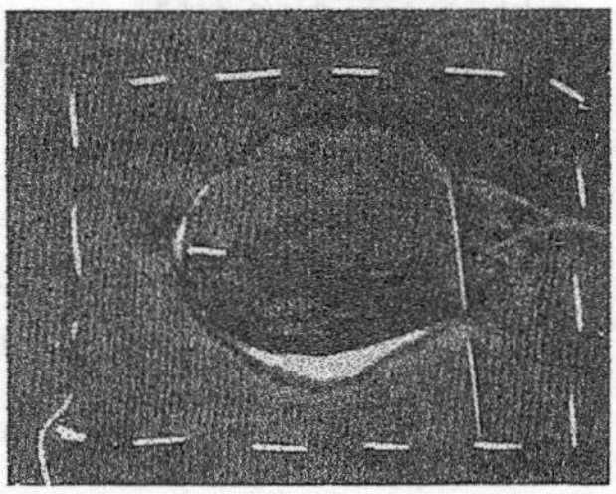
Fig. 59. Setting a Piece in a Stocking

Baste the part to be mended over a piece of paper and trim off the ragged edge. Cut a piece from a stocking-leg, matching it in color and texture, with the ribs running like those in the stocking, and conforming in shape to the hole, but a trifle smaller. Baste this piece into position on the paper, and join the two edges, the needle passing in close stitches, alternating, over one edge and under the opposite, until the piece has been securely and neatly worked into position. The stitch in this method will be seen to form a kind of lacing, which must be done evenly and closely, but not tightly enough to raise the edges. (See Fig. 59.)

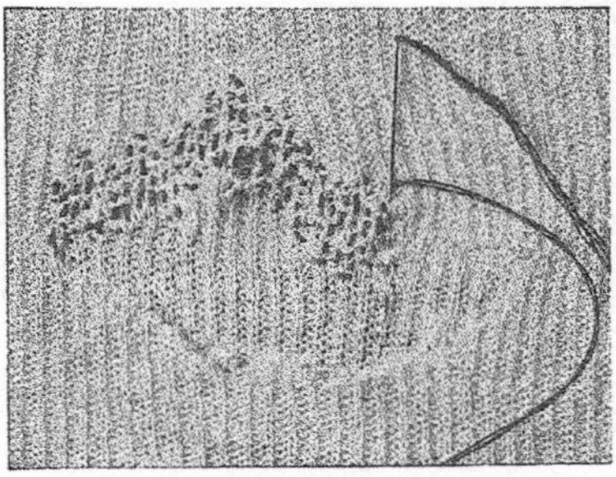
Fig. 60. An Underlaid Piece Darned In

An Underlaid Piece Darned In is a still better method of closing a hole when the stocking or garment is very loosely woven or knitted, in which case the use of a darning-egg would give it a baggy appearance. Do not trim off the ragged edges. Cut the underlying piece a trifle larger than the hole, but conforming to it in shape and matching it in color and texture. Baste the piece on the paper first, and then lay the hole over it. Or the torn piece may be stretched over an embroidery hoop and the patch basted to it. Run the darning-needle back and forth, over and under the lapped edges, closely weaving them together, keeping down all the loose ends. Fig. 60 shows the right side of the finished darn, a black thread having been used in the illustration to show the stitches.

A PATCH is generally used for mending flannel or heavy woven underwear, particularly if the garment is too much worn to warrant the time and work necessary for a careful darn.

A Flannel Patch is a piece of the material basted on the wrong side of the worn or torn part, and catch-stitched to the garment with small stitches all around the edge. The worn place, or the ragged edge of the hole, is then cut away from the right side, and the edge catch-stitched all around in the same manner. (Fig. 61.)

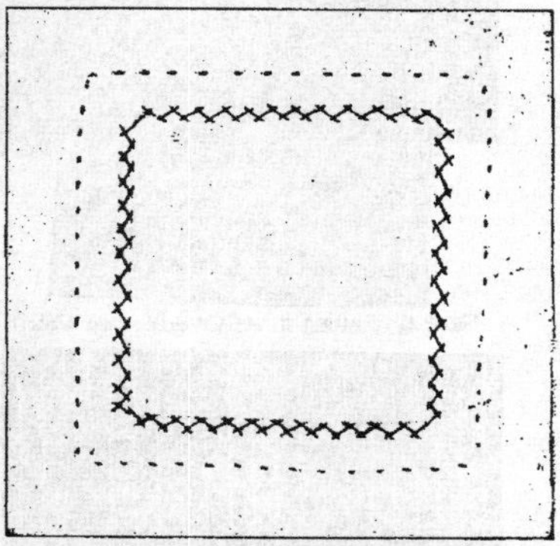

Fig. 61. Right Side of Flannel Patch

A Hemmed Patch is used—unless the hole is so small that it can be neatly darned—for mending material that requires frequent laundering, such as muslin underwear, bedding or household linen. If the material is striped or figured, the patch should be cut so that the lines will match. Pin the patch into position on the underside of the piece to be mended. Crease a seam all around and baste it down. Now cut out the worn part, allowing a narrow seam at the edge. Clip the edge a trifle at each corner, turn in the seam, and baste it down. Then with fine stitches sew the patch down all around on both sides of the material. (Figs. 62 and 63.)

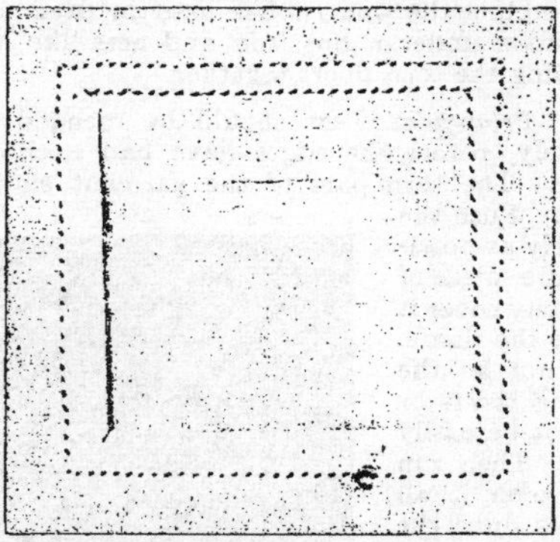

Fig. 62. Wrong Side of Hemmed Patch

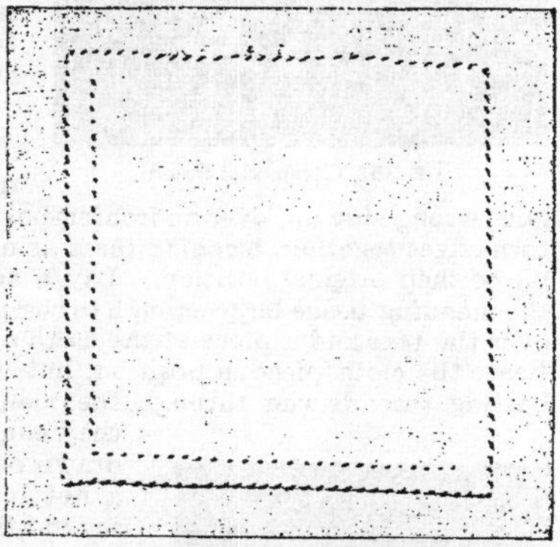

Fig. 63. Right Side of Hemmed Patch

An Overhanded Patch is used on material that is seldom washed, and where the raw edge on the wrong side is not objectionable. The sewing in this patch is not so noticeable as in the hemmed patch, for it has but one line of stitches. In cutting the patch be sure to match the stripe or figure. The piece should be large enough to cover the hole well, when it is basted over it with tailors' tacks. (Directions for tailors' tacks are given on page 22.) When the patch has been basted and cut apart, it will be seen that the exact outline of the patch has been marked on both the garment and the patch. The uneven edges are trimmed away leaving a narrow seam. (Figs. 64, 65 and 66, page 20.)

Fig. 64. Setting in an Overhanded Patch

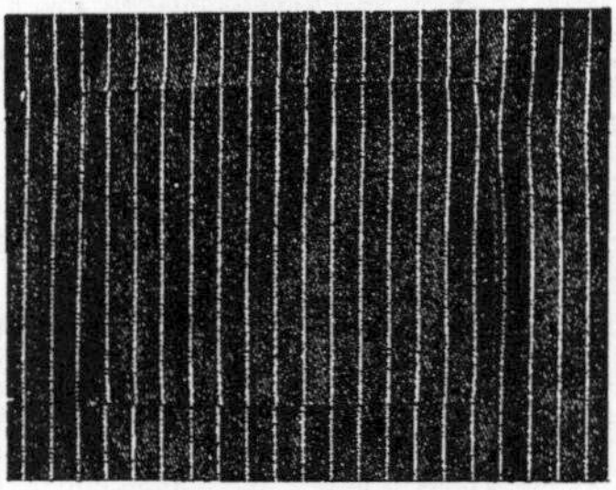

Fig. 66. Completed Patch

Notch the corners of the hole diagonally to the line of tacks, and trim off the corners of the patch. Turn the seam edges of both hole and patch toward the wrong side on the line of the tacks, and baste together. Then with small overhand stitches sew the patch in securely, being careful during the whole proceeding to keep the warp and woof threads of the material straight at the joining edges. Figs. 65 and 66 show both sides of the patch after it has been well pressed.

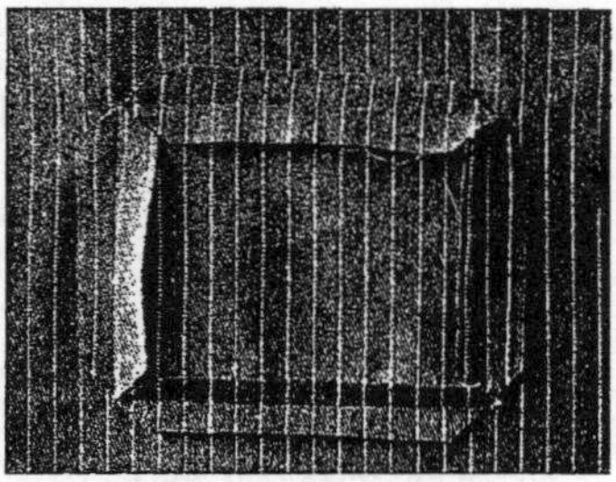

Fig. 65. Wrong Side of Patch

MENDING TISSUE, or TAILORS' TISSUE, as it is sometimes called, is a great convenience in cases of awkward rents or tears where patching would be undesirable. It is a semi-transparent substance, resembling the thin rubber used in dress shields. It melts under a hot iron and acts like a glue, holding the torn fibers together.

A Triangular Tear should be mended immediately, before the edges have had a chance to fray. The torn part of the garment should be laid, wrong side up, over an ironing-board. Push the torn edges together, bringing them as nearly as possible to their original position. Lay a square piece of the mending tissue large enough to completely cover it over the tear and a piece of the cloth over the tissue. Baste the cloth piece in position, but do not let the basting threads run through the mending tissue or they can not be easily drawn out. Then run a hot iron over it all several times until the two pieces and the ragged edges are nicely stuck together. Cut away all superfluous material around the edges. Fig. 67 shows a satisfactory result of this method of mending on the right side of the material.

Fig. 67. A Rent Repaired with Mending Tissue

Fig. 68. A Piece Set In

A Patch may also be set in with mending tissue in cases where it is undesirable to have any stitches showing. The hole is trimmed to a square or oblong shape, and a piece cut the same shape, but a seam's width wider all around. Lay the garment over an ironing-board, as directed above, and, between the edges of the hole and the lapped edge of the patch, lay strips of the mending tissue. Be careful not to have any of the tissue extending beyond the torn edge on the right side, as it will make an ugly mark after being pressed. Fig. 68 shows a hole neatly mended by this method.

STOTING is a process of mending much used by tailors, especially on closely woven or very heavy cloth that does not fray. The first illustration, Fig. 69, shows the cut, and in Fig. 70 is shown the position of the needle and thread in the process of stoting. Use either a thread drawn from the cloth, or a hair, to do the stoting.

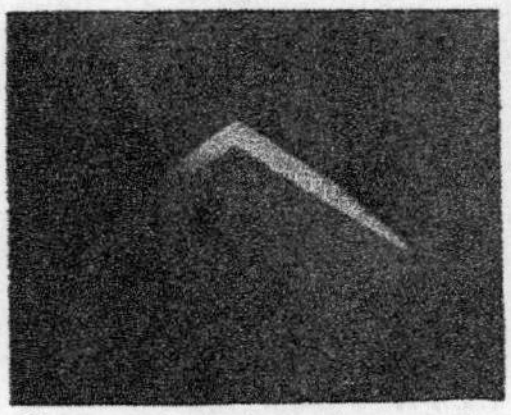

Fig. 69. A Cut in Heavy Cloth

Fig. 70. Stoting with a Hair

The part to be mended is basted smoothly over a piece of paper. The needle is inserted about half an inch from the torn edge, and run between the threads of the cloth, across the cut, to half an inch on the opposite side, and drawn through. Reinserting it, run the needle back on a somewhat slanting line and continue until the cut has been closed. Then repeat the same process, running the threads in the opposite direction. When pressed, this mending can hardly be noticed, but stoting can only be done over a clean cut or tear. On material that is not thick enough for the needle to pass between the weave, it must be done on the wrong side as lightly as possible.

CHAPTER IV

PRACTICAL AND ORNAMENTAL STITCHES

TAILORS' TACKS are used in cutting out garments to mark seams, perforations, etc. They are used to give a clean exact line for the sewing. When laying out the pattern on the material, mark all the perforations as directed in the pattern instructions with chalk and cut the pieces. Then with a double thread baste through both thicknesses of the cloth wherever it is marked, alternating one long and one short stitch. Leave the long stitches loose enough to form a loop under which a finger can be passed. (Fig. 71.) Then cut every long stitch and separate the two pieces, cutting the threads that still hold them together as you go along. There will then be enough stitches in each piece to indicate the sewing line plainly, and both pieces will be marked exactly alike. For waists or coats, or for any curved outline, the tack stitches should be quite short.

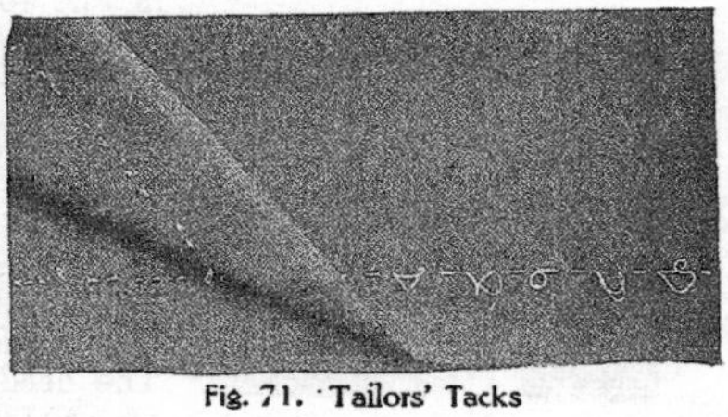
Fig. 71. Tailors' Tacks

In using tailors' tacks for marking long tucks or plaits in skirts, etc., the loose stitch may be an inch and a half long and not left in a loop, its length supplying the necessary thread for pulling through between the two pieces of cloth.

BAR-TACKS make a very neat and serviceable finish for the ends of seams, tucks and plaits, and the corners of collars, pockets and pocket laps of tailored garments. Fig. 72 illustrates the process of making the simple bar-tack, generally used as a stay for pocket openings. Mark the length desired for the tack; stick the needle through the entire thickness of the goods, down on one side, up on the opposite, and repeat several times, according to the required strength of the tack. Then without breaking off the thread, make one short stitch across one end of the long ones, and continue stitching closely all the way across, firmly covering the threads of the long stitches. Keep these cross-stitches close together, and while working, press the long stitches with the needle, to produce a cord-like effect.

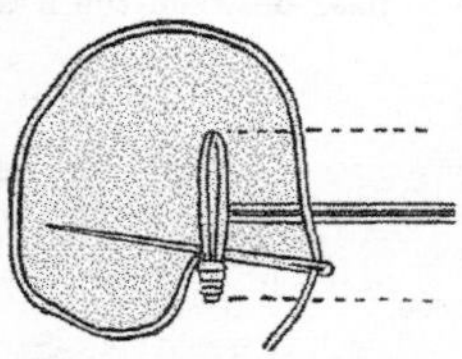
Fig. 72. Making a Bar-Tack

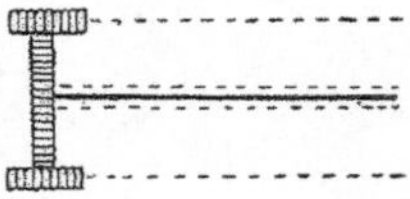
Fig. 73. Barred on Ends

On garments having a finish of machine stitches at pocket openings, etc., the bar-tack, with small bars crossing the ends of the plain bar, is more ornamental. (Fig. 73.) The process of making is similar to that of the simple bar-tack, with small bars worked in after the long one has been finished.

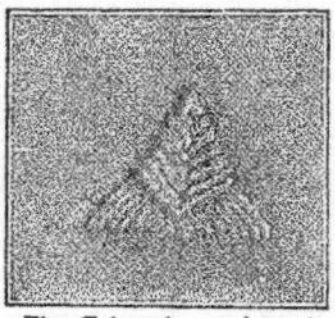
Fig. 74. Arrowhead

ARROWHEAD TACKS are used at the top or bottom of plaits and laps and at the ends of seams and pocket openings. (Figs. 74, 75, 76, 77.)

First make an outline of the arrow with chalk or pencil. Bring the needle up at point A, then take a small stitch at point B as shown by the position of the needle in Fig. 75. Bring the needle down at point C (Fig. 76), up very close to point A along the line

CA (Fig. 76), and take another stitch at point B close under the first one, and down very close to point C along the line CA. (Fig. 77.) The needle must go in on the chalk line BC and come up on the chalk line BA, keeping the outline of the triangle. Each successive stitch below point B will be a little longer than the previous one. Repeat this stitch until the entire space is filled. The finished arrowhead is illustrated in Fig. 74. on the preceding page.

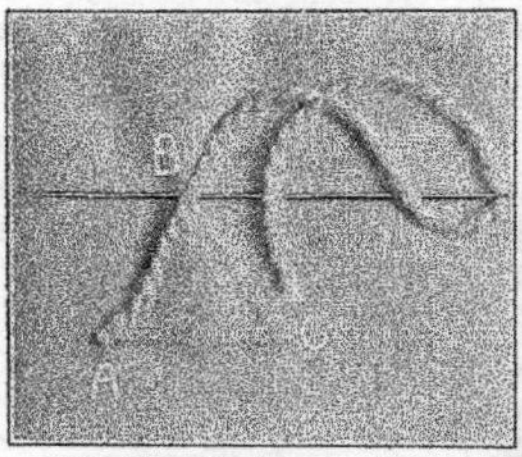

Fig. 75. Outline of Arrowhead

Fig. 76. Second Movement

THE CROW'S-FOOT TACK is the most ornamental of the fancy tacks ordinarily used at the ends of pocket openings and seams. It is illustrated in Fig. 78, with the detail of the stitch in Figs. 79 and 80.

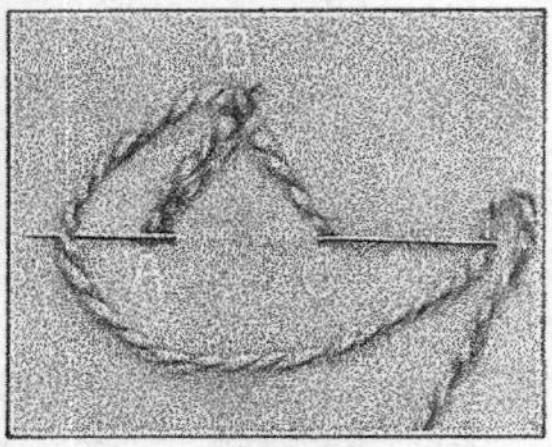

Fig. 77. Third Movement

Outline the tack with chalk or pencil. The dotted outline seen in Fig. 79 shows the correct design for the tack: Bring the needle up at point A, pass it down at B, and u again at B outside of and close to the stitch in line AB; then down at C, up at C outside of and close to the stitch in line BC, and down at A just outside the stitch in line AB, as illustrated in Fig. 79. Now bring the needle up on the dotted line AC out-

Fig. 78. Crow's-Foot

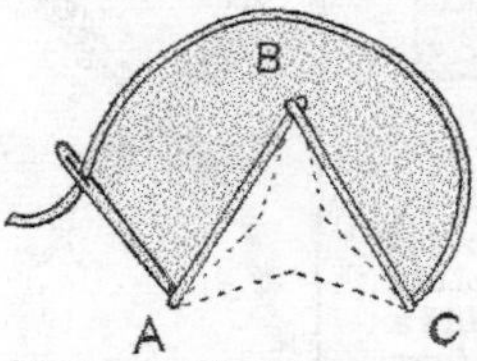

Fig. 79. Detail of Crow's-Foot

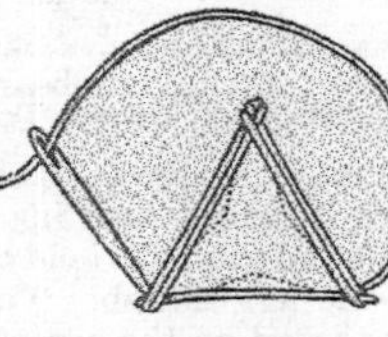

Fig. 80. Second Movement

side the stitch on line AC close to A; pass it down on dotted line BC outside the stitch on line BC close to B; up on dotted line AB outside both stitches on line AB close to B; down on dotted line CA outside the stitch on line CA close to C; up on dotted line BC outside both stitches on line BC; and down on dotted line AB outside both stitches on line AB, as illustrated in Fig. 80. Fill in the entire outline in this way until the completed foot looks like Fig. 78. It will be noticed in making this tack that all the stitches are taken on the dotted lines and always outside the made stitches, thus compressing the first stitches so as to curve the sides of the tack like the outline.

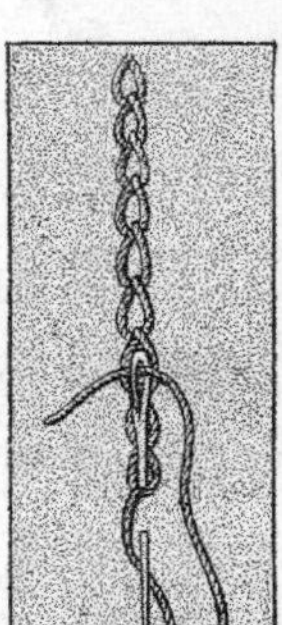

Fig. 81. Chain-Stitch

For working these ornamental tacks, coarse buttonhole twist or twisted embroidery silk is usually employed, and it is generally the same color as the material. With a little practise these tacks can be well made, and any of them will add greatly to the finish of the garment.

The crow's-foot is generally worked in scarlet or dark blue silk on the pockets of serge sailor suits. When it is used to finish the end of a plait in a skirt it is worked in floss the color of the dress.

A CHAIN-STITCH is, as its name implies, a row of stitches resembling the links of a chain. Bring the needle up from under the material, hold down the thread under the left thumb, and insert the needle in the same hole. Bring it up a stitch's distance below, on the upper side of the thread, thus forming a loop, or link. (Fig. 81, preceding page.)

THE FEATHER-STITCH is one of the most frequently used of all ornamental stitches, for it can be worked with the coarsest of yarn or the finest of silk or linen thread, according to the nature of the material on which it is used. It makes a most satisfactory trimming. The single, double and triple combinations are shown in Fig. 82.

Fig. 82. Feather-stitching. Butterick Transfer Design 3561

Run a colored thread along the outline to mark the center line or mark it with a transfer design. To make the single stitch, knot the thread and then bring the needle up through the material. Hold the thread down over the line with the left thumb. Insert the needle a little to the left of this line, and take a short, slanting stitch toward the right, drawing the needle out while the thread is held down smoothly by the left thumb. Then hold down the thread on the center line and take a stitch of equal length on the right side, and draw it out as before.

Fig. 83. Simple Design

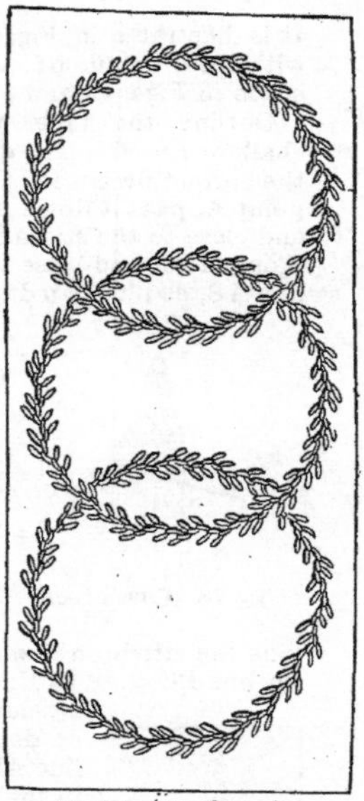

Fig. 84. Wreath Design

For the double combination, take two stitches to the left, and two to the right each time before crossing the center line; and for the triple combination, three stitches. The beauty of feather-stitching depends on its evenness. Material may be marked for feather-stitching by a transfer pattern. Figs. 83 and 84 show ornamental designs.

THE BLANKET-STITCH is used to protect the edges of heavy woolen materials, and prevent them from fraying. In working, do not use a knot, but secure the thread by one or two running stitches toward the edge. Then, holding the thread under the left thumb, insert the needle to the depth required and bring it up from under the edge, allowing the thread to lie beneath the needle, forming an edge. (Fig. 85.) This stitch may be worked into various ornamental designs if intended for decorative purposes. (Fig. 86.)

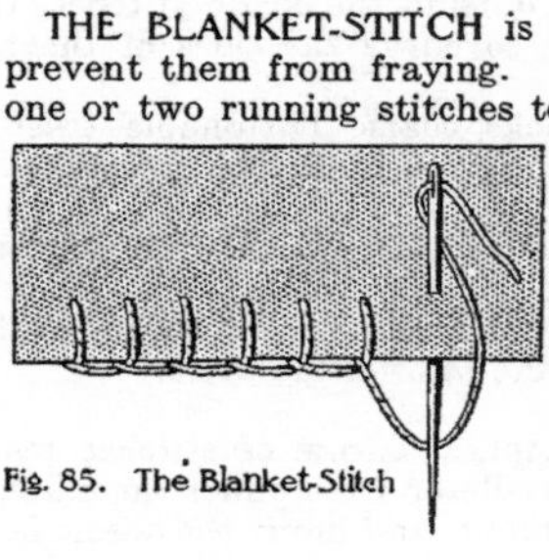

Fig. 85. The Blanket-Stitch

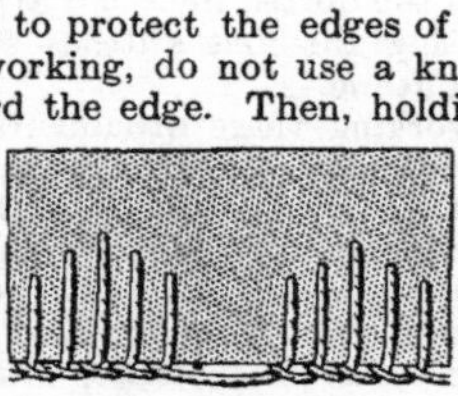

Fig. 86. Design used as Ornamentation

FOR EMBROIDERED SCALLOPS the material may be marked with a stamping pattern, which can be had in various sizes for various purposes—handkerchiefs, towels, sheets, table linen, etc. This marking should be half an inch from the edge of the material. The work is very simple and easy, even for an inexperienced needlewoman. Directly on the line run a row of chain-stitching which serves as a padding for the scallops. (Fig. 87.)

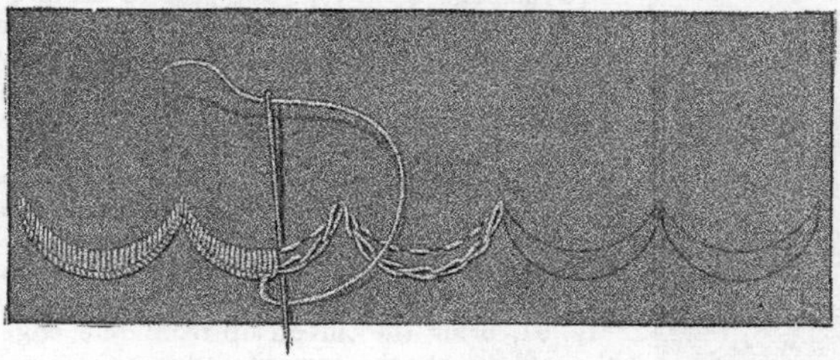

Fig. 87. Scalloped Edge. Butterick Transfer Design 2886

The buttonholing is worked closely with the needle inserted just above the line of running stitches and enclosing the line of chain-stitches. Use silk or cotton, whichever is best suited to the material. The outer edge of the material is cut away close to the embroidered scallops after the stitching has been finished.

FRENCH KNOTS, which are used in embroidery for the centers of flowers, etc., are made as illustrated in Fig. 88. After bringing the thread up through the material, take an ordinary back-stitch. Wind the thread or silk twice around the needle, draw it through, holding the coils down with the left thumb. Then insert the needle over the edge of the coils, in the same hole, thus making the knot secure. Do not cut the thread on the under side, but pass on to the next knot.

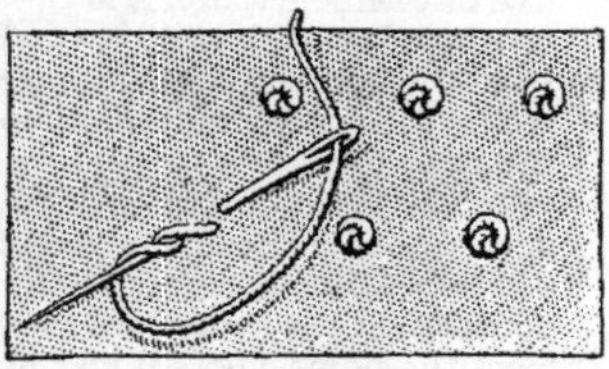

Fig. 88. French Knots

THE FAGOT-STITCH is a style of hand-made trimming that is always popular and attractive. (Fig. 89.). The simple beading stitch or any of the more elaborate stitches shown in the illustrations, which are very effective for trimming dainty lingerie, may also be used as a beading through which to run narrow ribbon.

For fagoting, the design of the work should first be traced on a piece of stiff paper. Or, as in the case of a yoke or collar where a fitted shaping is required, a fitted pattern should be cut of stiff paper, and the ribbon, braid or folds of the material basted evenly in position, following all the curves. When the fagoting is to be applied to the garment in fancy design, and the material underneath the stitches cut away afterward, the entire piece of work should be smoothly basted over paper, and the line of spacing which represents the fagot-stitching outlined with chalk or tracing cotton.

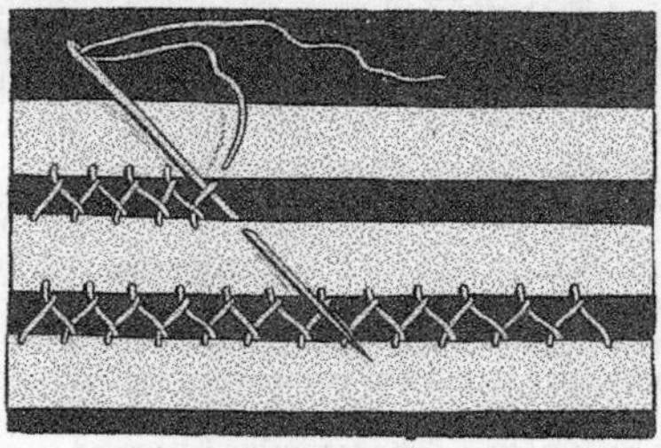

Fig. 89. Simple Fagot-Stitch

The Simple Fagot-Stitch is done by crossing first from left to right, and recrossing from side to side between the folds of the material, taking a small stitch in the edge. The needle in crossing each time passes under the thread of the preceding stitch, thus giving the threads a slight twist at the edge of the material. (Fig. 89.)

Simple Beading Stitches are illustrated in Fig. 90 on the following page. To make the upper design, a buttonholed bar, take a stitch directly across the space between the two folds and work the buttonhole stitch over the thread back to the starting-point. Then stick the needle into the edge of the fold near the hole of the first stitch, to keep the bar from twisting, and on the under side pass on to position for the next bar.

In the lower design the thread is carried across as in the other case, and, returning, one loose buttonhole stitch is made over the thread. Over this same loop, run two closer buttonhole stitches. Then make a second loose buttonhole stitch over the first thread, and again, as before, the two close buttonhole stitches over this loop. Catch the needle into the edge of the fold, and pass on to the next stitch. The link bar is not so difficult to make as it appears, and really can be done more quickly than the plain buttonhole bar.

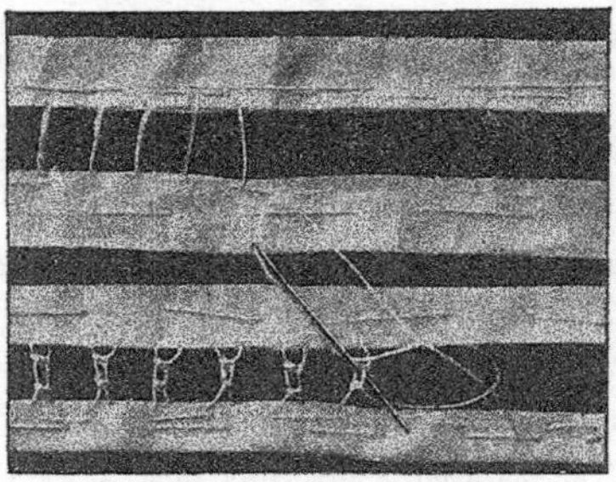

Fig. 90. Simple Beading Stitches

More Elaborate Beading Stitches are shown in Fig. 91. The upper design is a combination of the link bar (described in the preceding paragraph) run diagonally across the open space, and a simple twisted stitch run straight across from the apex of each of the triangles thus made.

To make the second design from the top in Fig. 91, bring the thread up from one edge of the fold over to the opposite edge, take a stitch from the under side and draw the thread taut. Then insert the needle three-eighths of an inch from that point, allowing the thread to form a tiny loop. Insert the needle again directly opposite the last hole, and from this point make five buttonhole stitches in the loop. Now catch up the edge of the fold just where the first plain stitch began, and on the under side bring it over to the second plain stitch, and draw it up for the next loop.

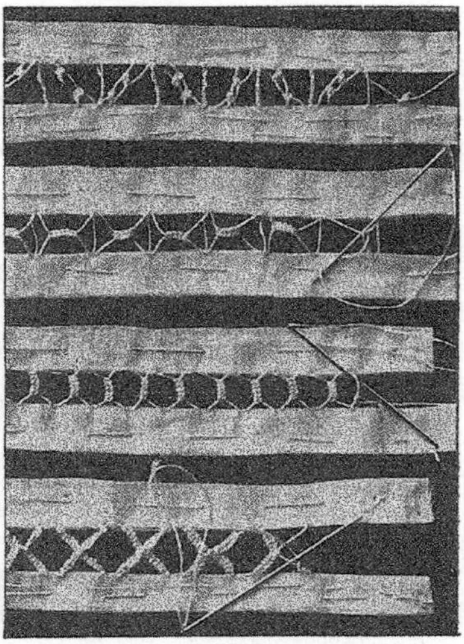

Fig. 91. Elaborate Beading Stitches

In the third design in Fig. 91, the thread is first carried across from one fold to the other and left rather loose. Then the thread is brought up through the same fold one-fourth of an inch from the point where it was just inserted. Make five buttonhole stitches in the loop formed of the thread in crossing, and insert the needle in the opposite edge. Now carry the thread over again to form the next loop, running the needle into the same hole. Bring it up one-fourth of an inch below this point, and continue as before.

To make the buttonhole cross-bar stitch illustrated in the fourth design of Fig. 91, first make a buttonholed bar as described in the paragraph on simple beading stitches, but do not draw it tight; rather let it curve a trifle. Then proceed as if for the next bar, but when crossing catch into the preceding bar at the center buttonhole stitch, and then continue to the opposite edge. Make an even number of buttonhole stitches on each side on this thread. Allow a small space between the cross-bars.

SHIRRING is made of successive rows of gatherings. It is used as a trimming. There are several different kinds of shirring, the use of which must be determined somewhat by the character of the material and the style of garment. Before beginning, it is best to mark the sewing lines with a colored thread, to be sure to get the rows even. This thread can be drawn out when the shirring is finished.

A Simple Shirring is shown in Fig. 92 on the next page. The top edge is turned in and the first row shirred in close to the edge. The thread should be amply strong, with a good big knot at the end; for if the thread is weak and breaks, or the knot pulls through, the shirring will progress slowly, and the material will suffer unnecessarily in the working.

Shirring can also be done very successfully on the machine, by using the gathering attachment. In that case it is especially necessary to mark the sewing lines before beginning, as the machine does the work so rapidly that one is more apt to get an irregular line.

Gaging or French Gathers is a style of shirring generally applied at the back of skirts, etc., where a quantity of material must be adjusted to a comparatively small space. (Fig. 93.) The stitches in this case are made evenly: long ones on the right side and short ones on the under side of the material. Each successive row of gathers has its long and short stitches parallel, respectively, with those of the preceding row. The threads are all drawn up evenly, and fastened at the ends.

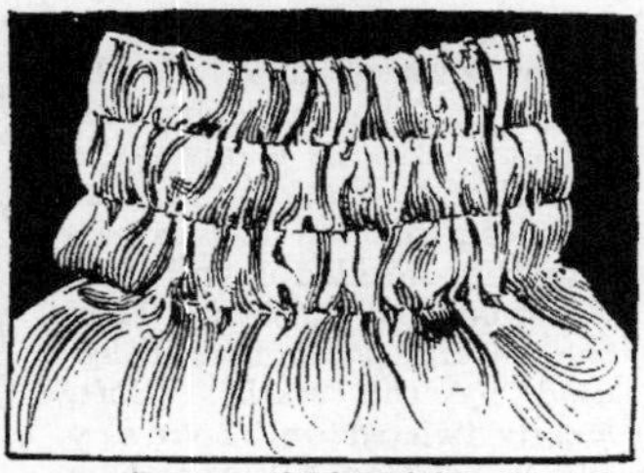

Fig. 92. Simple Shirring.

Tuck Shirrings should be made on the bias of the material. Baste the tucks in first, and then shirr along the line of bastings through both thicknesses of the material. Fig. 94 shows the tuck shirrings drawn up to fit over the shoulder. The length of the shirring thread determines the curve.

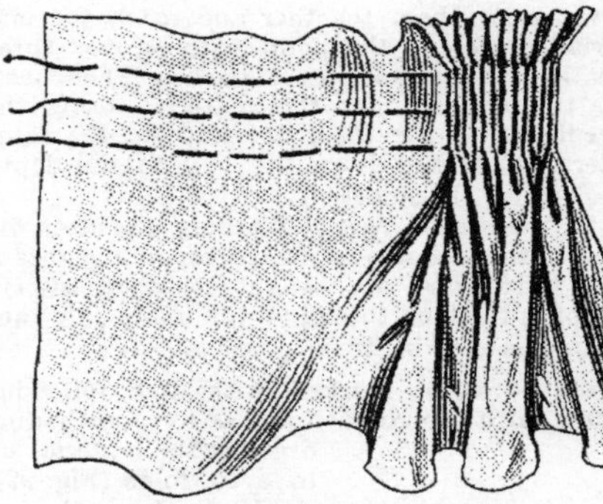

Fig. 93. Gaging or French Gathers

Scallops or Snail Shirrings are meant to be used as a band trimming. Make a narrow fold of the material, and run the shirring thread zigzag across from edge to edge. (Fig. 95.) As the work progresses, draw up the thread, when the fold will acquire a scallop edge on both sides. If a wider fold is used, two threads may be run in close together. This will produce a more even trimming and one that will be less perishable.

Cord Shirring (Fig. 96) is made much like the tuck shirring. Tiny tucks are basted in with a cord enclosed from the under side. (See Fig. 96, page 28.) Run in the shirring thread along the basting of the corded tuck, and when the entire number of threads have been run in, draw up the fulness.

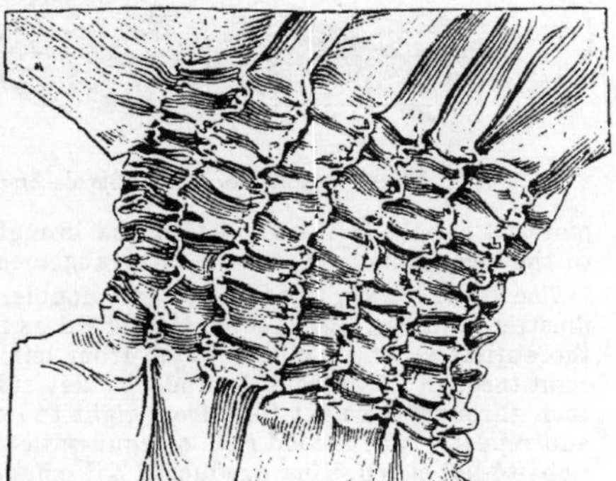

Fig. 94. Tuck Shirrings. Fitted Over Shoulder

SMOCKING (illustrated on two pages following) is a style of trimming particularly suited to children's dresses. It may be used in a pattern, forming yokes, etc. As a trimming it is sufficiently ornamental to make the addition of lace or other decoration quite unnecessary, and as an inexpensive trimming it can not be equaled. Delicate fabrics of cotton, wool or silk are best suited for this work, which is clumsy in too heavy materials.

Fig. 95. Scallops

To Prepare the Material for Smocking, spread it out on a table. With a transfer pattern mark the straight lines of dots spaced an even distance apart. (Fig. 97.) The rows of dots for the smocking are so evenly arranged that they form perfect squares. (Fig. 97.) Keep the lines of dots absolutely straight on the grain of the goods. When marking material for smocking by

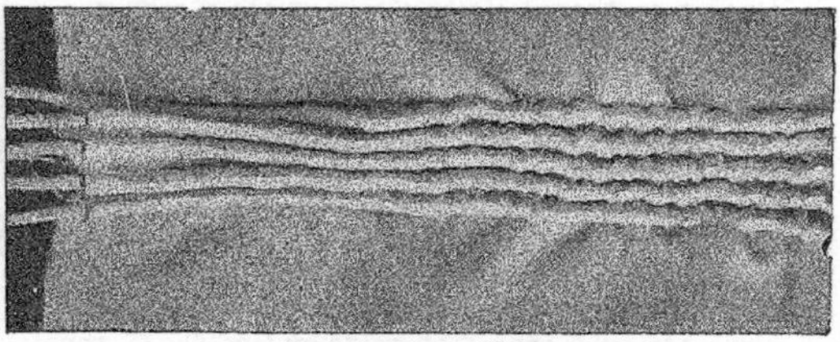
Fig. 96. Cord Shirring

a transfer pattern, use as many rows of dots as the width of the smocking requires. But it is always a safe plan to mark a row or two less, in case a change should be decided upon before the work is finished. Then the material will not be disfigured by the marks. Soft, loosely twisted embroidery silk is used on silk or woolen materials, and the best quality of French embroidery cotton on wash fabrics.

For the Simple Smocking, as illustrated in Fig. 98, take a thread and catch the material at the first dots of both the first and second rows; bring them together and catch the material securely at this point with two or three neatly made over-and-over stitches. Then, passing the thread under the material, bring the needle out at the third dot and do the same there. Continue down the row to the depth desired for the smocking.

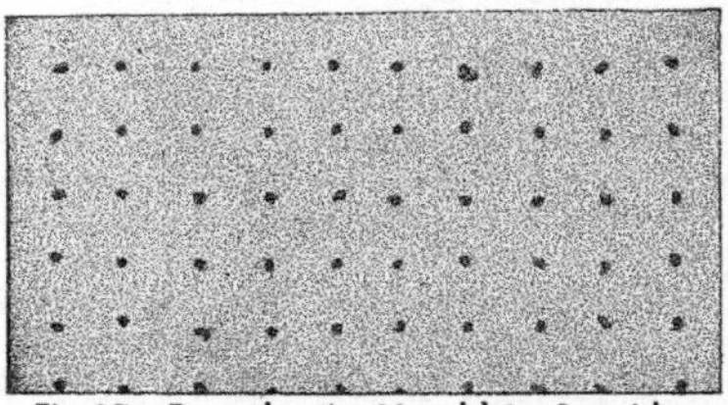
Fig. 97. Preparing the Material for Smocking

In the second row of stitching, the alternate dots of the second and the corresponding dots of the third rows are caught together, always keeping the long thread on the under side taut but not so it will draw, and making the stitches as even in size as possible.

In Fancy Smocking the material must, of course, be marked with dots following the pattern decided upon. The needle is first run through each dot as for a gathering, drawing the material up in even folds (Fig. 99), similar to the method of making French gathers.

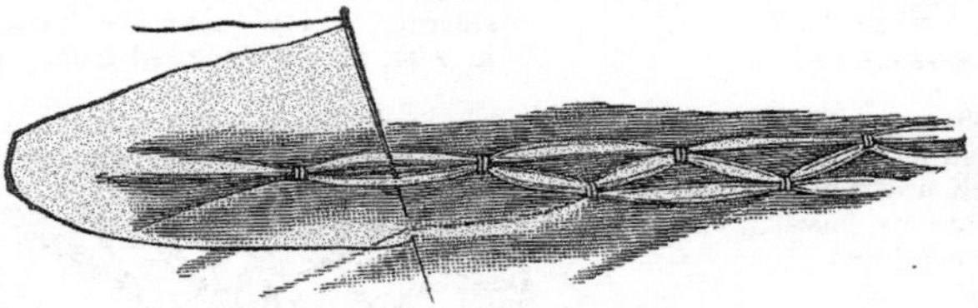
Fig. 98. Method for Making Simple Smocking

The Outline Stitch, as used in Fig. 100 is worked from left to right along the line of the gathering thread. The stitch is caught through from the under side of each small fold while the gathered material is held in the left hand, and brought up and over the edge of the first fold to the second one. A variety of arrangements can be used effectively in this way.

The Cable Stitch, used single and double, is illustrated in Fig. 101. Start the thread as for the outline stitch, taking a stitch from left to right through a fold from the under or left side; then through the next fold, from right to left, and repeat. The second row is begun with the right-to-left stitch, thus producing a V-shaped arrangement of the fold.

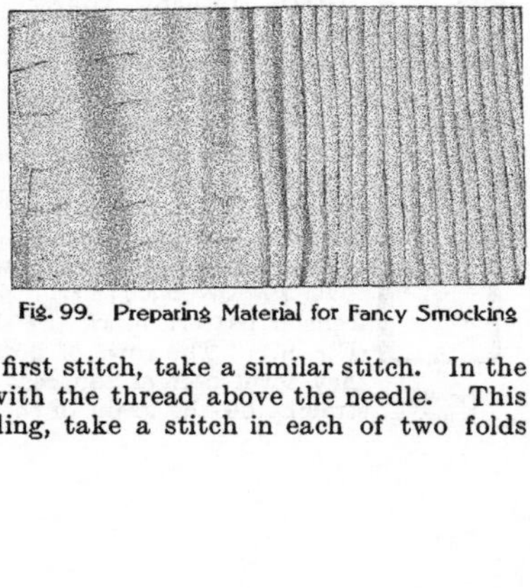
Fig. 99. Preparing Material for Fancy Smocking

The double cable stitch is simply two rows of the cable stitch run close together.

The Diamond Stitch is begun like the cable stitch. Take one stitch in the first fold, from left to right, with the thread below the needle. In the second fold, a little above the line of the first stitch, take a similar stitch. In the third fold take a stitch from left to right, but with the thread above the needle. This stitch forms the apex of the triangle. Descending, take a stitch in each of two folds from left to right, keeping the thread above the needle. The stitch in the third fold again has the thread below the needle, and the line of stitches again begins ascent. Continue in this way as far as the smocking is desired.

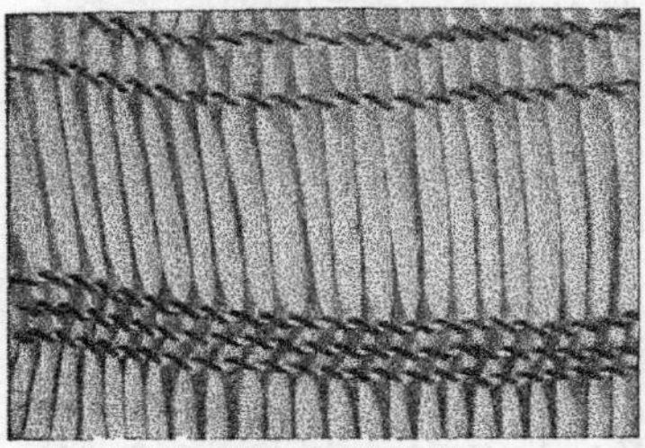

Fig. 100. Outline Stitch

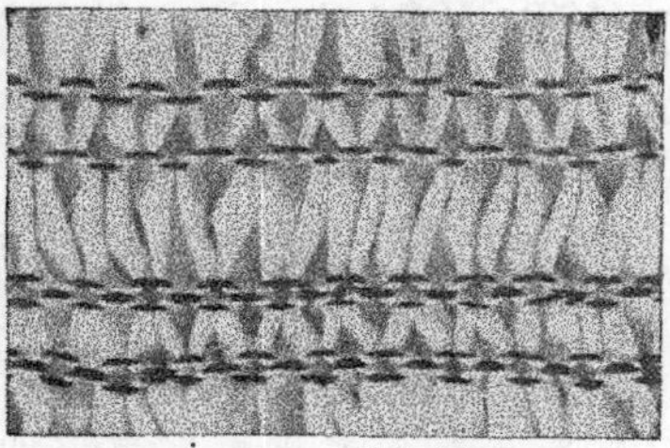

Fig. 101. Cable Stitch

The second row of zigzag stitches is put in so that the two will form a line of diamond-shaped figures which can be increased to any depth desired by additional rows of smocking. (Fig. 102.)

If a yoke or pointed effect of the smocking is desired, it can easily be accomplished by omitting as many diamonds as necessary to make the points, as one proceeds with the work.

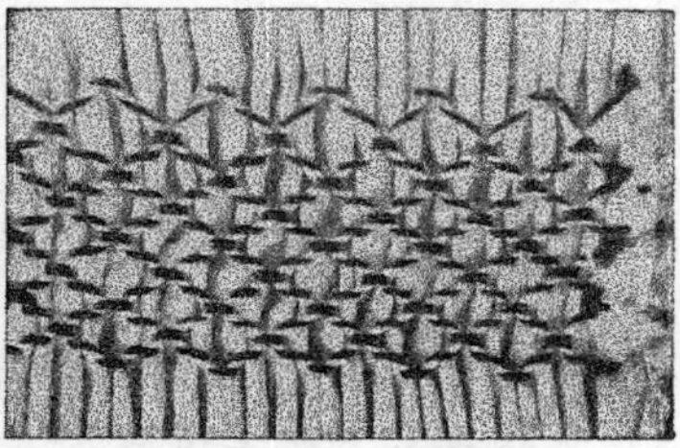

Fig. 102. Diamond Smocking

Smocking is not in the least difficult once the method has been thoroughly grasped. For some reason it is much more popular in England than in the United States. Abroad it is used a great deal for small children on little dresses of the simple smock order. They are very quaint and picturesque, extremely comfortable and becoming. Smocking done in colors on fine white batiste, silk mull, or nainsook makes pretty guimpes and dresses for children and very smart blouses for women.

CHAPTER V

BIAS TRIMMINGS

BIAS BANDS, folds, ruffles, facings, etc., must be cut on a true bias to give satisfactory results. For rounding corners or following curved lines, or making folds or ruffles hang gracefully, it is impossible to use successfully material that is cut on the straight of the weave. To maintain a perfect bias, the strips should be of equal width throughout their entire length.

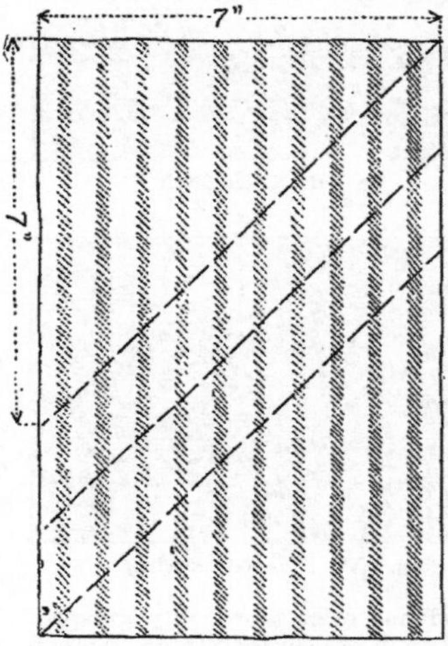

Fig. 103. Marking Material for Bias Strips.

Sometimes, in cutting, if the material is very pliable, the edges will stretch, and in time the cutting line will deviate from the original mark. It is well, in cutting many strips, to test the bias line occasionally, by laying the yard-stick across the material, and cutting a new edge if the old one is not even.

True Bias is obtained by spreading the material on the table and making a mark seven or eight inches from one corner on both the selvage and the cut end. Lay a yard-stick across the corner, touching both these marks, and draw a line. (Fig. 103.) Make as many marks on both edges as there are strips needed, marking them the required width. Then cut, carefully following the line and using sharp scissors.

When the material for the bias bands is alike on both sides, as in the case of corded silk, for instance, be careful to have the cut strips all on the same bias.

TO JOIN BIAS STRIPS, lay the two diagonal ends together as shown in Figure 104 and baste in a seam. (Fig. 104.) It will then be seen that when the joined strips are lapped back, the grain of both pieces runs correctly in the same direction. (Fig. 104 A.)

BANDS or FOLDS USED AS TRIMMING are made in a variety of ways. They may be lined, unlined, double of the material, or piped at the edges. Cut the band the required width, allowing for a turning at both edges.

The Unlined Fold, illustrated on the following page, has its lower edge basted up in a hem, and stitched evenly from the right side. The upper edge is turned over, and the band is then basted into position on the garment. The upper edge is stitched through the garment, making the one stitching serve two purposes. (Fig. 105.)

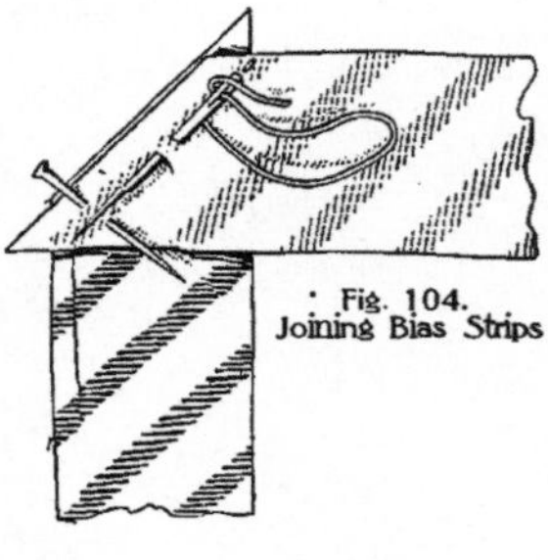

Fig. 104. Joining Bias Strips

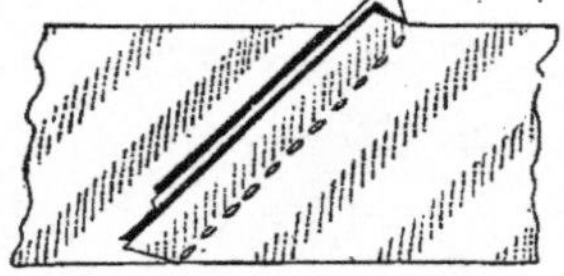

Fig. 104 A. The Seam.

The Lined Fold is finished before it is applied to the garment. Cut a strip of canvas or crinoline, as wide as the band should be when completed. Baste it evenly on the wrong

Fig. 105. Unlined Fold

side of the strip of material, catching both edges down over it. With the catch-stitch, fasten down the edges to the lining, and the fold is ready for use. (Fig. 106.)

The Piped Fold is one in which a cord or piping (see page 32) has been applied to the edges with one or more rows of machine stitching that give it a tailored finish. (Fig. 107.)

Double Folds are made of bias strips cut twice the width desired for the finished band. Fold them over on the center line and baste them flat. Turn the two raw edges in and baste them together. Then join them neatly with slip-stitches, and apply to the garment by hand. If machine stitching is desired, baste the fold in place first and then stitch. These folds are frequently used as a trimming in the place of tucks. (Fig. 108.)

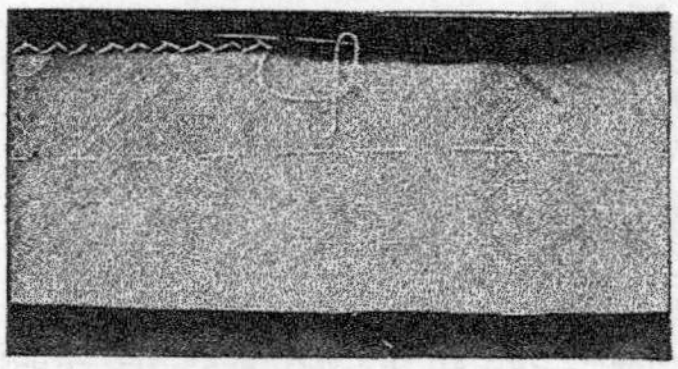

Fig. 106. Lined Fold

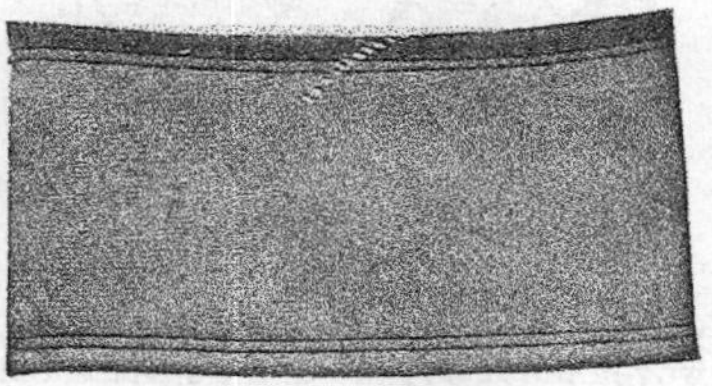

Fig. 107. Piped Fold

A Milliners' Fold is made by turning the top edge of the strip over one-half the width of the finished fold. Bring up the lower turned-under edge, covering the raw upper edge. Sew flat with fine running stitches. (Fig. 109.)

If the material is very sheer, it is a good plan to have a small strip of paper, not quite the width of the fold, to slip along within the fold as the work progresses. If pressing is necessary, use only a warm iron.

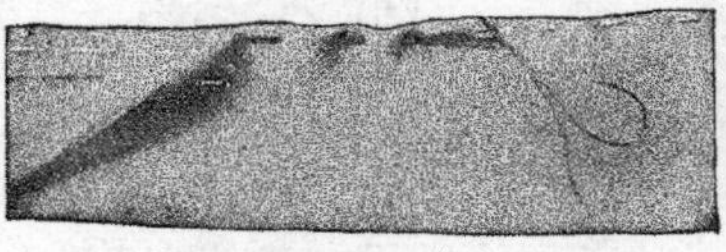

Fig. 108. Double Fold

Fig. 109. Stitched Milliners' Fold

Crêpe folds are cut on the straight of the goods, so that the crinkles will run diagonally.

Tailors' Straps are folded bands used to strap seams, or as an ornamental trimming on tailored garments. They may be cut on the bias, if of velvet or taffeta; crosswise if of woolen; lengthwise if of cotton materials. Fold the strip at the center and catch the raw edges together with loose whip-stitches as shown in Fig. 110. Spread out the fold and press it well. Baste into position on the garment and stitch by machine on both edges.

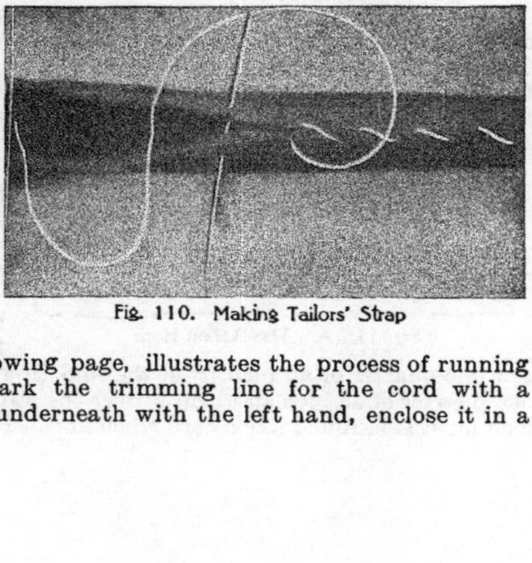

Fig. 110. Making Tailors' Strap

CORD PIPING is used to give firmness to an edge, or as a trimming for waists, skirts, etc. Fig. 111, on the following page, illustrates the process of running in a cord intended for a trimming. Mark the trimming line for the cord with a colored thread. Then, holding the cord underneath with the left hand, enclose it in a tuck, stitching with fine even running stitches as close to the cord as is possible.

In Fig. 112 is shown the cord run in a bias strip which is intended to be used as a facing for an edge. After the cord has been inserted, join the cording to the garment with the raw edge on the inside. The broad edge is then turned over one-quarter of an inch and hemmed down.

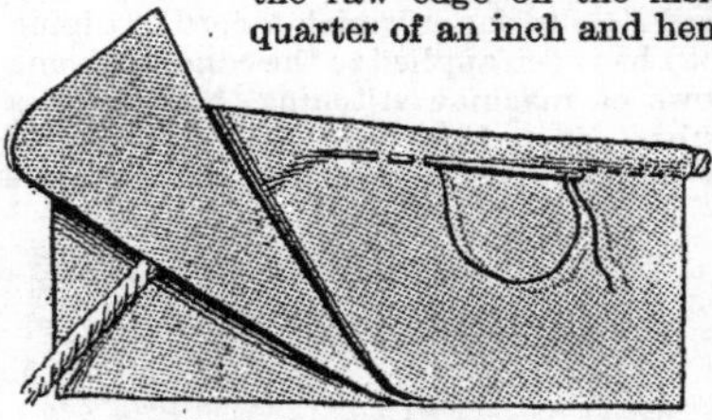

Fig. 111. Inserting Cord

PIPING is a finish much used in all styles of dressmaking. It is easy to make and very effective. Cut bias strips an inch and a quarter wide, if the material to be used for the piping is firm, as taffeta, etc. If a loosely woven material is used, the strips should be a trifle wider. Join all the strips, as described on page 30, and press the seams open. Then fold the strip over at the center line and baste it flat, being careful not to let it become twisted.

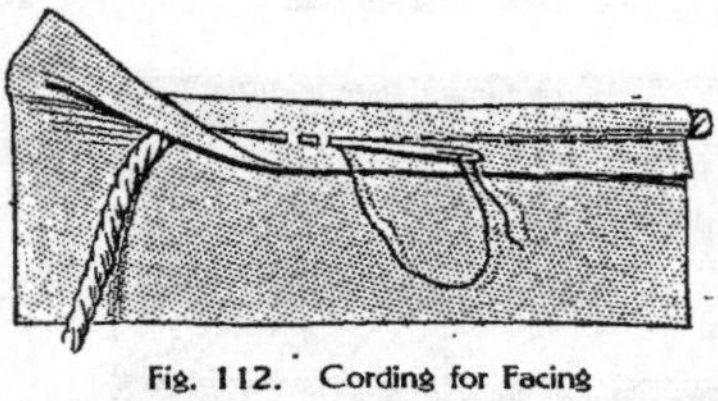

Fig. 112. Cording for Facing

Next prepare the edge of the material to which the piping is to be applied. If a stiffening is desired, cut a lining of crinoline or canvas three-eighths of an inch narrower than the pattern or the piece to be lined. Baste this lining into position as shown in Fig. 113.

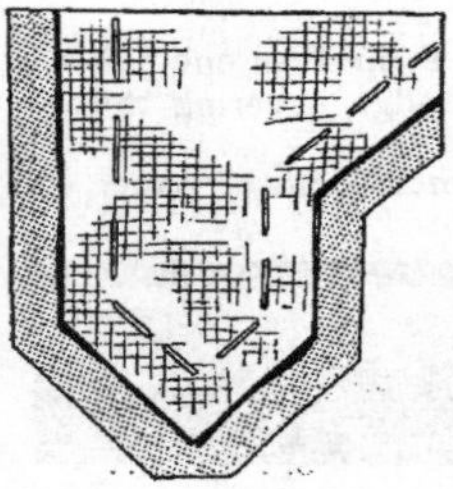

Fig. 113. Crinoline Basted to Material

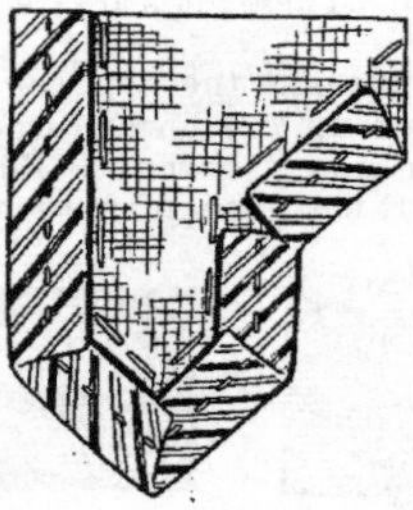

Fig. 114. Under Side Showing Piping Clipped at Corners

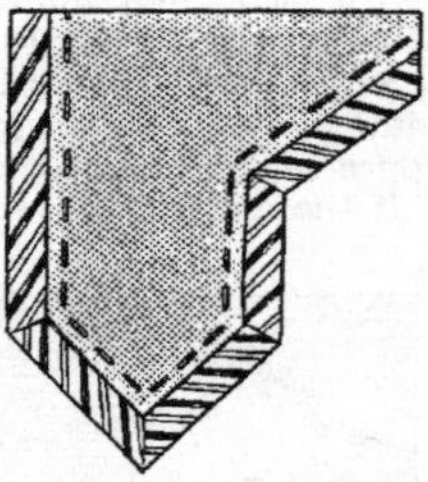

Fig. 115. Right Side of Completed Piping

If the edge forms a fancy outline, as illustrated here, turn the edges over evenly all around, clipping at the corners and folding in at the points where necessary. (Fig. 114.) Then run a basting thread an even width (about three-eighths of an inch) around the edge to serve as a guide. Next baste on the piping, following this line closely. Be careful to avoid any scantness at the points or bulginess at the corners. Fig. 115 shows the right side of a pointed edge neatly piped.

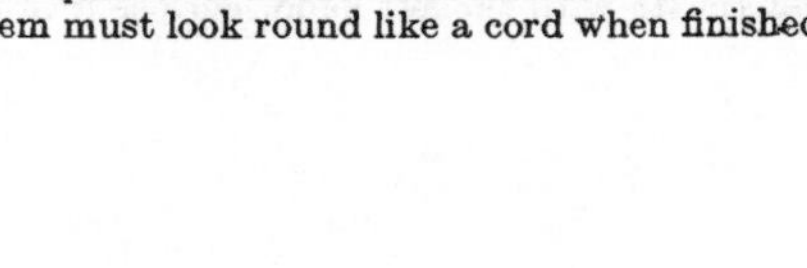

Fig. 115 A. The Rolled Hem

A ROLLED HEM makes a very pretty finish for bias or straight trimming-bands. It can only be used on an edge that is cut on a straight line. It can not be used on a curved edge.

An allowance of one and a half inches will have to be made on the edge for this hem. Fold the edge over on the right side and sew one-quarter of an inch from the fold (Fig. 115 A). Then turn under the raw edge one-quarter of an inch and hem it over the stitches on the wrong side (Fig. 115 A). The hem must look round like a cord when finished—not flat—(Fig. 115 A).

CORDING is a very useful trimming and is made with bias strips and Germantown or eiderdown wool. The bias strips should be about an inch and a quarter wide. Fold the strips lengthwise through the center and run a seam three-eighths or a quarter of an inch from the fold edge. With the strips still wrong side out, slip the ends of several strands of Germantown or eiderdown wool far enough into one end of the tube-like covering so that you can sew them securely to it. Then with the loop end of a wire hairpin push the wool farther and farther into the covering at the same time turning the covering right side out.

When cording is used to form a motif, stamp the motif on ordinary wrapping paper. The cordings are first basted in place on the design with the seam uppermost so that the right side of the motif will be next the paper. They are then sewed together at the points of intersection and contact.

CHAPTER VI

PLACKETS

UNDERWEAR PLACKETS are made in the following manner. If there is no seam, cut the opening in the garment the desired length. It should be long enough to slip easily over the head. Cut for a lap a strip of material lengthwise of the goods. It should be twice the length of the placket opening and three and three-quarter inches wide. Fold the ends together and crease through center; open and fold the sides together and crease. Cut out one section to within a small seam of the crease as shown in Fig. 116.

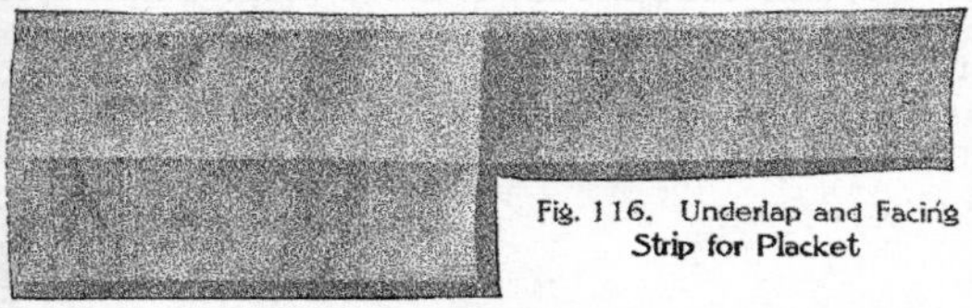

Fig. 116. Underlap and Facing Strip for Placket

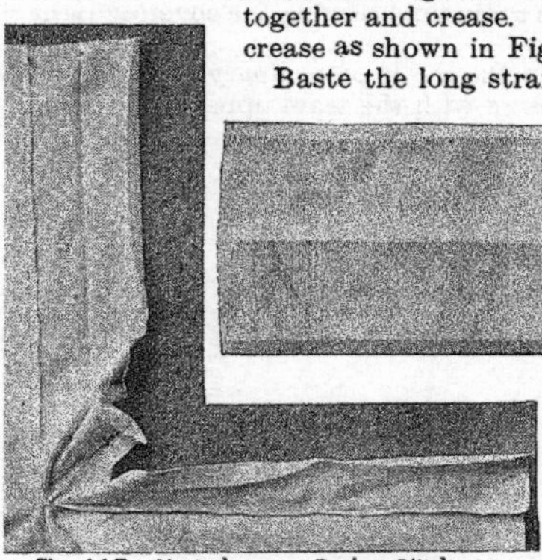

Fig. 117. Underlap and Facing Stitched to Placket Slit in Skirt

Baste the long straight edge of the lap to both edges of the opening, making a narrow seam. Run it almost to a point at the lower end of the opening. (Fig. 117.) Make a narrow turning on the three edges of both the narrow and the wide part of the lap. Double the wide part back (Fig. 118), baste the edge over the line of the sewing, and hem. This forms the underlap. Turn the narrow part back on the line of sewing, baste the free edge to the garment to form an underfacing, and hem. The end of the underlap is turned under, basted and stitched across. The finished closing is shown in Fig. 119. This placket has an outside row of stitching. It is usually employed for drawers, petticoats, etc.

Plackets such as are made for Unlined Dresses are shown in Figs. 120 and 121, on the following page. These illustrate the placket used on skirts of unlined dresses when the outside sewing would be an objection. Use a strip twice the length of the opening and three and three-quarter inches wide, without cutting away the section as in the first method.

The first sewing is made as in the first placket, then the free edge is turned under and hemmed close to the sewing. When this strip or lap is applied above the back seam of a skirt, it is set back an eighth of an inch from the stitching of the seam. One side is extended out to form the underlap, and the other side is turned under on an even line with the stitching of the seam. When the placket is closed, the entire lap is hidden as shown in Fig. 121.

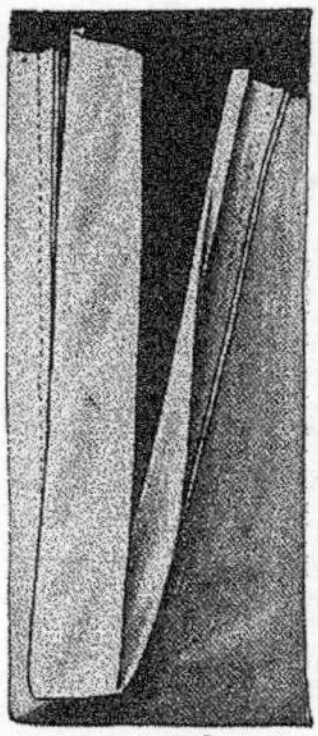

Fig. 118. Folded to Position

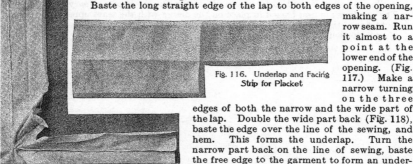

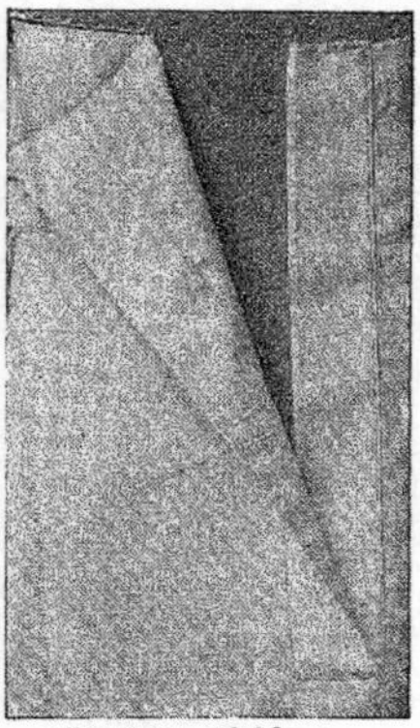

Fig. 119. Finished Placket

The Plackets for Cloth Skirts require neat and tailor-like workmanship. Great care must be taken in handling the edges of the

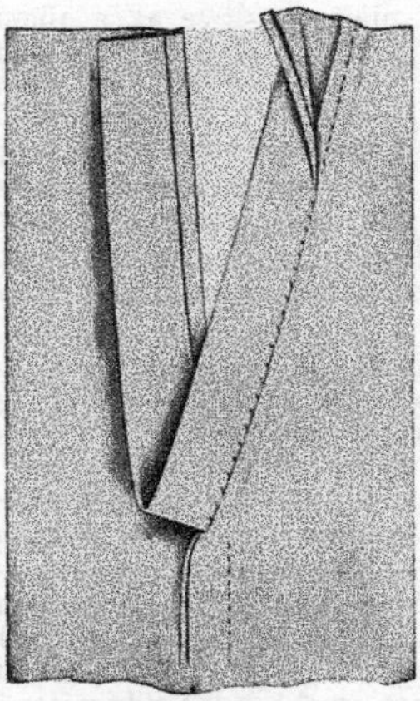

Fig. 120. Inside View of Continuous-Lap Placket

opening. They are generally bias, and stretch easily. If the upper edge becomes stretched it will bulge when the skirt is on the figure—a defect you probably have often noticed on other women. Hooks and eyes or patent fasteners should be placed sufficiently close together to prevent the skirt from gaping. Any stitching that shows through on the outside should be done evenly and with a suitable stitch and tension. Otherwise the placket-hole will have a careless appearance. A placket-hole should be ten or eleven inches deep unless the figure is unusually large and full, requiring a still deeper opening.

Fig. 121. Outside View of Continuous-Lap Placket

The design of the skirt regulates the position and finish of the placket. It may be at the center or side back, the front or side front.

A Placket-Hole at the Center of an Inverted Plait is shown in Fig. 122. The placket comes under an inverted plait at the center back of the skirt.

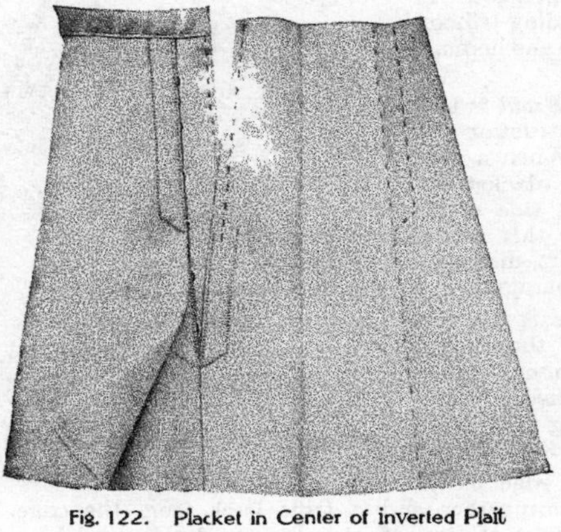

Fig. 122. Placket in Center of inverted Plait

The first step in finishing the placket of a skirt of this kind is basting a narrow strip of canvas or cambric along each edge of the opening, with the edge of the canvas three-eighths of an inch from the edge of the opening. The skirt edges are then turned back on the canvas and caught to it with small stitches. (Fig. 123.) Stitch the edges of the placket-hole and sew on the hooks and eyes as illustrated. Cover the canvas on the right side with a facing of silk. Sew an underlap of material an inch and a half wide, finished, to the left edge, and bind the raw edge of the lap with binding ribbon. (Fig. 123.)

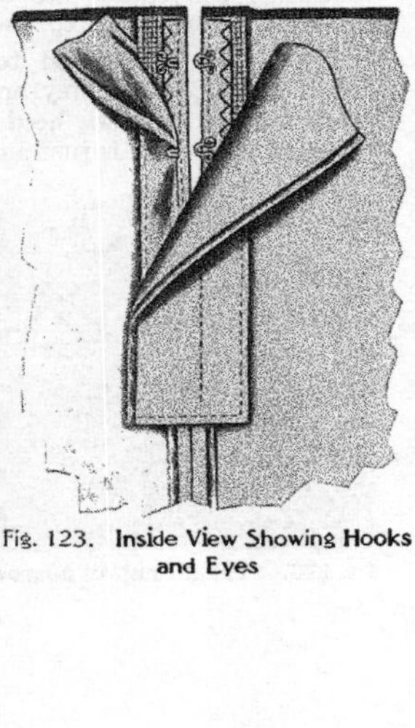

Fig. 123. Inside View Showing Hooks and Eyes

A Placket-Hole at the Right Side of an Inverted Plait is used on a skirt of heavy cloth that does not require the canvas reenforcement. Join the center-back seam to the top of the skirt and cut through the right-hand crease in the inverted plait to the regular placket depth. Bind both cut edges of the inverted plait with binding ribbon or a binding of thin silk. This method, as you see, allows

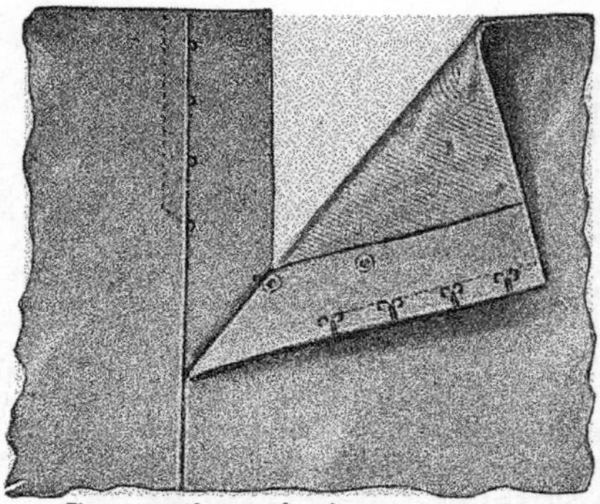

Fig. 124. Placket Showing Hooks and Eyes

the inverted plait to serve as a placket underlap. The outer left-hand fold of the plait should be stitched through all the thicknesses of the skirt, allowing the stitching to taper to a point. (Fig. 124.) The stitching on the right-hand side of the skirt leaves the under portion of the inverted plait free. Fig. 124 shows the position of the hooks and eyes and patent fasteners on this placket-hole.

The Placket-Hole at the Center of a Habit Back is practically the same as for the skirt with an inverted plait closed at the center-back seam. Face both edges of opening with canvas or cambric strips placed three-eighths of an inch from the edges which are turned back and catch-stitched to the canvas. (Fig. 123.) Stitch the edges of the placket-hole. Sew on the hooks and eyes, taking care that the stitches go no deeper than the canvas, for the sewing must not show through on the outside of the skirt. The same care must be taken in covering the canvas on the right side with silk, and in sewing on the underlap. The latter should be an inch and a half wide, finished. It is slip-stitched to the left hand edge of the placket. Its free edge should be bound with binding ribbon. The other edge should be turned under and hemmed by hand to the canvas. **(Fig. 125.)**

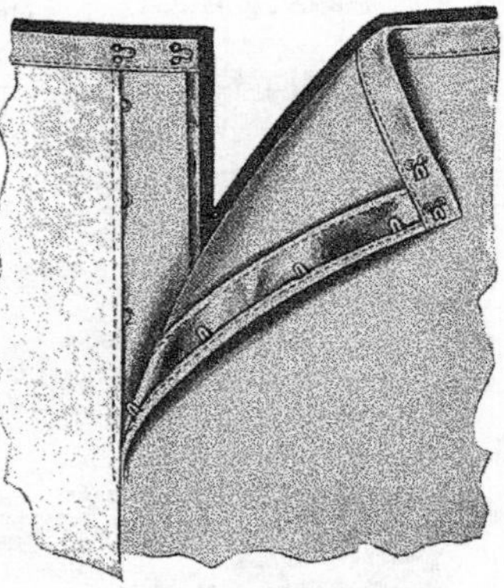

Fig. 125. Finished Placket on Habit Back Skirt

A Placket-Hole at the Side Back or Front is used quite frequently. So far as the construction goes a skirt can open at any seam. When a skirt does not open at the center back the placket-hole generally comes on a seam at the left side of the back or front. The placket-hole in this case is made exactly as in the habit-back skirt, directions for which are given in the preceding paragraph.

A Placket-Hole Under a Strapped Seam is shown in Fig. 126. The right-hand fold of the strap is stitched flat to the skirt. The left-hand edge of the strap is turned under and stitched to itself, following the same line of stitching that holds the rest of the strap to the skirt. **(Fig. 126.)**

The hooks are sewed to the left edge of the strap. Notice that they are set close together and a trifle back from the edge. A strap placket must be held firmly to keep the line of trimming absolutely straight. For the same reason it is just as well to add a row of patent fasteners just back of the hooks.

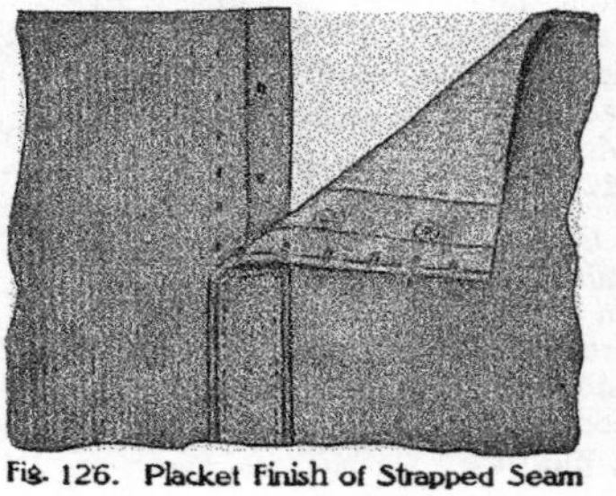

Fig. 126. Placket Finish of Strapped Seam

The underlap should be an inch and a half wide and an inch longer than the placket-hole, finished. It should be made of the skirt material faced with silk or with a light-weight lining fabric.

Lay the underlap on the under side of the skirt with the edges of the skirt and lap even. Join them with a generous seam. The depth of the seam will depend largely on the width of the strap. After stitching the seam, turn the seam edges back and hem them flat to the lap. The other edges of the lap should be bound with silk or binding ribbon. Blind loops are used instead of eyes and should be worked on the skirt in corresponding

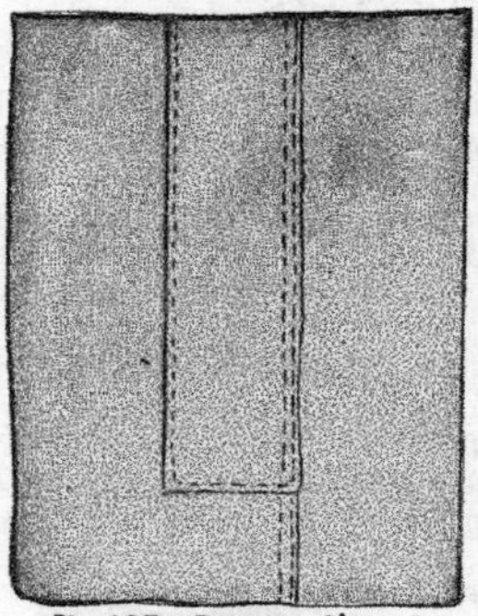

Fig. 127. Reverse Side of Underlap

positions to the eyes. The patent fasteners are sewed to the lap. (Fig. 126.)

The Placket-Hole in a Skirt Set in the Same Belt with its foundation skirt is made by the same methods as ordinary plackets. In such an instance, the placket opening of the skirt is finished separately. The edges of the placket opening of the foundation skirt are turned under three-eighths of an inch. The right-hand edge is hemmed under the bill of the hooks on the skirt, and the left-hand edge is hemmed against the edge of the underlap of the skirt placket.

This style of placket is not used as much just at present as in former years, when almost every skirt was made with either a lining or a foundation skirt. While we dispense with the drop skirt in all dresses of heavy materials, it is still used with all thin evening fabrics and with a good many light-weight materials such as voiles, etc.

Whatever kind of placket is used, one should be partienlarly careful to see that the hooks and eyes or fasteners are so arranged that they will keep the hole securely closed. Nothing looks worse than a gaping placket, and any woman who takes a pride in her personal appearance will pay special attention to this part of her dressmaking.

CHAPTER VII

APRONS AND FLANNEL PETTICOATS

ALL WOMEN need aprons, both for sewing and household use. For any one who has had little experience in needlework the making of a few simple, pretty aprons will make her familiar with the use of stitches and materials.

Two sewing aprons can be made from three yards of lawn thirty-six inches wide. Tear the goods into three equal breadths. If the edges are uneven, pull the crosswise threads into shape by stretching through the bias. From one length tear four strips, thirty-six inches long and six inches wide for the ties, and two lengths for the belt bands. The latter should be three inches wide and two inches shorter than the waist measure.

Take one of the remaining large pieces and turn up a four-inch hem at one end by folding over a narrow turning and creasing evenly. Make a second turning four inches wide and crease. Baste along the line of the first turning and hem neatly with small even stitches, using fine cotton and a small needle.

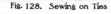

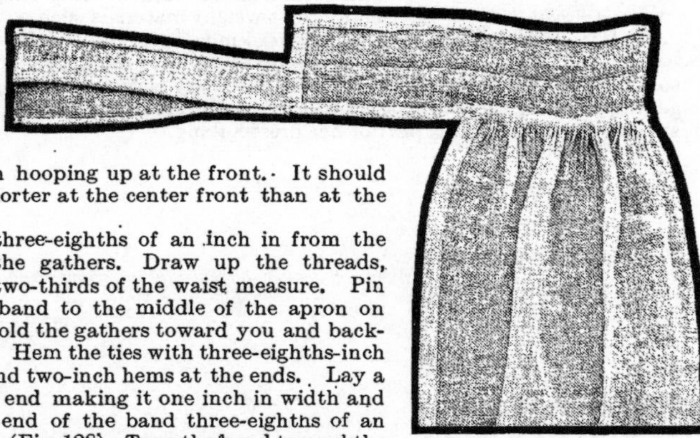

Fig. 128. Sewing on Ties

Beginning with the selvage, slope the apron off a little at the top to keep it from hooping up at the front. It should be one-half inch shorter at the center front than at the sides.

Gather the top three-eighths of an inch in from the edge and stroke the gathers. Draw up the threads, making the apron two-thirds of the waist measure. Pin the middle of the band to the middle of the apron on the right side. Hold the gathers toward you and backstitch to the band. Hem the ties with three-eighths-inch hems at the sides and two-inch hems at the ends. Lay a plait in the upper end making it one inch in width and back-stitch to the end of the band three-eighths of an inch from the edge. (Fig. 128). Turn the band toward the wrong side of the apron, turn in the raw edge three-eighths of an inch and hem to the gathers, covering the line of sewing. Turn in the ends of the band and hem them to the ties. Overhand the remaining spaces on the band.

The apron may be finished without ties by cutting the band one and one-half inches longer than waist measure. Turn in three-eighths of an inch at each end and overhand all around. Make two buttonholes at one end and sew two buttons at the other end.

A FLANNEL PETTICOAT or UNDERSKIRT is an excellent garment for the inexperienced needlewoman to practise on.

Select a good pattern and cut as directed in the instructions. If the pattern allows for no hem, each gore must be cut about three inches longer at the bottom. Baste the seams, matching the notches, and backstitch them. Leave a ten-inch opening at the back for a placket, which can be finished with featherstitched hems as shown in Fig. 129. The seam edges may be catch-stitched as shown in Figs. 11, and 12 on page 5.

The bottom of the skirt may be finished with a scalloped edge as shown in Fig. 87 on page 25. Or, the hem may be turned up on the right side, made into a French hem, and finished with a row of featherstitching as shown in Fig. 131. If this latter finish is desired, the seams must be stitched to within twice the depth of the finished hem, as illustrated in Fig. 130. Clip the seam at this point to the stitching, turn the lower edges toward the right side and stitch the remainder of the seam. Press open, turn the hem to the right side, baste and featherstitch. Gather the top of the skirt, or, lay the fulness in an inverted plait at the back.

Pin the belt to the top edge, on the outside of the skirt with the marks indicating the middle of the belt and the middle of the skirt edge together, and the ends of the belt extending three-eighths of an inch beyond the hems of the placket. Distribute the gathers evenly, baste and backstitch the skirt to the belt. Turn the belt toward the wrong side, make a narrow turning on its wrong edge and hem it over the seam, covering the raw edges. Turn in each end of the belt three-eighths of an inch and finish with over-and-over stitches.

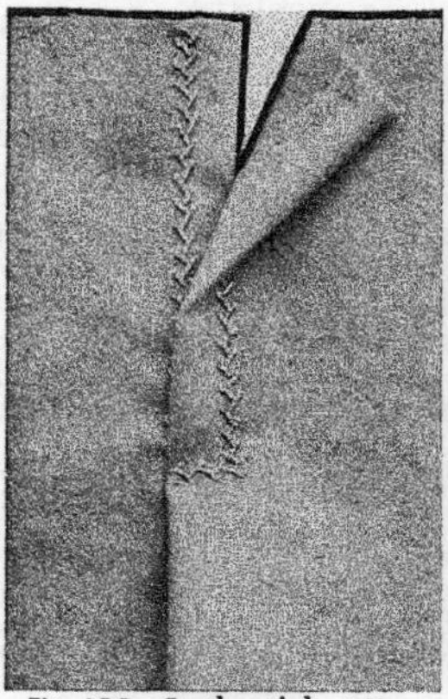

Fig. 129. Featherstitched Hem at Placket

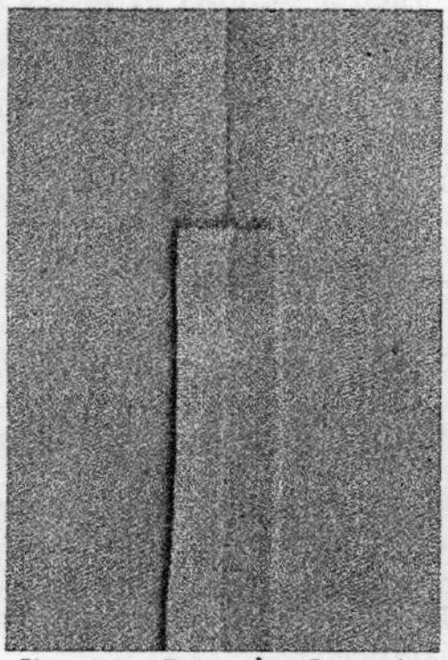

Fig. 130. Reversing Seam for French Hem

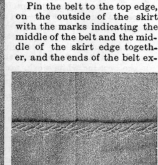

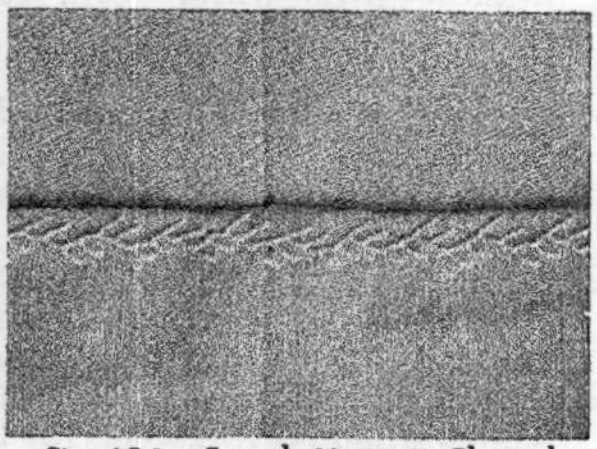

Fig. 131. French Hem on Flannel Skirt

CHAPTER VIII

MAKING AND FINISHING UNDERGARMENTS

ALTHOUGH there is a particular daintiness and charm about hand-made underwear, much fine and beautiful work may be done on the machine. The saving of time is so great that when a number of pieces are to be made this method is usually given the preference. A few of the smaller pieces—a corset cover, chemise or a pair of drawers—can easily be made by hand, but the amount of work on gowns, petticoats or combination garments inclines one toward the machine method.

One must understand something of the mechanism of the machine. It must be kept clean and well oiled. The number of the thread, the size of the needle, the length of the stitch, and the adjustment of the tension must be adapted to the material. No. 80 cotton is the best for white work, except for tucks and hems and all outside stitching on very sheer and fine materials, when No. 100 or No. 120 may be used. Every make of machine has a table, giving the sizes of needles that should be used with certain number threads, which it is wise to follow. Remember that a sewing-cotton requires a looser tension than silk.

The hemming and tucking attachments are great time-savers, but many women prefer to gather ruffles, puffs, etc., by hand and stroke them.

No raw edges of material are left at the seams in lingerie. All edges should be joined with veining or finished in French or felled seams. The French seam is used at what may be called the regular seams—those joining together the gores or the front and back portions of the garment. A felled seam is used to piece the material in cutting unusually wide garments—drawers, for instance.

Both the felled and the French seams are illustrated and explained in Chapter I, "Sewing Stitches."

The daintiest and at the same time the most effective trimming for lingerie is hand embroidery. It is used on all the most beautiful French underwear, and is very lovely to look at, and yet adds very little to the cost of the garment. It is the only trimming that does not wear out, and it never requires mending. For every-day wear the simple scallops and eyelets which can be used in place of beading are very satisfactory. More elaborate designs can be used on finer lingerie for evening wear, etc. One can get very beautiful effects by combining hand embroidery with lace.

THE PETTICOAT is a simple garment which even the beginner on the sewing-machine can undertake. With dress skirts that fit smoothly about the hips the fit of the undergarments is an important matter.

Select a good pattern, in a suitable number of gores. A seven-gored pattern is preferred for a stout figure, as it gives two more seams for fitting.

For Cutting, arrange the pattern pieces economically on the material, following the instructions carefully. Allow a two and one-half inch hem if it is not provided for in the pattern.

Baste the gores together with a three-eighths of an inch seam. In basting a petticoat always begin at the top with small, close stitches, for the greatest strain in fitting comes at the waist and hips. Below the hips the basting stitches may be larger. Be careful not to stretch the bias edge of the gore, as this is often the cause of the seams not being put together correctly.

Try on and make any necessary alteration in the fitting. Stitch one-quarter of an inch outside of the bastings. Remove the bastings and reverse the seam, stitching a second time where the first row of bastings was made, making a French seam, as shown in Fig. 15 on page 5.

The Placket is made at the back with a continuous lap three-quarters of an inch wide, finished as shown in the process of making on page 35.

The petticoat may be finished at the top with a narrow bias facing which allows it to drop below the waistline. If fulness is used, it can be gathered or laid in plaits at the back and the bias facing is basted to the right side of the skirt, turned over to the wrong side and stitched down by machine. The method for applying a facing is shown in Fig. 137.

A Yoke which insures a better fit to the outer skirt is often used instead of a facing on underskirts and drawers. The yoke pattern should be bought by the same measurements as the skirt. If the waist and hip measure are disproportionate, order the pattern by the hip measurement nearest your own and alter it at the waistline. The yoke patterns are cut in one piece, either with or without darts.

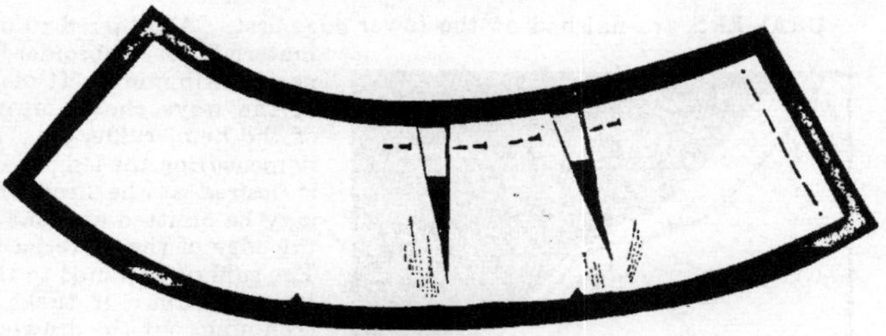

Fig. 132. A Circular Yoke Fitted to a Large Waist.

The yoke may be fitted by the darts if there are any. In case there is none, cut a trial yoke from coarse cambric before cutting out the real garment. Mark the center front with a colored thread and fit the yoke. If the waist is too small, slash the yoke down from the waist wherever necessary and pin a piece of cambric at each slash to hold it to the correct size as shown in Fig. 132. Use this fitted yoke as a pattern from which to cut the real yoke. Do not alter any of the notches in the lower part of the yoke, as the changes at the waistline do not affect the construction of the rest of the garment.

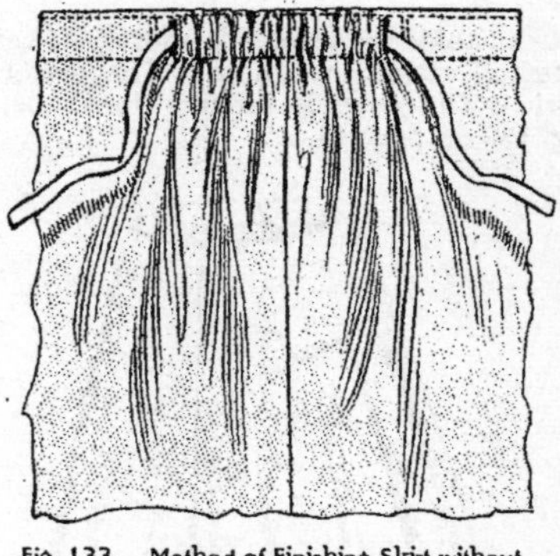

Fig. 133. Method of Finishing Skirt without Placket.

If the waist measure is smaller than that of the pattern, pin little darts into the cambric yoke to make it fit. This process will repay the slight trouble involved by giving a smooth and comfortably fitted garment. Two pieces should be cut from muslin by the yoke pattern, one to be used as a facing or lining.

If the yoke is not provided in the pattern, measure down from the waist to yoke depth and cut off the top of the skirt, making the cutting three-quarters of an inch above the lower edge of the yoke.

A Silk Petticoat may be finished at the top by a method which dispenses with a placket. (Fig. 133.) The entire upper edge of the skirt is finished with a bias facing. Stitch the facing to the skirt with the seam on the wrong side, turn the facing over and stitch directly on the edge; the remaining edge is turned in and stitched down flat. At the back, where the fulness commences, cut a slit in the skirt at each side.

The slits should be worked like buttonholes. Insert a tape or drawstring through one buttonhole and draw it over a short distance beyond the buttonhole on the opposite side. Tack it firmly. A second tape is put through the buttonhole near the last tacking and brought out through the one on the opposite side, where it should be tacked firmly just beyond the buttonhole. (Fig. 133.)

The Hem is turned up at the bottom, or a narrow ruffle is put on as shown in Figs. 38 and 39 on page 11, making the skirt three-quarters of an inch longer than the desired length. Gather the ruffle, quarter it, and stroke the gathers. Measure up from the bottom of the skirt the exact depth of ruffle and crease, folding in the right side of skirt. Insert the ruffle and stitch three-eighths of an inch from the crease. Fold the tuck back and make a second stitching along the fold. This uses up the three-quarters of an inch which was added to the length of the skirt.

DRAWERS are finished at the lower edge first. A gathered ruffle of either the plain material or embroidered edging makes a pretty trimming. It may be added in either of the ways shown on page 11. The depth of the hem, ruffle, etc., must be considered in measuring the length. If a row of insertion is desired at the head of the ruffle, the hem may be omitted and the insertion applied to the edge of the material with a French seam. The ruffling is joined to the insertion also in a French seam. If tucks are to be used as trimming, cut the drawers sufficiently long to allow for them. One-eighth inch or finer tucks in clusters of three or five are effective, either with or without an insertion of lace or embroidery between the clusters. All the edges are joined in felled seams.

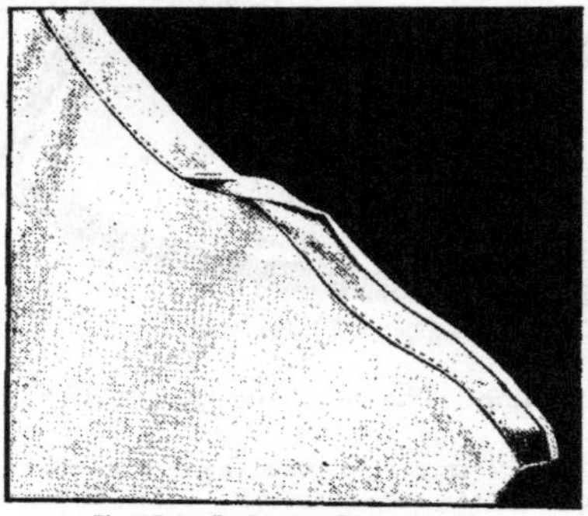

Fig. 134. Facing on Open Drawers

Open Drawers are made with the seam running from the front belt to the back, not joined, but hemmed or faced, as the pattern provides. If a facing is applied, stitch it to each leg portion from the waist to the front around past the joining seam, easing the facing on the curve, and continuing it up the back edge to the waist. Turn in the free edge of the facing and hem it to the inside of the garment. The manner of applying the facing is shown in Fig. 134.

In Fig. 135 is shown a pair of drawers that can take the place of a short petticoat, as they are cut in circular shape and fall quite full about the knees. The material is fine nainsook, long-cloth or French cambric. The yoke is circular in shape, and should be fitted to the figure as shown in Fig. 132 on page 41.

The lower edges of the drawers are turned up in narrow hems and the lace edge is inserted in the manner shown in Fig. 34, page 10. The lace may be fulled very slightly by drawing the strong thread which will be found in the top edge of nearly all laces. This will keep the lace from hooping; at the same time it is not full enough to look like a ruffle. Or, the lace edge may be whipped on to the edge of the hem by hand.

The rows of lace insertion are then applied in even rows. Measure with a notched card as shown in Fig. 24, page 7. Baste close to the edge of insertion. Turn to the wrong side and cut the material to within a narrow seam of the bastings. Turn in a very narrow hem which must come exactly under the edge of lace so that the work may be turned to the right side and the lace stitched on by machine, at the same time sewing in the narrow hem. An illustration of this method is given in Fig. 135.

Fig. 135. Circular Drawers on Fitted Yoke

If the ruffle at the lower edge of the garment is straight, the lace edge and insertion may be applied as illustrated in Figs. 34 and 35, on page 10. There are different ways of fitting the drawers at the waist. (Fig. 136.) If there is fulness at the top of the drawers, gather the top of the drawers according to the instructions given with the pattern, and stroke the gathers. The right side is lapped across the left at the front. The center front of both the yoke-pieces is marked with a colored thread, and the lower edge of one yoke is basted in a seam to the gathered top of the drawers, matching the notches in both, and making the seam toward the outside. The garment may then be tried on, to see if the distribution of the gathers is correct.

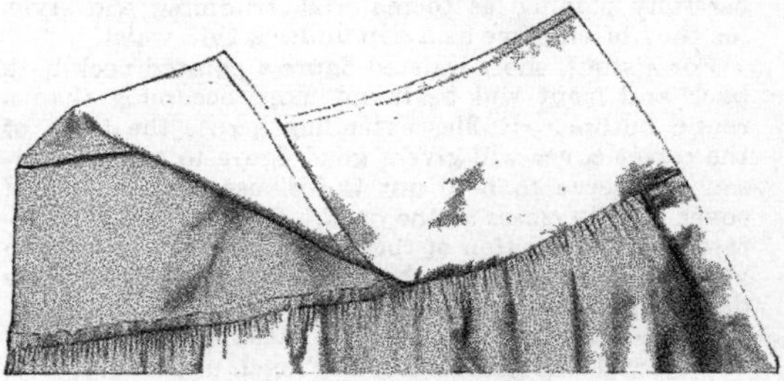

Fig. 136. Yoke Sewed to Drawers

The drawers portion may need raising a little into the yoke at either front or back if the figure requires it. After any needed alterations are made, the seam is stitched. The second piece is then placed even with the one joined to the drawers, but toward its wrong side—that is, the inner side of the garment—and a seam is stitched around the top or waist edge that will hold the two yokes together. The one on the inside (that has not been seamed to the drawers) is then turned over toward the outside, covering the top of the seam just made. Its lower edge is turned under a seam's width and is basted and afterwards stitched on, on the outside, to cover the seam joining the top of the drawers to the first yoke. This process may be readily understood by examining Fig. 136.

Drawers are sometimes fitted with darts instead of a yoke. In this case the darts are closed with felled seams, and the plaits laid in the back to hold the fulness in place are often stitched down a short distance on each fold edge. The waist edge of the drawers is finished with a bias facing. Fig. 137 illustrates the upper portion of a pair of drawers showing the first row of stitching. Clip the seam at the curves, turn over the facing and stitch at the top and bottom, as shown at the right-hand side of the illustration. The drawstrings or tapes are put in, one on each side, and sewed firmly. Or, the drawers may be fastened by a button and buttonhole. If preferred, the fulness, instead of being laid in a plait, can be gathered by the drawstring. Insert the tape and fasten the ends securely where the gathers begin.

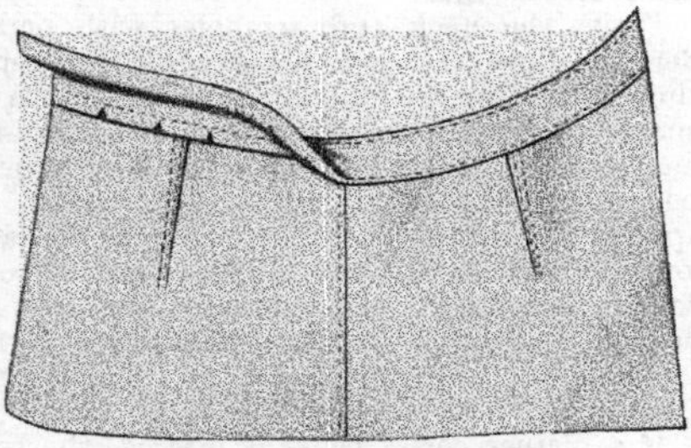

Fig. 137. Facing at Top of Drawers

Drawers cut in this way are not at all difficult to fit. There is just one point that needs the same care in these garments as in the skirt, and that is the adjustment to the figure that has very full abdominal development and is flat at the back. In such a case, if the drawers are cut exactly by the pattern, they will draw from the back to the front. If the waistline of the drawers is raised a little in the back, to counteract this tendency the entire garment will be made shorter. The correct way is to allow an extra inch or two at the top on the fronts in cutting, tapering the allowance away to nothing just over the hip. In patterns for the larger waist measures a moderate allowance is made at the abdomen, but when the development is unusually large, it is better to make a still greater allowance in cutting.

For Closed Drawers, cut the slits at the side like the pattern and finish with a continuous placket. The two parts are seamed together with a flat-fell and the top is gathered. The lap at the front of the opening is turned under at the joining, and the one at the back extends out to form an underlap. The facing or yokes are attached in the manner illustrated on page 43. A button and buttonhole is used for fastening the front of the drawers to the back.

If worn with a waist, buttonholes only are needed in the ends of the bands, and at the center front and center back.

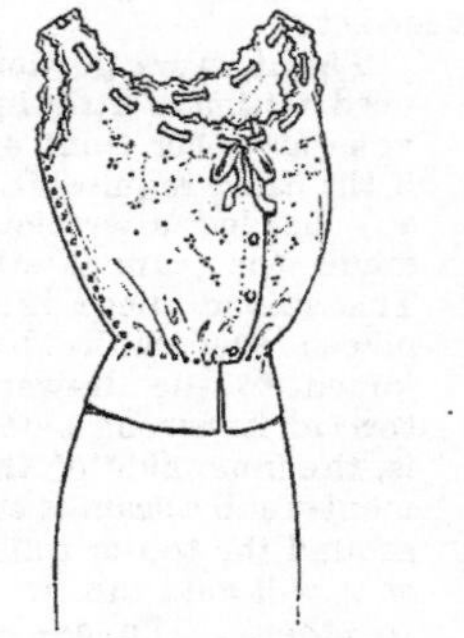

Fig. 138. Hand-Embroidered Corset Cover

CORSET COVERS have the widest range of design and style among undergarments. They should be carefully planned as to material, trimming and style, for they often serve as a slip under a thin waist.

For a stout, short-waisted figure a pointed neck both back and front will be found more becoming than a round outline. Ruffles extending across the front of the corset cover will give a good figure to a slight person and serve to hold out the blouse. This style of cover usually closes at the back. The pattern is perforated for the position of the ruffles. Corset covers can very easily be made by hand, and they are extremely dainty, pleasant handwork.

Hand-made underclothes are steadily gaining popularity with the general use of French underwear. Its very simplicity expresses refinement and daintiness. Very narrow tucks, insets of lace and motifs of hand embroidery are used as trimming.

A dainty corset cover may be made of either nainsook or cambric. The under-arm and shoulder seams are put together with veining or stitched with a French or felled seam. If a peplum is used, it is fitted like the yoke of drawers. Gather the corset cover at the waist as directed in the pattern instructions, and sew it to the peplum in a French seam. Or, the seams may be turned from the inside, and a narrow bias strip basted on and stitched over the seam. This bias seam is hemmed over as a narrow facing. If preferred, the waist may be gathered into a strip of beading and sewed on in a French seam. The bottom edge has a narrow hem.

Finish the neck and armholes with embroidered scallops as shown in Fig. 138. Buttonhole tiny slashes for the ribbon draw-strings. A few sprays of flowers scattered over the front or a monogram in hand embroidery makes a pretty trimming. Medallions may be purchased and applied if the hand embroidery seems too laborious. Valenciennes insertion inset in the fronts, combined with a little embroidery in a fancy design, makes a dainty trimming. Several methods for applying laces, etc., are given in Chapter XV, "Unlined Waists."

If a plainer corset cover is desired, the top is hemmed and beading and lace overhanded to it as a finish. A very narrow bias facing is basted around the right side of the armhole, stitched, basted over on the wrong side, and stitched again. Care must be taken in basting on the bias strip to give plenty of ease around the curve of the armhole so that it will not draw when turned over. The lace edge should be sewed on the armhole after it is faced.

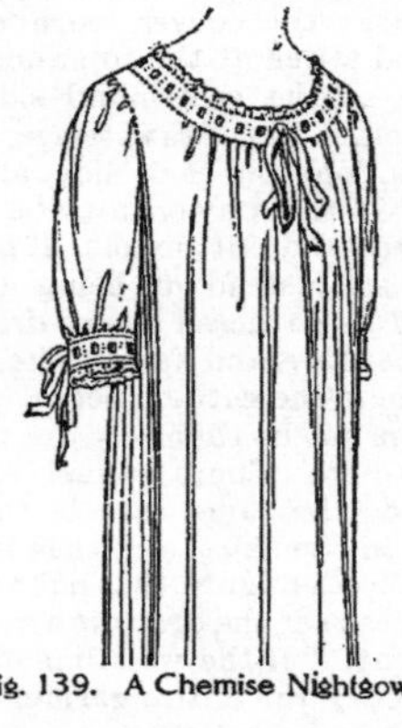

Fig. 139. A Chemise Nightgown

COMBINATION GARMENTS dispose of much of the useless material about the hips and waist, are excellent for stout figures, and give a better fit to the one-piece dress.

If the corset cover and skirt are cut in one, the garment is basted and carefully fitted and stitched in French seams. If cut separately, each is fitted and them basted together with the seam toward the outside, which is afterwards covered with narrow beading. The skirt is closed directly in line with the closing of the corset cover. The skirt opening is made the necessary length and finished like the placket for underwear, which is shown in the process of making on page 34.

NIGHTGOWNS may be made of cambric, nainsook, long cloth, dimity or cross-bar materials, and trimmed with lace, embroidery, or a touch of handwork. The parts are joined by French seams and a hem turned up at the bottom.

The Chemise Nightgown slips over the head and may be gathered into a fitted yoke or finished with an insertion or beading. (Fig. 139.) It may also be gathered into a binding of sheer lawn, trimmed in any pretty fashion. The binding should be about three-quarters of an inch wide after it is joined. The ribbon is run through it instead of through a beading. If desired, beading or narrow insertion may be used for attaching this binding to the gown. Beading is inserted between the turned-in edges of the binding and all three edges held together with one row of stitching. The beading is then joined to the garment in a tiny French seam. The ends of the binding are made to meet in front so as to form openings through which the ribbon is passed.

In a High-Neck Gown the opening is cut as directed in the pattern instructions. The edges are usually turned under for hems, the right lapping over the left and machine-stitched across the bottom. Another kind of finish for the neck is a strap, yoke-shaped to fit the neck of the gown smoothly. It gives a simple method of closing, one side entirely covering the other. The strap may be trimmed with feather-stitching or hand embroidery. When the yoke is not lined, the outer edge is turned under in a narrow hem. A buttoned through closing is better for this style than the fly. The neck decoration is usually repeated in the sleeve.

The Sleeves are gathered twice at the top. Baste the seam in the armhole with the seam toward the outside and stitch close to the edge. Now turn the seam and stitch again, having the finished seam at the inside of the garment. Care must be taken that the gathers are evenly distributed between the notches of the pattern, and drawn down straight from the first stitching.

CHAPTER IX

INFANTS' CLOTHES

AN INFANT'S WARDROBE should be characterized by extreme daintiness of materials, trimming and workmanship. Baby clothes are not subject to sudden changes of style, but there are improvements instituted from time to time, primarily with a view to insuring greater comfort to the child in the wearing of the garments and to making the process of dressing an infant a less tedious operation. Buttons and buttonholes are not desirable, except on the dresses, slips and outer garments.

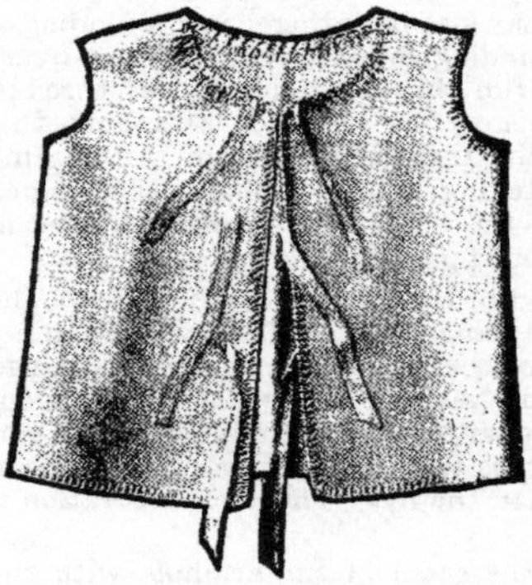

Fig. 140. Flannel Shirt with Crocheted Edges

SHIRTS should be made either of softest baby flannel, or of fine linen, nainsook, etc. Every stitch should be made by hand.

In the Flannel Shirt it is necessary to exercise great care in finishing all of the seams, hems and turnings as flatly as possible, as otherwise they are likely to render the child uncomfortable. The shoulder and under-arm seams should be pressed open, after stitching, and both seam edges catch-stitched on the inside of the garment.

Double turned hems are frequently dispensed with on the front and lower edges of shirts. In some cases the flannel is turned only once and a loose buttonhole or crochet-stitch in soft Saxony wool or silk floss is made over the edge. This finish is shown in Fig. 140.

Fig. 141. An Infant's Linen Shirt

A Linen or *Nainsook Shirt* is made with felled seams. The front and lower edges are finished with a hem, and the neck and armholes with narrow bias facings of the material. Around the neck the facing serves also as a casing for the drawstring. If fine lace is used as trimming, the armhole edges are not faced, but are merely rolled and the lace is whipped to them. (Fig. 141.)

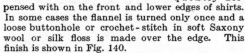

Fig. 142. A Flannel Band

A FLANNEL BAND for an infant is shown in Fig. 142. It is of flannel twenty-seven inches long and about six inches wide. All the edges are turned over on the outside, one and a quarter inches and catch-stitched. (Fig. 142.)

A PINNING BLANKET or BARRIE-COAT is used in place of the flannel petticoat. After the skirt portion is cut, the front and lower edges are turned in hems and feather-stitched on the outside. (See Fig. 143 on the following page.)

The body is cut from fine cambric, and though the edges may be bound or faced, it is better to make the body double. Join the shoulder edges of both the outside and inside, and press the seams open. Lay the two body portions evenly together, with the shoulder seams of both toward the outside. Stitch a seam around the upper edge and across the lower edge to the notches. The ends are left open until the tape is inserted. The body is stitched between the notches after the skirt is joined to it. After they are stitched, the two body parts are turned to bring the seam edges inside. The edges at the pointed ends are turned in and the end of the piece of tape is slipped into each opening. Gather the skirt and join it to the body as shown in Fig. 143. Baste around the armhole about one inch from the edge to keep the two portions evenly together. Clip the raw edges and turn one in a seam's width and baste it; then turn the other edge in and baste it to the first. Stitch by machine or overhand the two folded edges together to finish the armhole. The edges of the body portion should be basted and then featherstitched. Baste about an inch each side of the perforations that indicate the opening to be made at the left side. Cut through the perforations and bind the opening with soft ribbon or silk tape. If preferred, the skirt may be mounted on a straight band, made double, instead of on the shaped body. The straight band can be lapped and hemmed.

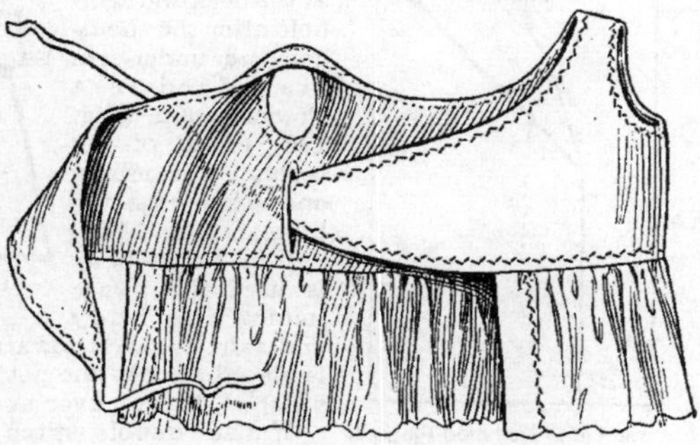

Fig. 143. A Pinning-Blanket with Tie Ends

AN INFANT'S PETTICOAT is finished according to the material of which it is made. *The Flannel Petticoat* has the seams stitched and finished as shown in Figs. 11 or 12, on page 5. The bottom of the skirt may be embroidered in scallops, or the hem finished as shown in Fig. 131, page 39.

A flannel petticoat which hangs from the shoulders and has no separate body or placket is shown in Fig. 144. It is fastened on one or both shoulders by ribbons or buttons and buttonholes. The neck and armholes of this style of petticoat are usually bound with ribbon or tape, though a scalloped edge worked with white embroidery silk makes the little garment much prettier. If it is to be embroidered do not cut out the neck and armholes, but mark the outline of the pattern with a colored thread. The design can then be stamped along the outline and cut out after the embroidery is done.

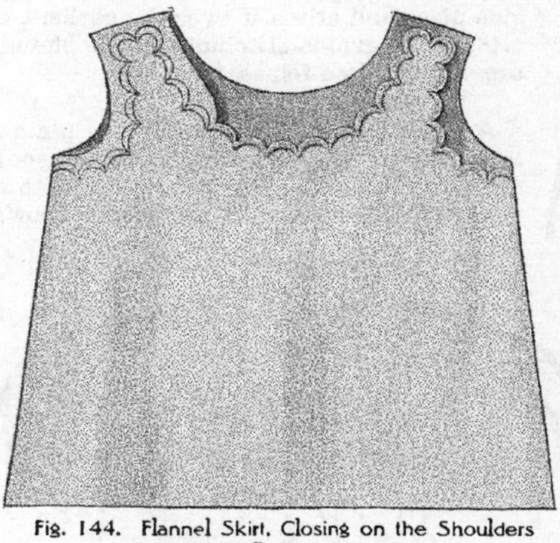

Fig. 144. Flannel Skirt, Closing on the Shoulders
Transfer Scallop Design 10420

The under-arm seams are finished in the regulation manner with catch-stitching or featherstitching before the embroidery is begun.

The Nainsook or *Cambric Petticoat* is finished in French seams. The lower edge of the skirt may be finished with a deep hem or with tucks, insertion and edging. The upper edge is gathered with fine stitches and joined to the body after the placket has been hemmed with a very narrow hem on one side, and one three-quarters of an inch wide on the other. Lap the wide hem over the narrow (Fig. 145), and tack firmly at the bottom

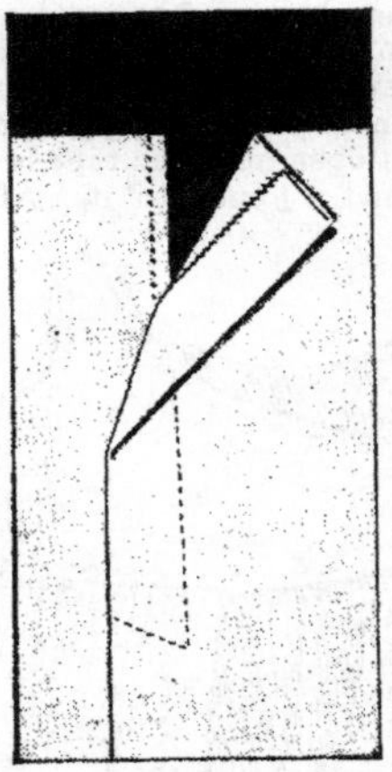

Fig. 145. Hemmed Placket

of the placket with two rows of machine stitching, preferably running slanting.

The body is either cut single and faced at the neck and armhole after the shoulder and under-arm are joined in a French seam (Fig. 146), or cut of two layers of cambric, one serving as the lining. (Fig. 147.)

Fig. 146. Petticoat Joined to Single Body

If a single body is used the seam joining the body and skirt is made toward the inside. A bias strip of cambric is placed next to the petticoat in the same seam, which is then stitched, turned over and hemmed to the body.

If made double, stitch the under-arm seams of both outside and lining; place the right sides of the material together and stitch all except the lower edge and shoulder seams. Clip the curved edges, turn the body right side out and crease along the sewing line. It may be stitched again on the outside to strengthen the edges and hold the seams in position. The top of the petticoat is gathered and basted to the lining with the seam toward the inside. Turn this seam up on the body; turn in the edge of the outside piece and stitch it over the gathers, covering all previous stitchings. The shoulders are stitched in a fell seam.

Fig. 147. Petticoat Joined to Double Body

A SLIP is invariably made very plain and loose, of fine, sheer Persian lawn, nainsook or dimity. It should be put together with narrow French seams. In the model shown in Fig. 148, the neck is finished with a bias binding. A narrow tape is run through the binding so that the neck can be drawn up to the right size when the slip is worn. Make an eyelet in the outside of the neck-binding just in front of the underlapping hem. Pass the ribbon through this opening so that it will meet the other end that comes from the opening of the overlapping hem.

The neck and sleeves, which should be gathered into narrow bands at the bottom, may be edged with a frill of lace. The back is cut down through the

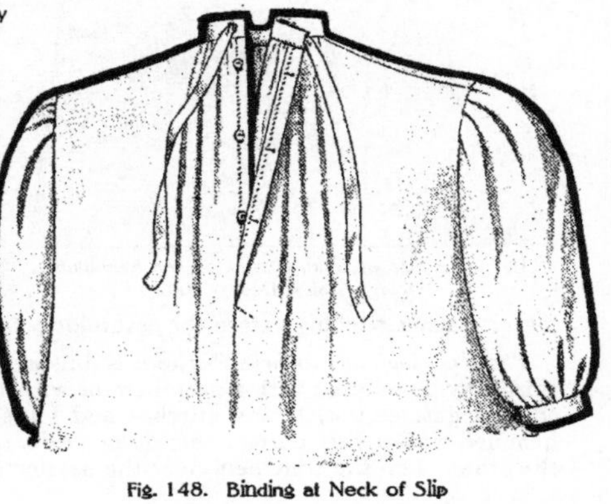

Fig. 148. Binding at Neck of Slip

center to the depth given for the opening in the pattern instructions. Each edge of the opening is finished with a tiny hem. A plait is then made deep enough to bring the opening back one-half inch from the edge. It is held in place by a slanting row of stitching at the end of the opening. (Fig. 149.)

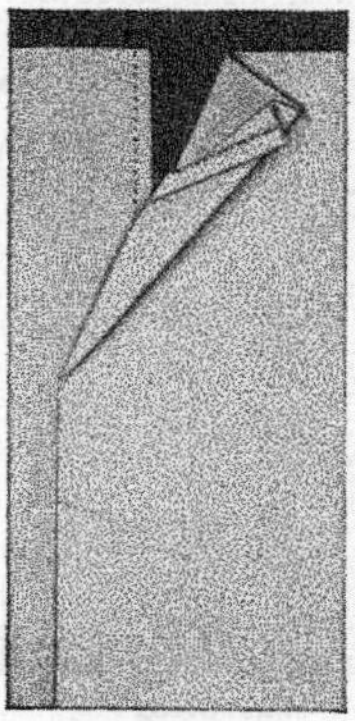

Fig. 149. Finish at Closing

THE KIMONO or WRAPPER is a very practical garment and may be made of flannel, cashmere or any light-weight woolen material. A very pretty little garment may be made of French flannel, dotted or plain, with a shaped band of contrasting silk or flannel. (Fig. 150.)

The garment is collarless, and the neck and front edges, as well as the sleeves, are finished with shaped bands. The band is basted to the inside of the wrapper, along the neck and front edges. After it is stitched on, the band is rolled over on the outside of the wrapper and basted in such a manner that it extends a trifle beyond the joining seam. The other edge of the band is turned in and basted flat to the material and is held in position by a simple featherstitch. When a straight band is used, one long edge is joined to the wrapper with the seam toward the outside; the other edge is then turned under and basted over the seam as shown in Fig. 151.

Fig. 150. Applying a Facing

French knots and various fancy stitches, scallops or little trailing vines of embroidery can be used very effectively in the trimming of these wrappers. Silk or satin ribbon may be used for the straight band. Some of these kimono wrappers are lined throughout with soft India silk. The wrapper design mentioned above is perforated in the correct length for a house sack. This convenient little garment is made like the wrapper in every particular, except the length.

A dainty little sack is made of white cashmere lined with pale pink India silk. Both the outside and lining portions are cut exactly alike, the seams stitched and pressed open. The sack and lining are then basted together, with seams turned toward the inside. The sleeve portions are gathered separately at the top. Sew the outside material of the sleeve in at the armhole. Turn the raw edge of the sleeve lining under, gather it and hem to the armhole. A tiny turnover collar may be added with the same kind of finish. The edges of the sack may be turned in and secured with a row of featherstitching, or they may be buttonholed together by a scalloped edge. Both finishes are shown in Chapter IV "Practical and Ornamental Stitches."

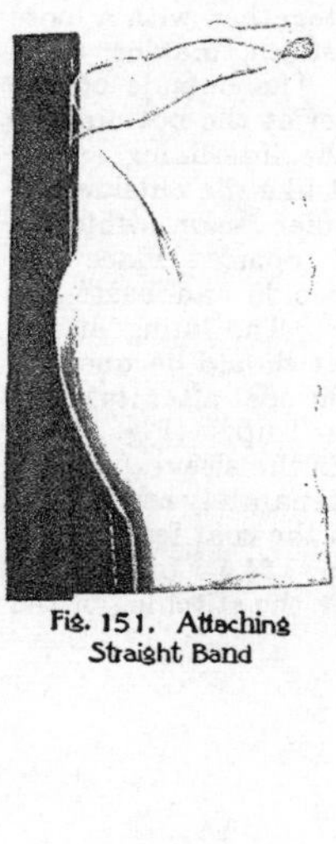

Fig. 151. Attaching Straight Band

THE DRESS is made practically in the same way as the slip. Nothing but the finest material should be used, batiste, nainsook or sheer linen. Simple designs with a few hand-run tucks, a bit of embroidery, featherstitching or drawn-work make a far daintier gown than heavy material, lavishly trimmed with lace or machine embroidery. There are many excellent patterns for baby dresses, and one who has the time and taste to spend on the layette will find it a fascinating occupation.

A Dainty Yoke may be made by over-handing alternate rows of lace insertion and embroidery together. Fine tucking rolled and whipped to lace insertion, also makes a pretty yoke. Narrow veining or hemstitched beading as shown in Fig. 152, joins the yoke to the dress. It is rolled and whipped on, or sewed in a tiny French seam. The shoulder seams are joined by beading, which is also used as a finish for the neck and sleeves.

If the Skirt is made of flouncing with an embroidered or hemstitched edge, the fulness under the arm is usually disposed of in an inverted plait. This plait takes the place of a gored seam and enables one to keep the outlines at the bottom perfectly straight. The edges are joined at the back to a convenient depth for the opening and a placket is finished as shown in Fig. 148.

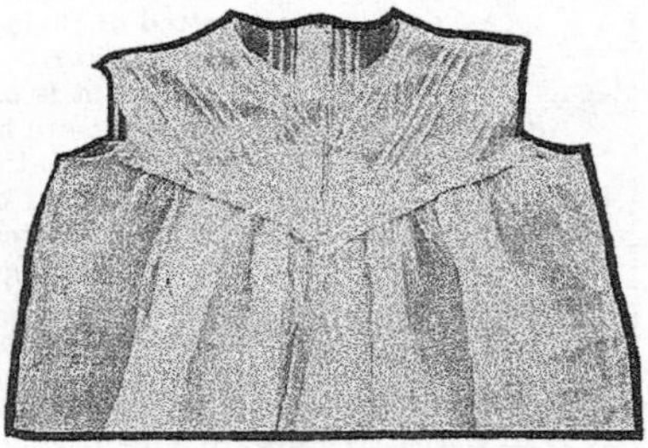
Fig. 152. Yoke for Infants' Dress

In Cutting a dress from any plain material, follow the instructions on the pattern. The concealment of the back seam is usually arranged for under the plait. The edge may be hemmed by hand, tucked or ornamented in any way desired. The placket opening is cut and finished in the center of the back piece.

Some of these patterns are arranged so that the material may be cut with a bias seam under the arm, if it should be desired, which gives the garment a curved lower edge.

THE CLOAK and OUTDOOR GARMENTS are made more or less elaborately according to one's taste and needs. White is generally used and daintiness and simplicity are the most desirable characteristics. In summer, pretty little cloaks are made of piqué and cashmere. The lower and front edges may be hemmed by hand or held in place by feather-stitching on the outside, or the hem may be stitched by machine. The same finish is carried out at the neck and wrist. The buttonholed edge is a suitable finish for piqué.

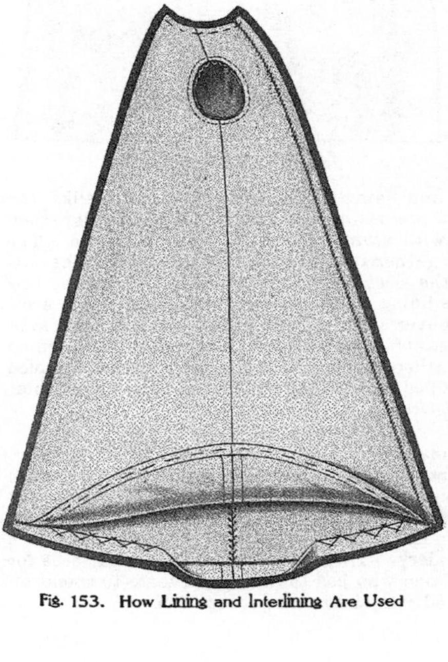
Fig. 153. How Lining and Interlining Are Used

Even for colder weather cashmere may still be used with a warm interlining. Bedford cord and broadcloth make excellent coats. Wool wadding or a soft flannel are best for the interlining. It should be cut without the seam and hem allowance Instead of making the regular seam, draw the shoulder and under-arm edges together with a loose overhand or ball-stitch, making them lie perfectly flat. The outside of the coat is turned under at the bottom and catch-stitched to the interlining.

The Lining is cut like the outside and seamed in a regular seam, which is afterward pressed open. Place the seams toward the inside and baste the lining to the coat. The lining at the bottom of the coat should be one-half inch shorter than the coat after its lower edge has been turned up. (Fig. 153.)

Place the lining in the sleeves; gather sleeve and lining separately at the top. Stitch the sleeve in the coat leaving the lining loose. (Fig. 154.) Later it is hemmed down over the stitching of the armhole.

The Collar is made unlined, with a facing of the lining material. It is stitched to the neck of the coat, and the lining of the coat hemmed against this stitching. If the coat has a cape it is sewed on like the collar. The edge of the collar, the wrist and the cape may be trimmed with fancy braid, lace or handwork.

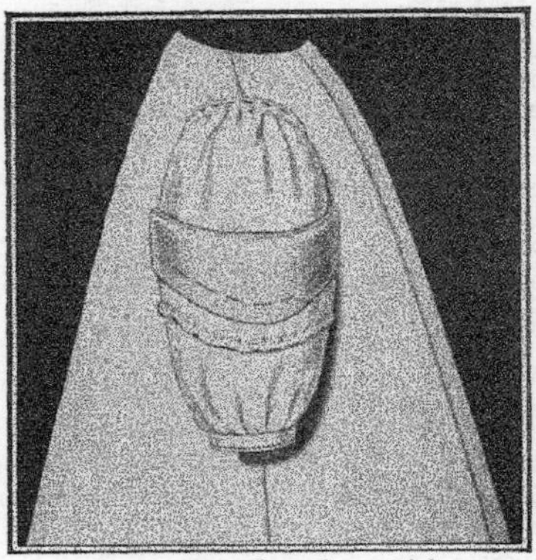

Fig. 154. Detail of Sleeve Lining

The cloak is preferably lined with soft China silk, and if wool wadding is used, the wool is picked away from the cheese-cloth around the seams to avoid bulkiness at these points.

LITTLE SHOES and SLIPPERS made of a washable material are a pretty part of the layette. The piqué or other material is cut according to a slipper pattern, following the directions given on the pattern envelope. The sole is cut from silesia or some other stout lining fabric. The sole and upper part of the shoe should be lined with flannel. The outside material and the flannel lining are seamed separately and the seams pressed open. They are then basted together with their edges even. The upper and lower edges of the slipper are bound with a bias seam binding. The upper part and the sole are overhanded together on the wrong side and the shoe is turned right side out. The ankle straps are lined with cambric. Work the buttonhole in the right hand strap of one slipper and in the left hand strap of the other. Flat bows run through tiny buckles, or rosettes of baby ribbon, can be used to trim the bootees.

CHAPTER X

CHILDREN'S CLOTHES

CHILDREN'S CLOTHES should be made very simply. Use a good quality material and suitably childish colors. The one-piece dress is an accepted style for small boys and girls, and can be made of wool, linen or cotton materials. Directions for finishing dresses made of sheer materials will be found in Chapter IX, "Infants' Clothes." For instructions on the making of a sailor or naval suit, see Chapter XI.

THE RUSSIAN DRESS has a side-front closing, and the buttonholes may be made through the material or in a fly applied underneath the overlapping edge. Patterns for this style of garment are to be had either with or without plaits. A good design for little folks is a perfectly plain dress confined at the waist with a belt of leather or of the dress material. An inverted plait is sometimes allowed at the under-arm seams, which gives extra fulness to the skirt. The neck and wrists, and sometimes the closing edges, are usually finished with narrow bands.

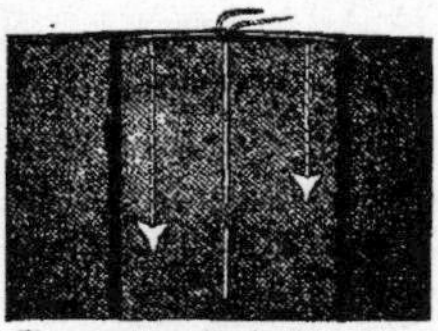

Fig. 155. Stitching on Box Plait Finished with Crow's-Foot

A Plaited Design is very becoming to little girls. The front and back portions of the dress are laid in plaits which are stitched only to the belt line. The closing is arranged under one of the plaits, either at the front or back. Before cutting out, place the front and back of pattern on the material, and if piecing is necessary, plan to have the joining concealed under a plait. Mark all perforations and notches plainly on the material. To make the box plaits, bring the lines of perforations together; baste and stitch through them. Bring the center of the plait over the line of stitching and spread it to form a box plait. Baste the plait in position along both folds and stitch it down, if desired. A crow's-foot (Fig. 155) worked at the end of each row of stitching may be used. The method of making a crow's-foot is given in Chapter IV, "Practical and Ornamental Stitches."

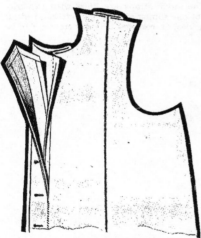

Fig. 156. Laps Finishing Closing Edges

The Closing, cut under a plait and finished with laps for buttons and buttonholes, is shown in Fig. 156. The slash for the opening was made under the plait a seam's width from the sewing. The laps are made double, and when attached should be a little narrower than the plait which covers them. By referring to the illustration, the method of joining the laps to the edges of the opening will be readily understood.

A Buttonhole Fly is provided in some patterns by a hem allowed under the plait. The edge is turned under once, and basted as for a hem, but not stitched. The raw edge is not turned in a seam, but is inserted in the box plait and secured with the one stitch-

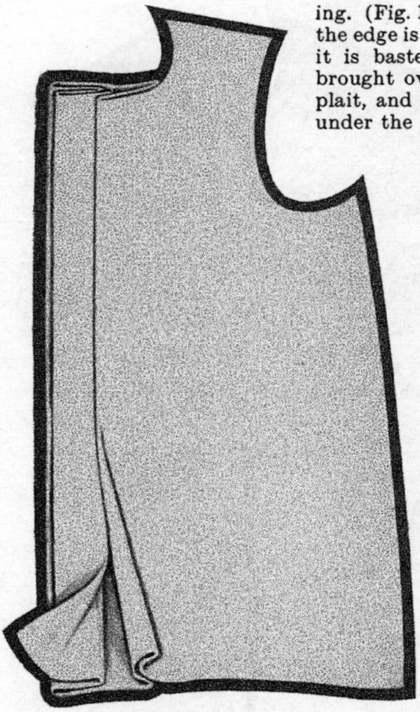

Fig. 157. Hem Used as Fly Under Plait

ing. (Fig. 157.) If the hem is not allowed on the pattern the edge is brought over to the line of perforations, where it is basted and stitched. The center of the plait is brought over to the line of stitching forming the box plait, and is then basted in position. To the raw edge under the plait, stitch a lengthwise strip of material cut to extend to within one-quarter of an inch of the outer edge of the plait, to form the fly for the buttonholes. Hem the free edge of the strip against the line of sewing. Instructions for the most suitable finish for each garment will be found on the pattern. The button side of the garment can be finished with a hem or an underlap. (Fig. 158.)

A Yoke can be joined to the front of a dress as shown in Fig. 159 on the following page. Cut the yoke and turn the edge under a seam's width, clipping the edge where necessary to make it lie flat. Baste the yoke over the top of the front of the dress. To the wrong side, baste a bias strip of material with its edges turned under. Place two rows of stitching across the yoke, stitching from the outside. They will catch through the bias facing that is basted underneath, and which covers the seam, making a neat finish on the inside. This finish is desirable for a summer dress, as it makes it unnecessary to line the yoke. If a lining is used, however, it is cut like the yoke pattern, and the top of the dress portion is enclosed between the turned-under edges of the yoke and its lining.

Sleeves are made in various ways. They may be gathered at the wrist and set into a cuff or wristband, or the lower part of the sleeve may be stitched in plaits forming its own cuff. After laying the plaits according to the pattern instructions, baste them flat to the sleeve and stitch through both plait and sleeve. Stitch the seam of the sleeve at the openings, with the extensions beyond the edges of the seam. On the front edge this extension is turned under for a hem, and on the other extension a tiny hem is turned in along the upper end and the long side. This extension is meant for an underlap. Underface the wrist as shown in Fig. 161. Close the opening with buttons and buttonholes. (Fig. 162.)

A Cuff, if one is used, is made of two pieces of material cut from the cuff pattern. These two pieces are basted together, with the right sides facing each other. The stitching is made close to

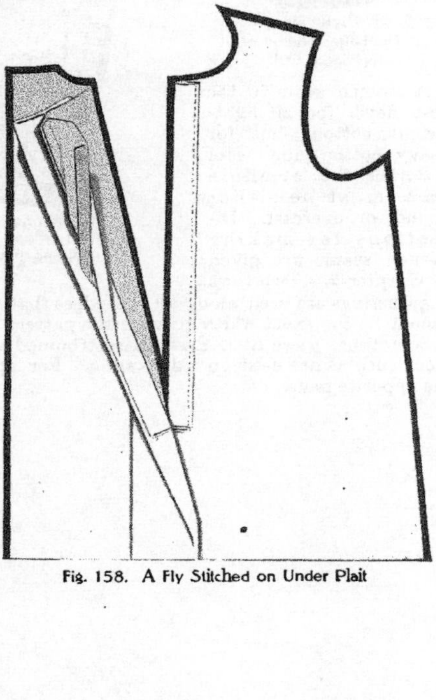

Fig. 158. A Fly Stitched on Under Plait

the edge, and runs around the two ends and the lower edge. The cuff is then turned right side out and carefully basted so that the stitching will come in the crease. Join the upper edge of the cuff portion to the lower edge of the sleeve, with the seam toward the outside. The other cuff portion is turned under and basted over the seam. Stitching at the edges, around all four sides, finishes the cuff.

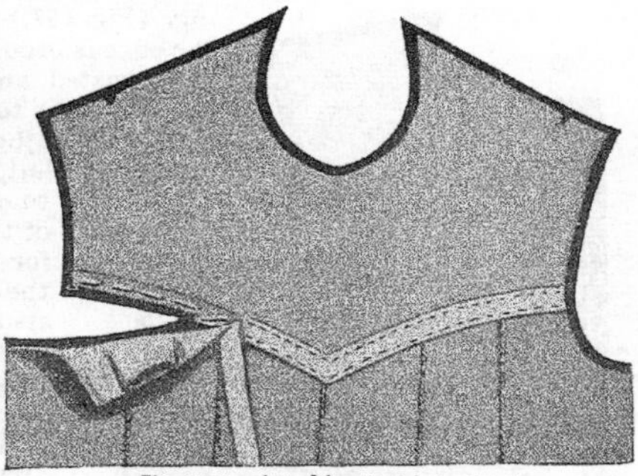

Fig. 159. Attaching Yoke to Front

Buttons and buttonholes are also used in closing the cuff, which is made to lap the width of the extension. Fig. 160 shows the cuff basted to the sleeve in preparation for stitching. If the sleeve has a box plait extending to the top, gather the sleeve from the edges of the plait to the notches, but do not gather the sleeve across the box plait.

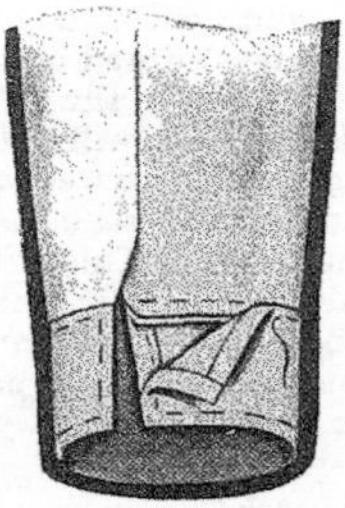

Right Side
Fig. 160. Method of Applying a Cuff

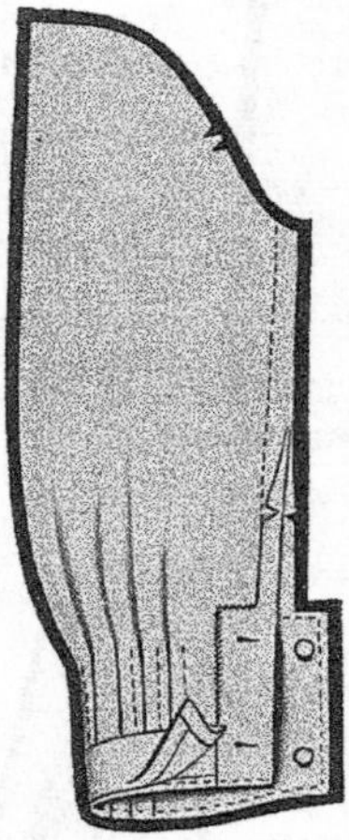

Wrong Side
Fig. 161. Method of Finishing Sleeve

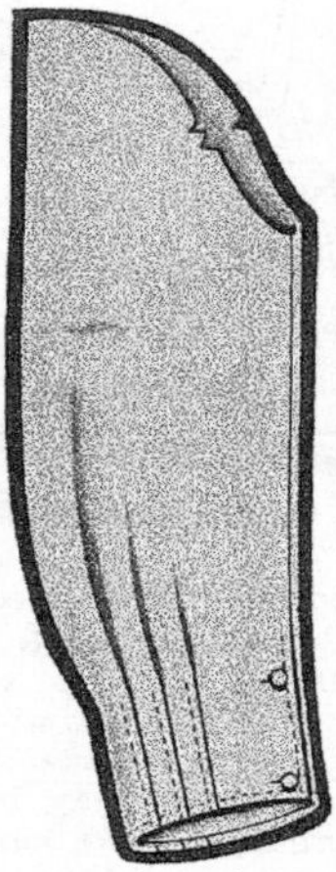

Right Side
Fig. 162. Finished Sleeve Closed

A French seam is the best finish for all light-weight cottons, but for heavy cotton and wool materials the armhole seams must be either bound or overcast. Directions for making French seams are given in Chapter I. Two rows of gatherings are used along all the edges that are to be gathered. The finished hem should be the exact width given in the pattern instructions.

Sometimes these little dresses are trimmed with an embroidered star or other emblem such as are used on sailor suits. For appropriate designs for this purpose see the opposite page.

CHAPTER XI

SAILOR OR NAVAL SUITS

ALMOST invariably the small boy and girl, if given any voice in the choosing of their clothes, will select the suit that looks most like a uniform. Probably this is the reason why the styles permitting the use of brass buttons, emblems or insignia meet with such general and long-continued favor.

EMBLEMS and CHEVRONS in the various groups, or sets of anchors, bars, eagles and stars, finished and ready to sew on, can be bought, but they are never as satisfactory as the designs that can be stamped on the dress itself. Sometimes the figures are worked in the center of a piece of broadcloth or linen, which is cut square or oblong, or possibly in shield shape, and attached to the sleeve with a row of catch-stitching.

Fig. 163. Emblems and Chevrons

The mother who makes her children's clothes is sometimes confronted with the problem of selecting some kind of an embroidered emblem, and for this reason we offer the different combinations illustrated above. The chevrons or stripes are not padded but should be made of strips of scarlet three-eighths of an inch wide, separated one-fourth inch and sewed on flat with an overlock stitch of scarlet silk on the edges.

In working the specialty marks and eagles, an easier plan than the one of cutting the figures out of pasteboard and working over them, is to baste a piece of canvas or crinoline on the wrong side of the material, and work right through it, cutting the edges of the canvas away after the figure has been completed.

Light-weight twisted embroidery silk, mercerized cotton, or a linen thread may be used to advantage, for in this work smoothness is the most desirable feature, and the threads should all be placed in such a way as to lie next to one another, but not overlap.

On suits of galatea, chambray, linen or any of the pretty cotton materials used for children's clothes, the work may be done with cotton, either plain or mercerized. This thread is more suitable than silk for suits which need frequent washing. The sleeve emblem may be repeated on the front of the blouse or shield, or a simpler design—a star or anchor, for instance—may be used if preferred.

THE SAILOR or NAVAL SUIT is one of the most attractive costumes for young girls for any season of the year. This type of dress makes excellent school and play dresses. The blouse is particularly good for gymnasium suits. There are many modifications of the sailor dress, and a great variety of patterns.

Dark navy-blue flannel and bleached cotton drill are the materials used for these blouses or overshirts, as they are called. According to the regulations governing the uniforms of officers and enlisted men of the navy, the dark-blue flannel blouses are trimmed with white linen tape, while the cotton drill blouses are made with sailor collar and cuffs of dark-blue flannel, which are also trimmed with the tape.

In adapting this style for misses' and girls' wear, it is not necessary to be governed absolutely by the ironclad rules regarding color and material which are observed in the navy. Besides the regulation navy-blue and white, brown, gray and red, and the unbleached "khaki" shades are considered quite correct for sailor dresses. Serge, cheviot, prunella cloth and panama suiting are appropriate woolen materials, while linen, duck, piqué, gingham, galatea, etc., are a few of the suitable wash fabrics.

The selection of the emblems for the "rating badge" on the sleeve of the blouse makes quite an interesting study. The navy regulations state that the rating badge shall be made of the garment material, its decoration to consist of a spread eagle above a specialty mark, and a class chevron.

Fig. 164. Boatswain's Mate First-Class

Fig. 165. Rating Badge for Chief Master-at-Arms

For blue clothing, the eagle and specialty marks should be embroidered in white, and for white clothing they should be worked in blue silk. The naval uniform regulations further order that the rating badge shall be worn by all petty officers of the starboard watch on the right sleeve, midway between the shoulder and the elbow; by all petty officers of the port watch the badge is on the left sleeve. This statement eliminates any doubt as to the correct placing of the rating badge, as, in accordance with these instructions, either sleeve is correct. The chevrons show the class of the officer, while the specialty marks indicate his position in the marine service.

In using these emblems on a girl's blouse, it is a pretty fancy to select the specialty marks worn by the father or brother who is enlisted, or even an insignia indicating the trade or professional calling followed by a male member of the wearer's family, such as engineer, electrician, printer, carpenter, plumber, machinist, etc. The emblem may be placed on the shield also, and a five-pointed star should be embroidered on both corners of the collar. Excellent transfer stamping patterns can be purchased for the emblems, stars, etc.

TO MAKE THE BLOUSE, baste the seams with notches matching, and try the blouse on, either by slipping over the head or lapping the fronts, as directed in the pattern instructions. If a yoke-facing is used, the under-arm seams are left open to facilitate the work. The shoulder seams of the blouse are joined with the seams toward the outside; those of the yoke-facing toward the wrong side. Stitch and press the seams open.

The lower edge of the yoke is turned under a seam's width. If the yoke has a curved lower outline, the turned-under portion at the fullest part of the curves must be slightly eased, while at the sharp points it must be slashed as shown in Fig. 166. Lay the blouse flat on the table, spread out its entire length. Place the yoke on the blouse so that the shoulder seams come exactly together and the yoke lies smoothly on the blouse. Pin the yoke to hold it in place, then baste and stitch it to the blouse.

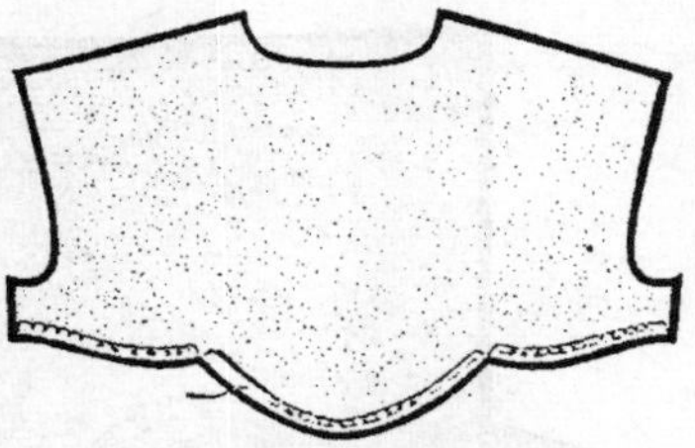

Fig. 166. Turning Edge of Yoke

Plaits are made in the regulation sleeve by creasing from the perforations at the bottom to the corresponding perforations at cuff depth. These creases are brought over to the position marked by perforations and the plaits are stitched along the fold edge before the seam is closed.

The illustration below shows how the blouse may be laid out on the table for convenience in joining the sleeve. Baste the sleeve to the yoke with the usual three-eighths-of-an-inch seam and then stitch it. Turn under the armhole of the blouse three-eighths of an inch, baste it over the seam, and fell it down. Make a second stitching on the body of the blouse one-quarter of an inch from the seam. The under-arm and sleeve seams have been left open until now, making the work easier to handle and also making it possible to sew the rating badge on the sleeve properly.

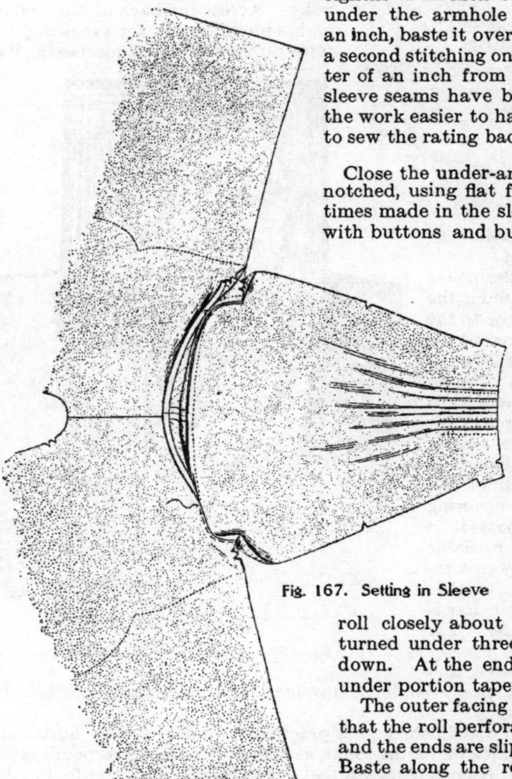

Fig. 167. Setting in Sleeve

Close the under-arm seams and the sleeve seams as notched, using flat felled seams. A placket is sometimes made in the sleeve at the wrist, which is closed with buttons and buttonholes. The method for making this style of sleeve, with and without a cuff, is given in Chapter X, "Children's Clothes."

A hem is turned at the bottom of the blouse, and, if the pattern instructions direct, an elastic is inserted to hold the blouse in place.

THE COLLAR is joined to the neck with the seam toward the inside. (Fig. 168.) The collar is marked with notches showing where it joins the blouse, and, in basting it on, the edge should be stretched between the notches to fit the corresponding edge of the blouse thus causing the collar to roll closely about the neck. The outer edges are turned under three-eighths of an inch and basted down. At the end of the slash in front, the turned-under portion tapers away to a point.

The outer facing is placed on the collar so carefully that the roll perforations will come exactly together and the ends are slipped under the fronts. (Fig. 169.) Baste along the roll perforations. The neck edge of the facing is stretched sufficiently to make it lie smoothly when the collar is rolled back. After pinning the collar facing around the neck and down the

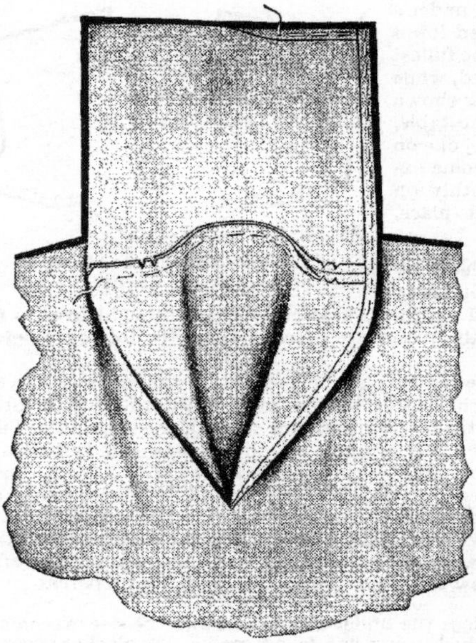

Fig. 168. Basting on Collar

front, roll the collar and facing over at the perforations, and roll the fronts back to the single perforations near the front edge. Put your hand under the collar and smooth it outward, so that it does not wrinkle on the collar facing.

Turn the edge of the collar facing under, even with the collar. Baste the collar and the facing together across the bottom and sides, up to the seam joining the collar and blouse. From that point down, take out the pins that hold the collar facing to the blouse.

The collar facing is trimmed with three rows of linen tape, set its own width apart and stitched on both edges. If you sew the tape on the collar facing after the latter is on the blouse, the stitching will show on the front of your yoke. Across the back of the collar it makes no difference, for the facing is on top, and the stitching underneath. Baste the linen tape carefully to the collar facing and stitch it on both edges.

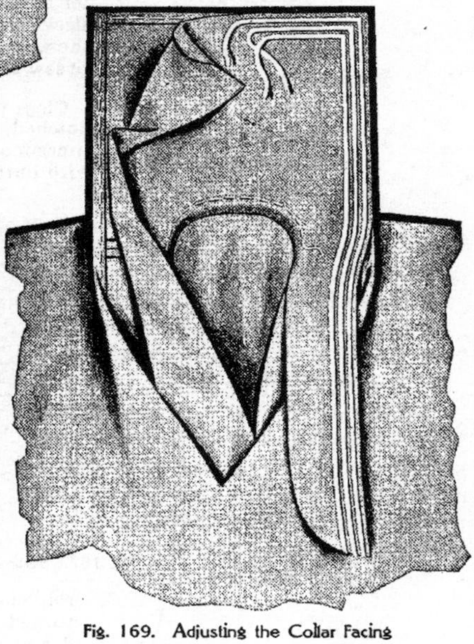

Fig. 169. Adjusting the Collar Facing

After it has been stitched, the collar facing can be basted in place under the front. A row of stitching as close to the edge as possible should run around the entire outer edge. The inner edge of the collar facing must be turned under three-eighths of an inch. Wherever it is necessary, it must be clipped, or eased, like the edge of the yoke. After the edge is turned under, it is basted to the blouse. Across the back of the neck it is felled to the blouse, covering the seam, but down the fronts it is stitched with two rows of machine stitching, which makes a pretty decoration on the front of the blouse. Another method of attaching a sailor collar is given in Chapter XXII, under "*The Russian Blouse Jacket.*"

The shield is cut in one piece and may be simply hemmed, or, if preferred, lined throughout with lawn or cambric. It is trimmed with an emblem or star.

After both blouse and shield are finished, it is practical to make a few buttonholes along the neck line of the body part, under the collar, sewing buttons in corresponding positions on the shield to prevent it from shifting around out of place. A crow's-foot may be made at the lower end of the neck opening in front.

THE NECKERCHIEF or TIE worn with the blouse by a sailor of the navy is made of a perfect square of black silk tied in a square knot, leaving ends from four to six inches long. This square piece is folded diagonally and then rolled up, with the two overlapping corners folded into the material and held together by an elastic, as shown in Fig. 170, while the other corners are tied at the lower end of the collar in a square knot, with a corner extending from each side. By studying Fig. 171 the method of tying a sailor's knot will be easily understood.

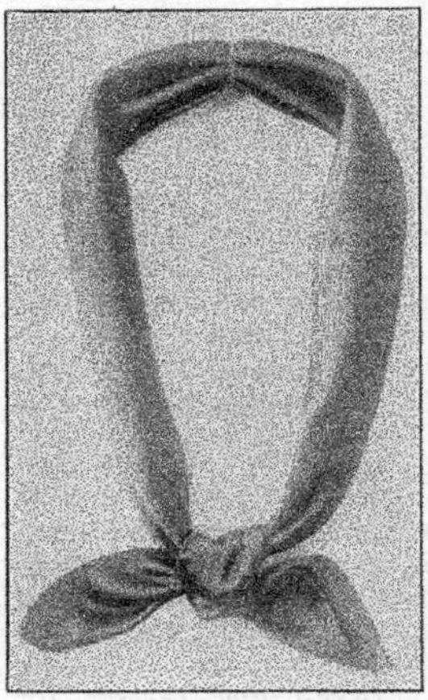

Fig. 170. The Neckerchief Tied

TO MAKE THE SKIRT, lay the pattern pieces on the material, paying due attention to the perforations indicating the grain of the goods. The skirt length should first be ascertained, and, unless allowance is made for a hem, sufficient length should be added when cutting.

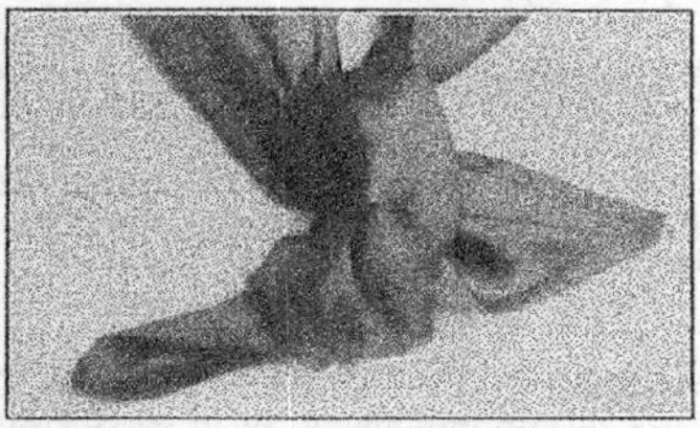

Fig. 171. Detail of Tying Knot

If front openings are desired, and are not provided for in the pattern, both edges of the front gore are underfaced to the depth of a placket opening, with a straight strip of material about one and one-half inches wide. The front edge of each side gore should have an underlap to the same depth, which should be about one inch and a half wide when finished.

Join the gores together with stitched, felled seams, continuing the stitching along the opening. Baste the hem. If the skirt is to be plaited, the plaits will give sufficient material for the underlap. See Chapter XXI, "Skirts." After the skirt has been fitted, the plaits are stitched near the edge down to the required depth.

For a back lacing, the back plait is stitched separately from the skirt and the fold edges worked with six or eight eyelets, done in the same manner as instructed on page 15. A black silk lacing or silk tape is laced through the eyelets. The navy regulations demand that the finished lacing appear like Fig. 173.

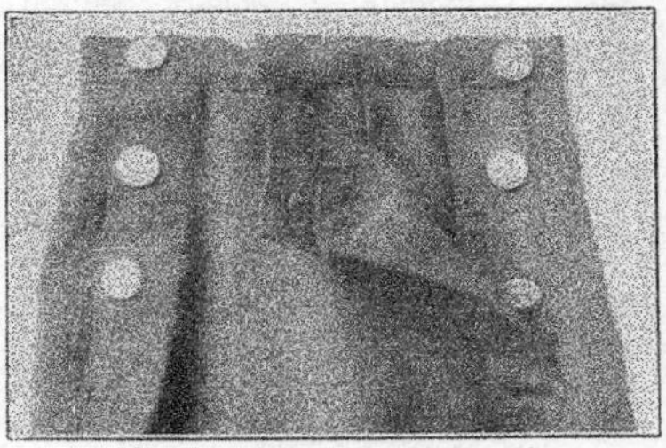

Fig. 172. Front Placket of Skirt

The upper edge of the front gore is finished with a straight belt two inches wide. A continuous belt of the same width is attached to the side and back gores of the skirt. The belts are cut single and lined, with an interlining added if it is necessary. Three buttonholes are made at each side of the front gore, two on the skirt part and one on the belt as shown in Fig. 172. The sailor blouse may be used with a boy's suit. Instructions for making trousers will be found in Chapter XXIII.

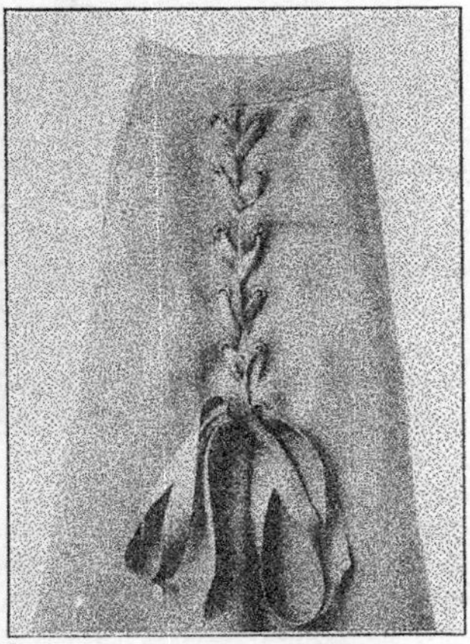

Fig. 173. Regulation Naval Lacing

CHAPTER XII

AN EFFICIENT EQUIPMENT FOR DRESSMAKING

DRESSMAKING, like any other form of work, will give the best results when it is done with the best equipment. "Best" does not mean the most expensive. A three-dollar pine table of the right height and size for sewing and cutting is a better table for dressmaking than a fifty-dollar mahogany sewing-table just big enough to hold your scissors and work-basket.

THE SEWING-ROOM. Every woman who sews or who has sewing done at home should have a light, well-equipped sewing-room. It need not be large, but it should have a good light by day and the artificial light should be properly placed and shaded. The floor should be covered by a clean sheet or linen drugget—sometimes called a crum-cloth. This covering keeps light-colored material from becoming soiled, and also enables you to leave the sewing-room in perfect order at the end of the day, for all the scraps and threads can be picked up in the cloth.

The room should be furnished with comfortable, straight chairs and a table large enough to lay out a skirt or coat for cutting and sewing. If it is a regular sewing-table you can keep your shears, pins, etc., in the drawer. The table should have a smooth, hard, even surface and should be of comfortable height, so that you can sit at it with your feet under it as you would sit at a writing-table. Never sew with your work on your lap. It makes you sit in a fatiguing position, strains your eyes and back, and stretches and crumples your work. Lay your sewing on the table, letting the table support its weight. A big chest of drawers is useful. Keep one drawer for buttons, boxes, hooks and eyes, bones, etc., another for patterns and a third for left-over pieces of materials. Keep all pieces of material as long as the garment is in use, in case you wish to mend or alter it. There should be hooks on the wall, coat and skirt hangers, and a silkoline curtain to draw over dresses, etc., that are left hanging overnight.

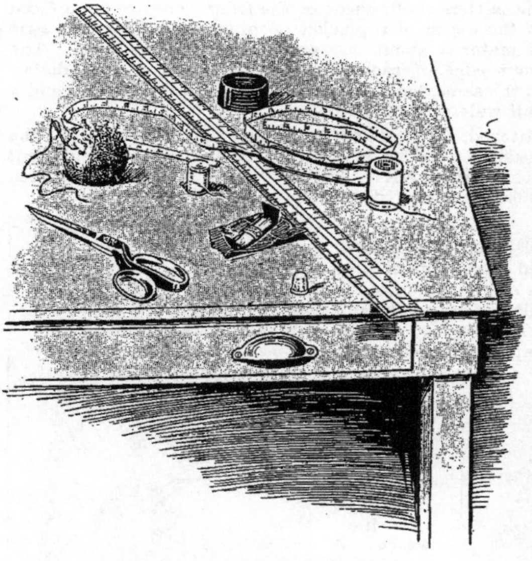

Fig. 174. The Sewing Equipment

SHEARS AND SCISSORS. Dressmaking shears should be about nine or ten inches long. Never use scissors for cutting. The shears should be kept well sharpened so that they will cut a clean, even edge and not fret and chew the material. The best shears for dressmaking are known as the "bent" shears. (Fig. 174.) They are bent in this way so as to raise the material as little as possible in cutting and so prevent the under layer from slipping in cutting two thicknesses of material. A good pair of bent shears can be had for a dollar and a quarter. Do not buy a cheap, poor pair. Good steel will last for many years. Do not use your shears for cutting threads, etc. You will need a pair of scissors and also a pair of buttonhole scissors.

WEIGHTS. When your material is laid out smoothly on the table for cutting it should be held in place by four round iron weights weighing one or two pounds. (Fig. 174.) You can get them at the stationer's and they cost about fifteen cents apiece. Or you can use the same sort of weights you use for your kitchen scales.

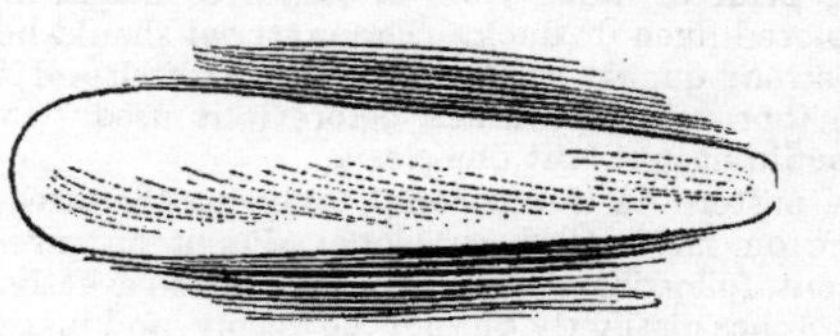

Fig. 174A. The Sleeve-board

PINS, NEEDLES, ET CETERA. Clean, unbent pins are important. Small pins are better than large, and fine steel pins should be used on silk or any material that will mark. Never push a pin through a fabric. Use the points only and take up as little of the material as possible.

You will need a thimble that fits correctly, needles of all sizes, basting cotton, different colored cottons for marking tailor's tacks, chalk, a yard-stick and a tape-measure. Learn to use your tape-measure accurately, for one of the points of fine dressmaking is the difference between an eighth of an inch and a quarter, a quarter of an inch and three-eighths.

IRONS. You should have either an electric iron and two ordinary irons; or else three ordinary irons. The two extra irons are used to hold the third in an inverted position in steaming velvet. An eight-pound smoothing-iron is the most satisfactory type for pressing.

IRONING-BOARD. Skirts and coats can be pressed on your long laundry ironing-board or on your sewing-table. Seams should be pressed over the curved edge of an ironing-board so that the seam edges will not be marked on the garment.

A SLEEVE-BOARD which can be used for sleeves and short seams can be made from a board two or three feet long, and tapering from five or six inches in width at one end to three inches at the other. (Fig. 174A.) The ends and edges should be rounded and the board should have an inner covering of flannel or a similar wool material, and an outer cover of smooth cotton cloth. (Fig. 174A.)

A TAILOR'S CUSHION is used for pressing darts and curved seams. (Fig. 174B.) It is ham shaped and is stuffed tightly with cotton rags. Cut two pieces, eighteen by fourteen inches, making them narrower at one end. (Fig. 174B.) Round off all the edges. Stitch the seam with a close stitch.

THE SEWING-MACHINE should be of a good, reliable make. You will get full directions with it, and in using it be careful to observe the correct tension, length of stitch, etc. Tucking and gathering, etc., can be done on a machine.

THE DRESS-FORM. It is necessary in dressmaking to have a perfect duplicate of your own figure on which you can try your clothes as you make them.

Buy a dress-form one size smaller than your bust measure. If you have a thirty-six-inch bust, buy a thirty-four-inch dress-form. It should have an extension stand that can be lowered to your skirt length. The stand should be on casters so that you can move it around and turn it easily. It is

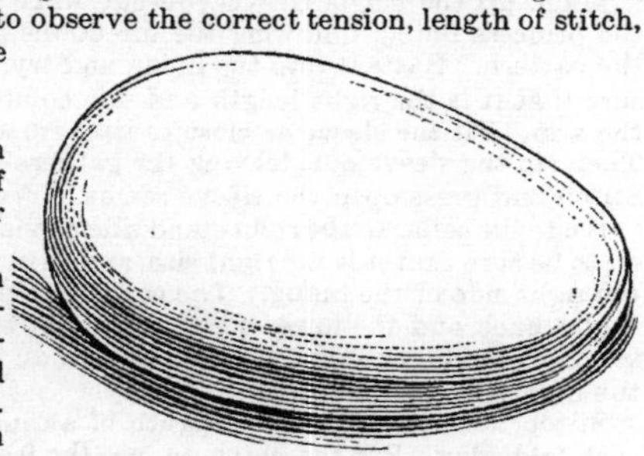

Fig. 174B. The Tailor's Cushion

Fig. 175. The Padded Dress-Form

not necessary for you to have a wire skirt frame.

Buy a princess lining, buying it by your bust measure. If you are long or short waisted, round-shouldered or over-erect or have any other slight peculiarity of physique, alter your pattern according to the instrucions in Chapter XIV, "The Use of Butterick Patterns."

Cut the princess lining from unbleached muslin or natural-colored linen or duck. The material should be of a firm, strong quality so that it will not stretch and it should be thoroughly shrunken before it is used. In cutting the lining out, cut one sleeve.

Lay the pattern on the material, following the directions given on the pattern envelope. Pin it on carefully and cut, following the edges of the pattern exactly. Clip the notches distinctly but not too deeply, and mark the working perforations with tailor's tacks, using different-colored cottons for the different-size perforations.

Put the lining together according to the illustrated instructions given in the pattern, making the closing at the center front.

Try the lining on with the fold edges of the front opening just meeting.

The lining should be tried on directly over your corset so as to get as close a duplicate of your figure as possible. In using the finished dress-form remember that it represents your figure without lingerie. If you wear heavy, clumsy underwear you should put it on the form in fitting. If you wear fine, close-fitting lingerie it will not be necessary to do so, as the lingerie will not alter the size or shape. Pin the fronts carefully and be sure that the neck edges are even.

Make the necessary alterations at the outlet seams, fitting the lining very carefully. Be sure to have the neck and armhole exactly right. Remove the lining and if you make any alterations baste them in and try on the lining once more to be sure that it fits perfectly. Stitch the seams through the bastings. If you can't remove them afterward it doesn't matter in this case. Press the seams open. It is not necessary to bind, or overcast or bone them. Run a strong basting around the armholes and neck to keep them from stretching.

Make up the single sleeve you cut with the rest of the princess lining, following the directions given with the pattern. Baste it into the lining and try it on to be sure that it is the right length and sets comfortably on the arm. Fit the sleeve as close to the arm as possible. Then rip the sleeve out, leaving the gathers at the top. Stitch and press open the sleeve seams.

Baste the collar to the right-hand side of the lining, try on to be sure that it is the right size, and then stitch it to the right side of the lining. The collar closing is at the center back and the lower edge on the left side will be sewed to the lining later, three-eighths of an inch below the neck edge of the lining.

Stitch the fronts about an eighth of an inch back of each fold edge. Put the lining on, pin the fronts evenly together and have some one turn up the lower edge of

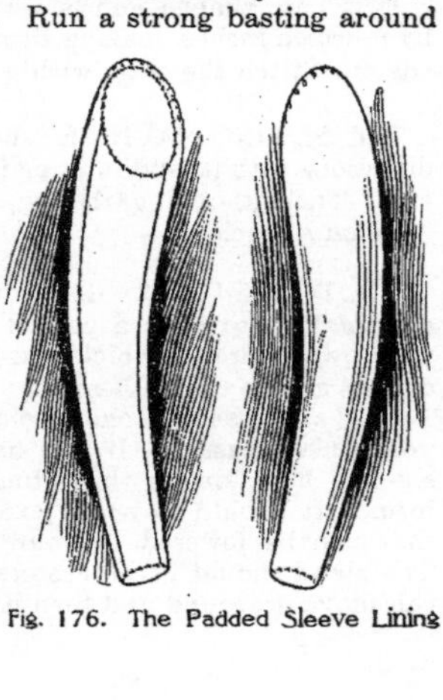

Fig. 176. The Padded Sleeve Lining

the lining. (See Chapter XXI, Skirts.) Take the lining off and face it with a bias facing three inches wide, stitching the upper edge of the facing flat to the lining.

Mark the waistline by a line of colored thread through the waistline perforations.

Place the lining on the dress-form, leaving the front edges open temporarily. Pad between the lining and the form with tissue-paper, cotton rags or wadding until it fits perfectly. Be careful in padding not to stretch or draw the lining or to let the padding get in bunches. Pack it until the front edges just meet and then pin them together. Then sew them with an overhand stitch. (Fig. 175.) If you have prominent or uneven hips or a round abdomen, place the wadding where it is needed. When you pad below the waistline, pin the wadding to the form so that it will not slip. When you have padded the front out to its right proportions, turn up the lining and cover the padding at the hips with a thin piece of lining material, tacking the covering to the dress-form.

Fell the left side of the collar in place and overhand its back edges together.

Place a piece of lining material inside each armhole, turn in the armhole edges three-eighths of an inch and fell them to it. (Fig. 175.)

For a figure that varies quite decidedly from the average it is better to use a special dress-form. Alter your pattern and make up the lining as described in the earlier part of this chapter. Send your finished lining to a firm that makes dress-forms and have a special form made from it, but a size smaller than your lining. When you get the form, put the lining on it and pad it as already described.

Or a woman of this type of figure can get an adjustable dress-form. Get it a size smaller, adjust it to represent your figure, cover it with your lining and pad it as directed here.

A woman who sews for a number of people will have to use an adjustable form with a fitted lining for each person she sews for. Mark these linings distinctly with name of the person for whom it was made. The form will have to be adjusted and padded each time a lining is used.

In using a dress-form, the skirt can be put on the form and the form placed on the table. It is easier to work with in this position.

In fitting a coat the form should be dressed with the waist and skirt over which the coat will be worn.

THE SLEEVE-FORM. Take the finished sleeve of the lining and pad it firmly and evenly. Place a piece of lining material over the padding at the wrist, turn in the wrist edges three-eighths of an inch, and fell them to the piece of material. (Fig. 176.)

Slip a piece of lining material in the armhole of the sleeve. Turn in the edge of the under portion of the sleeve three-eighths of an inch and fell the fold edge to the lining material. (Fig. 176.) Pad the upper part of the sleeve until it looks as nearly as possible like the arm. Turn in the upper edge of the piece of lining three-eighths of an inch and fell it to the upper part of the sleeve. (Fig. 176.)

You can use the sleeve-form for either the right or left arm and you will find it very useful for trimming or draping sleeves.

CHAPTER XIII

CUTTING MATERIALS, SPONGING, ETC.

THE NAP or PILE in all *woolen* cloths should invariably run toward the bottom of the garment. (Fig. 177.) The cutting line of perforations in the patterns, and the directions for their use must be carefully followed. In waists and skirts that are to be cut bias, special instructions for placing the cutting perforations are given with the pattern. Fig. 178 shows a pattern laid on material that has no nap.

When Velvet or *Plush* or any velvet material except panne velvet is used, the pile should run upward, just as the pile of the fur does in a garment of sealskin. When in these fabrics the pile runs upward its tendency is to fall outward, thus bringing out and enhancing its depth of color; while when the pile runs downward it is more liable to flatten, just as fur will when stroked, and its richness and intensity of color are rendered less apparent, and therefore less effective.

Panne velvet, the one exception to the above rule, should be cut with its pile running downward.

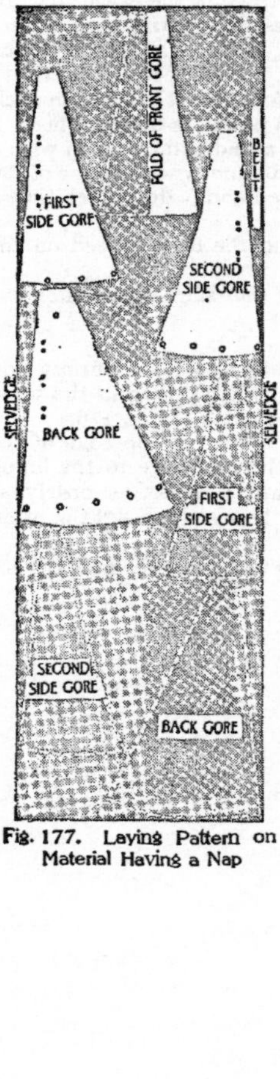

Fig. 177. Laying Pattern on Material Having a Nap

In Adjoining Sections, great care should be taken to have the nap or pile run in the same direction. Otherwise the different reflections of light caused by the varying directions of the nap will make the garment appear as if made of two shades of goods.

An Irregular Plaid can rarely be used on the bias, consequently the ways of making it up are limited. A dress made of irregular plaid requires more material than one made of regular plaid. The darkest stripes should run across the bottom with the lighter tones up, as the shading in this direction is better.

It must always be borne in mind throughout the cutting, that all pieces of the pattern, or lining, must be placed with the upper part in the direction for the top of the material. An amateur had better use an even plaid.

The most satisfactory results are obtained by folding the material and pinning through both thicknesses as for a seam, then turning over on the right side and noting the effect. In this way it may be easily ascertained which stripe, plaid or figure it will be best to use for the center of the front and back, respectively. Be careful, in replacing the goods, not to lose the original position.

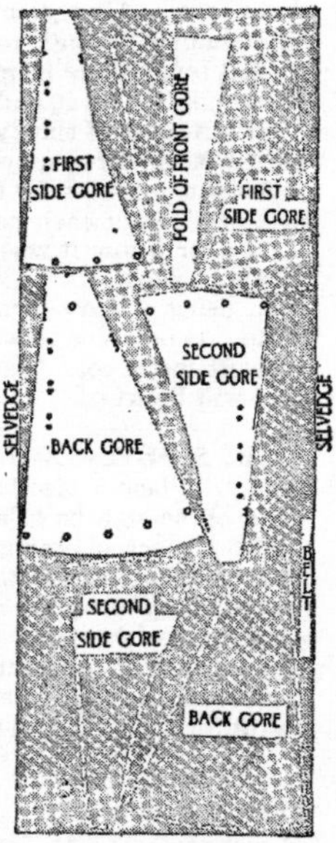

Fig. 178. How Pattern May Be Laid When Material Has No Nap

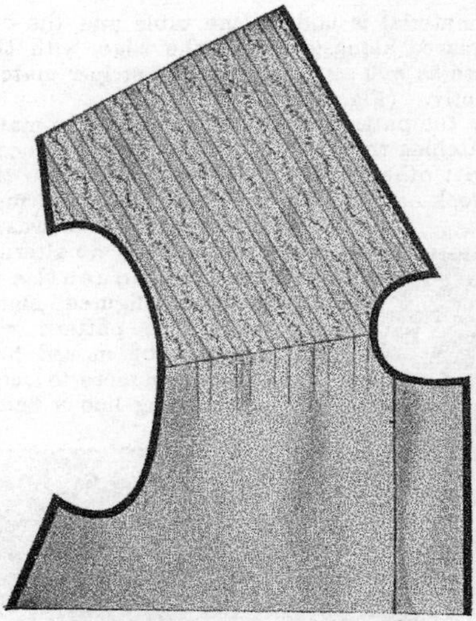

Fig. 179. Marking Pattern for Matching Stripes on Shoulder

THE PLAID WAIST should be cut in as few pieces as possible and can be made either on the straight or the bias of the material. Match the heavy lines wherever the waist is joined, either at the under-arm or shoulder.

With the present style of stretching the back of the draped waist, little difficulty is experienced in the making. Having chosen the stripe that is most suitable for the center of the back, select also, for the crosswise stripe, a position which will leave the best effect on the figure. For the front, arrange the plaid so that when the waist is closed the center will form a succession of perfect blocks. Other ideas may be considered for the front closing; this is simply a matter of choice, since the lines across the front must match. In any event, the crosswise plaids of the front must be on a line with those of the back, so that when the under-arm seam is joined the crosswise stripe of both will match perfectly. (Fig. 180.)

The chief difficulty in the making of a striped or plaid waist lies in the accurate matching of the stripes. In using a new pattern, cut and fit the lining first. Then if any alterations are necessary they can be repeated in the pattern of the outside waist before cutting the material.

When making a waist of striped material the only place where the stripes must match is at the shoulder seams—unless, of course, the stripes in the material run bias or the waist itself is cut on the bias. In the latter case the general principles given in the preceding paragraphs on cutting materials can be followed.

In a plaid waist the vertical lines at the shoulder seams and the crosslines at the under-arm seams must match. (See Fig. 180.) If the waist closes in front, the back should be cut out first. Pin the back to the pattern of the front at the shoulder edge. Mark the stripes with a pencil on the pattern of the front where they intersect the shoulder seams. (Fig. 179.) Lay the pattern of the front on the goods so that the stripes of the material correspond to the stripes marked on the pattern. Then cut out the fronts. In Fig. 179 the seam edge of the pattern is folded under to show the way the stripes should match when the shoulder seam is closed.

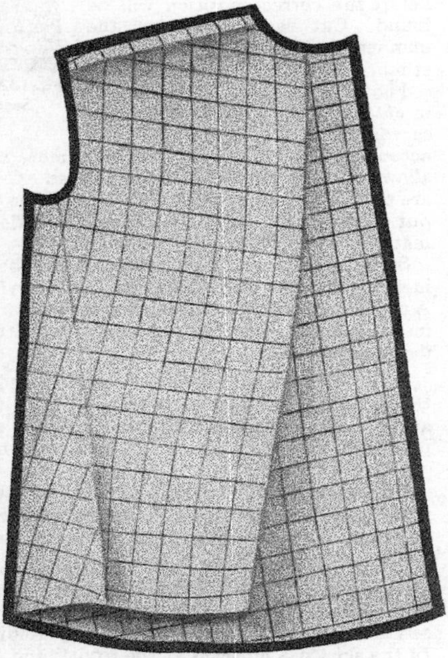

Fig. 180. Matching Cross Stripes at Under-Arm Seam

IN CUTTING THE SKIRT of plaid, place the chosen line or plaid exactly in the center of the front gore, or, if the skirt is circular, directly down the center of the front. After the front is cut, the

Fig. 181. Matching Plaid at Side Seams of Skirt

uncut material is laid on the table and the cut front placed alongside, near the edge, with the crosswise as well as the lengthwise stripes matching exactly. (Fig. 181.)

Place the pattern of the side gore on the material, matching the front, and if the position is correct, cut; otherwise move the front gore to the next block or plaid on the material. This may necessitate some waste, but there is no alternative. Frequently, in plaid or figured materials, the pattern will have to be moved half a yard or more to a corresponding line or figure before the correct position will be found. Cut each gore after the manner directed, and baste and stitch.

Fig. 182. Center Back or Front Seam of Circular Skirt

Fig. 183. Center Front or Back Seam in Skirt of Plaid

Fig. 181 shows a material of plaid, in cutting which a waste was necessary in order to match the plaid. On account of this waste in matching, more material must be allowed for the making of a plaid dress. Care and attention are necessary in making up plaids, for no costume is well put together unless the different portions are carefully matched.

Stripe, check and plaid materials can be used effectively in a circular skirt with a bias seam down the front. (Fig. 182.) A two-piece pattern is suitable for such a skirt, and full directions are given in the pattern instructions showing how to place the pattern on the material in order to obtain a desirable bias.

It is better in cutting a skirt of plaid or stripe, to cut one side first, then, removing the pattern, lay the section just cut upon the material, and carefully match the plaid at all points before cutting the opposite piece. When both sides are joined, the prominent lines in the plaid should have a mitered effect, as shown in Fig. 183.

FIGURES and FLOWERS must also match perfectly. Unless one line of flowers is up and the next down, as usually occurs, one position will have to be selected for the top. Generally the stems of the flowers run downward.

When cutting a garment where several breadths of silk must be joined (a circular skirt, for instance) it is most important that the pattern or figures on the material should be matched. Often this can not be done when the breadths are simply joined at the selvages. Cut the front gore first by folding the silk lengthwise through the center (if the skirt has no seam at the front), and laying the front edge of the pattern even with the fold. If there is a decided figure in the silk, fold this front breadth so the figures will balance and not make the skirt look onesided.

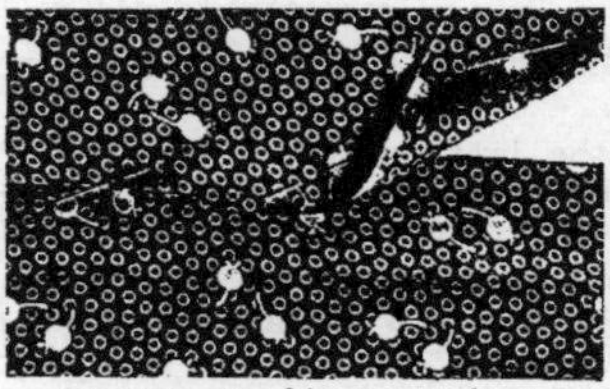
Fig. 184. Matching the Design in Figured Silk

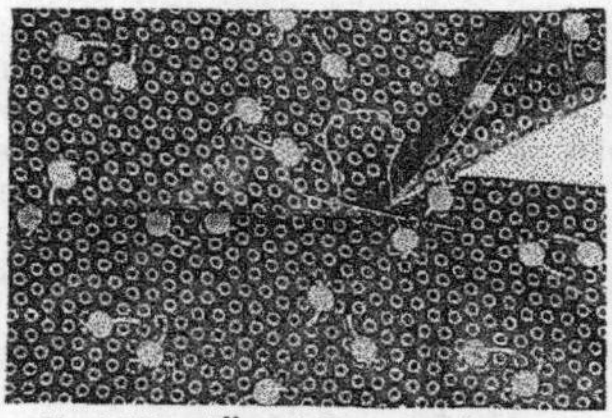
Fig. 185. Slip-stitching the Breadths Together

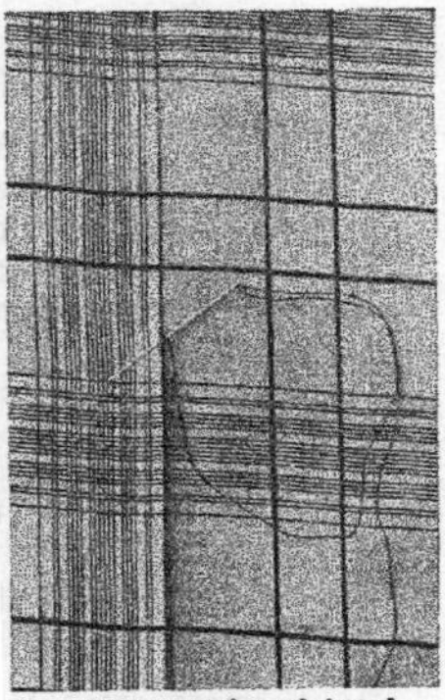
Fig. 186. Matching Plaid When Piecing is Necessary

Lay the paper pattern out on a table; place the front gore upon it and match the figures of the silk at the edge of the second breadth to those at, or near, the edge of the first. It will sometimes be necessary to lap the second breadths considerably over the first, as shown in Fig. 184, in order to find the corresponding figures. Turn under the edge of the second breadth and pin it to the first. The gore may then be cut according to the pattern. Proceed in the same way to join the breadths for both sides of the skirt.

Slip-stitch the breadths together, from the outside by slipping the needle along, inside the fold edge of the upper breadth, and then taking a stitch in the under breadth, as shown in Fig. 185. When the skirt is turned wrong side out, it will be found that the slip-stitching from the right side forms the basting of the seam. Material will give more and match better if the selvages are cut off.

SPONGING is one of the most important steps in both dressmaking and tailoring.

Almost all woolen materials should be carefully sponged before they are used. A few very thin, open-meshed fabrics cannot be sponged on account of the shrinkage, but in most cases the sponging is advisable. If you are in doubt take a small piece of the material and experiment with it. To a certain degree it prevents spotting from rain, etc. For sponging, one must have a large-sized table, an ironing-blanket and a strip of heavy unbleached muslin or drilling one yard wide and two yards long. The ironing-blanket must be laid on the table without a wrinkle. The selvages of the material should be clipped or cut off and the material should be laid face down on the blanket. Wet and wring out the strip of muslin, lay it over the material, and press it with an iron several times. Then remove the muslin and press the material itself until it is dry. Sponge a small portion of the goods at a time and work slowly and carefully.

In sponging material of double width, let it remain folded with the right side turned in during the sponging. If the material is very heavy, it may be turned to the other side and the sponging repeated.

Wash materials of the linen order should be shrunken—dipped in water, wrung out and pressed dry—before they are made up. Fine mulls, flowered organdies, swisses, etc., should not be shrunken for they are not as pretty afterwards as they were before.

CHAPTER XIV

THE USE OF BUTTERICK PATTERNS

BUYING A PATTERN—In home dressmaking, the first principle of success is to start with the right size pattern. The wrong size pattern means a waste of good material and an unnecessary amount of fitting. · It only takes a fraction of a minute to be measured, and it saves you the possibility of any trouble and extra work.

You ought to be measured each time you buy a pattern. Don't be measured over old corsets or a carelessly fitted dress or a house gown. Put on the corsets you are going to wear under the new dress. Lace them properly. It may make a difference of one or two inches in your waist and hip measure. Have your measurements taken over a waist and skirt.

Your bust measure should be taken easily, but not snugly, over the fullest part of the bust, close up under the arms and across the back. (Figs. 187A and 187B.)

Your waist measure should be taken snugly, but not tightly, at your normal waistline. Don't think because you are going to buy a pattern with a raised waistline that you should take your measure at your raised waistline. *The waist measure given with any pattern is the measure of the lower edge of the finished belt which comes at the normal waistline.* (Figs. 187A and 187B.)

Your hip measure should be taken easily, but not snugly, seven inches below your normal waistline. (Figs. 187A and 187B.)

Your arm measure should be taken easily around the arm, just below the armhole. (Fig. 187A.)

In buying a pattern for a skirt have both your waist and hip measures taken carefully. Compare your measurements with the table of waist and hip measurements given on the pattern envelope. Buy your pattern by the measure recommended on the pattern envelope.

After you have bought your pattern, buy your material, guided by the quantities given on the pattern envelope.

In buying material for a ladies' dress or skirt, remember that the pattern does not allow for a hem. If you wish to hem the skirt you will have to buy a little more material than the pattern calls for. A facing can often be cut from the left-over scraps of material if you prefer to face the skirt.

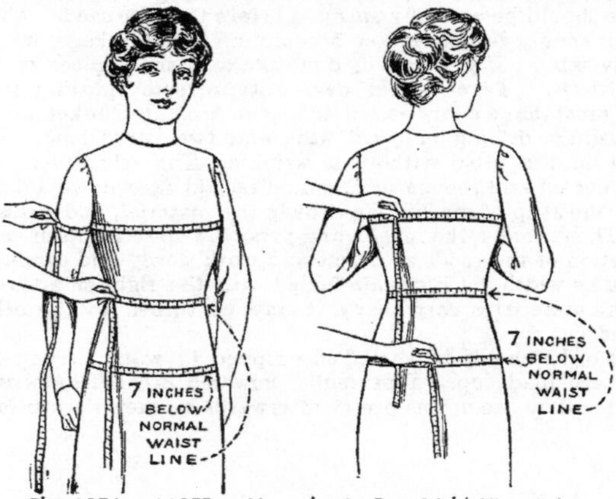

Figs. 187A and 187B. Measuring the Bust, Waist, Hip and Arm

When you get your pattern home, open it, and identify each piece from the illustration on the back of the envelope. Read the instructions carefully, and go over the illustrated instructions. You will see that they are very simple, and with the illustrations are extremely easy to follow. Butterick patterns have these illustrated instructions.

The pattern is marked with a few clear, unmistakable symbols that show you exactly how to cut and put the dress together.

Fig. 187C. A Line of Large Double Perforations is Always Laid on the Material Lengthwise and Parallel to the Selvage.

Large double perforations invariably mark the cutting line. (Fig. 187C.) They are always used in a series that form a straight line. (Fig. 187C.) When you have your material laid out, ready for cutting, these large double perforations are always laid lengthwise of the material. (Fig. 187C.) Every piece of material has two dimensions: Crosswise—which is from selvage to selvage; and lengthwise—which is the length of the selvage. The large double perforations are laid on the material parallel to the selvage, so that each one of these large double perforations is the same distance from the selvage as all the other large double perforations.

It is extremely important to get these large double perforations straight, and not bias, on the material. If they are laid on straight, the garment will be easy to make, and will wear nicely. If you put these perforations on carelessly, so that instead of being parallel to the selvage they run bias, the garment will pull and twist and stretch. It will be found an aid in cutting correctly if a ruler or yardstick is laid on each piece of the pattern, its edge touching each of the perforations that indicate the way the pattern should lie on the goods, and a heavy pencil mark made along the line formed by the ruler. This question of the grain or thread of the goods is a very important one. Some skirts are cut with one straight and one bias edge on each gore; others have two bias edges, for it all depends on the design of the skirt. The only safe plan to follow is the line of perforations marking the grain of the pattern. Measure from each end of the line to the selvage of the goods, and move the pattern until both ends of the line are the same number of inches from the edge.

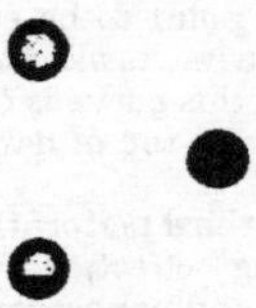

Fig. 187D. Large Triple Perforations.

Large triple perforations are also always used in cutting. (Fig. 187D.) They are always laid on a lengthwise fold of the material. In some cases they can also be laid on a crosswise fold. The pattern instructions tell you whether you are to lay the large triple perforations on a lengthwise or crosswise fold.

Small double perforations are always used to mark the normal waistline in skirts, blouses, coats, etc. (Fig. 187E.)

Large single perforations (Fig. 187F) and small single perforations (Fig. 187G), either alone or together, are used for different purposes, which are explained in the instructions.

Notches (Fig. 187H) are used to mark seam edges and to show which edges come together. Edges marked with corresponding notches are put together in a seam, with the notches matching.

Fig. 187E. Small Double Perforations.

USING A PATTERN FOR CUTTING is explained fully on the pattern envelope. In most cases, when the two sides of a garment are exactly alike, the pattern is given for one-half the garment. Each piece of the pattern is cut twice or double to make the complete garment. In cases where the two halves of a garment are not alike, for example, when a skirt is draped on the left side and not on the right, the pattern is given for the entire garment. In every case the pattern explains which pieces should be cut twice or double, and which should be cut once and singly. A front-gore pattern is usually laid on the folded material with its front edge on the fold, thus cutting it double. Two side gores can be cut either singly, making two cuttings, or once with the material doubled so that the two are cut at once. In a skirt with an irregular front closing, each half of the front is cut separately. Before cutting your material, be sure that the pattern is the right length and proportion for you. If you are shorter or taller than the average figure, the length of the pattern can be altered as directed on the pattern envelope.

Fig. 187F. A Large Single Perforation

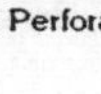

Fig. 187G. A Small Single Perforation.

If your figure is out of proportion in any way, large or small in the bust, etc., the pattern should be altered according to the directions

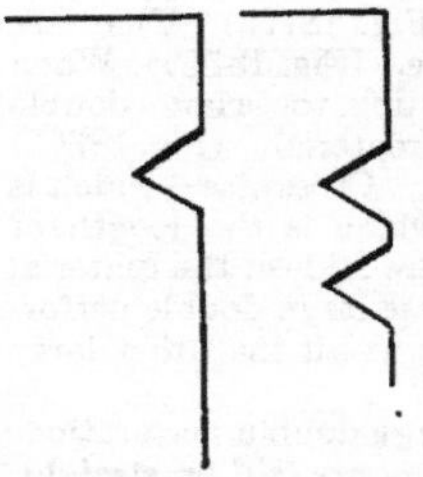
Fig. 187H. Single and Double Notches

given in this chapter, which covers the alterations for different types of figures.

Cutting—In laying a pattern on material for cutting, arrange the pieces so that they will cut to the best advantage without wasting your material. Follow the pattern instructions in regard to the position of the cutting perforations. (Figs. 187C and 187D.) Pin the pattern in place with fine small pins placed as close together as necessary to hold the pattern firmly. Do not push the pins through the material recklessly, but take up as few threads as possible so as not to mark the material.

Cut out the garment with bent shears (Fig. 174, page 60), following the pattern edges exactly, and cutting a clean, even line. Mark the working perforations with tailor's tacks (Fig. 71, page 22), using different colored cottons to indicate the different size perforations.

Putting Seams Together—The seam edges are marked with notches (Fig. 187H), showing which edges come together. Outlet seams are marked by large single perforations (Fig. 187 F) and the basting on these seams should be through these perforations. Ordinary seams are not marked by perforations, but are sewed evenly three-eighths of an inch from the seam edge.

Darts are marked by V-shaped lines of perforations. A dart is made by folding the garment so that the two lines of dart perforations come together.

Fig. 187 I represents the easy curve commonly followed in terminating darts in waist patterns. The picture shows the effect when the material is folded with the corresponding dart perforations matching, according to the pattern instructions. The point to be emphasized here is that the line of the dart seam should follow the reversed curve, toward the point running into the folded edge, almost in a line with the fold. When this curve is followed, the "pouting" effect (as it is called by professionals), often seen at the top of darts, is avoided.

Fig. 187 J shows the line of the dart seam running straight from the third perforation from the point of the dart to this point. This is the cause of the "pouting" effect, which, as explained in the preceding description, is easily avoided. It is an ugly and unnecessary fault.

Although the darts in skirts are reversed, this caution should be observed, as the points should be finished perfectly, to avoid this same pouting effect already referred to.

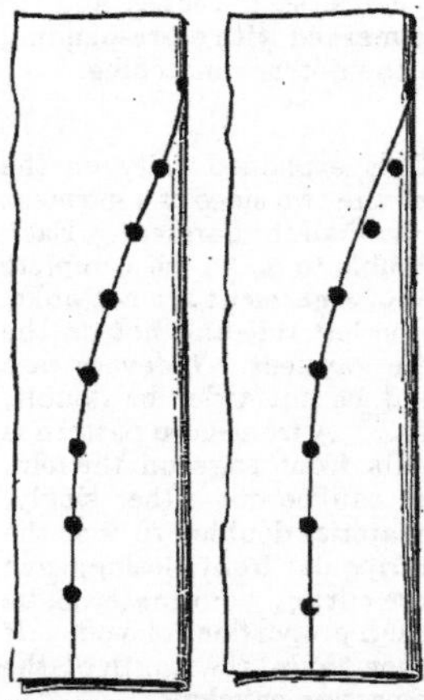
Figs. 187I and 187J. Right and Wrong Methods of Terminating Darts

THE BEST METHOD OF ALTERING PATTERNS—Butterick patterns are so carefully planned that it is unnecessary for most women to change them in order to secure an absolutely satisfactory fit. At the same time, for figures varying from the average in waist lengths, sleeve lengths, skirt lengths, bust size, waist size, hip size, etc., the patterns can be easily changed to suit individual peculiarities of form by following these instructions.

It is easy to lengthen or shorten a waist, sleeve or skirt without in any way detracting from the original lines, if the work is done at the right time and in the proper way. A woman sometimes spends a long time endeavoring to fit a waist cut the normal length to a long-waisted figure, and the result is unsatisfactory because the lines of the seams and the proportions of the waist are not what they were designed to be, a very slight change sometimes destroying the effect of the whole garment. Fitting an average-length waist pattern to a short-waisted figure is another difficult thing for an amateur to do. By carefully studying these illustrations, methods and principles, one can alter patterns satisfactorily for all types of figures.

A knowledge of the proportionate measurements used in making patterns is very necessary for the dressmaker,

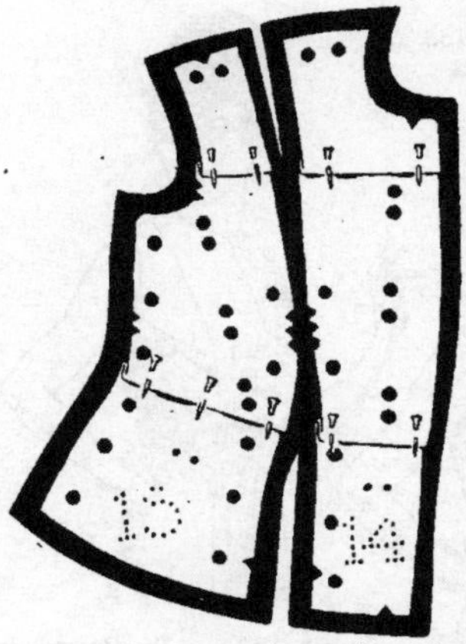

Fig. 187. To Shorten the Waist Lining

whether professional or amateur. A comparison between these measures and those of the person to be fitted should be made before cutting into one's material.

FOR ADAPTING PATTERNS TO LONG OR SHORT WAISTED FIGURES, the first step should be to read the pattern instructions carefully. Then open the pattern, and, referring to the instructions, identify each piece by its number and description. Before cutting the material, the figure should be measured from the collar seam at the back of the neck to the waistline and from close up under the arm to the waistline.

Make a note of all the measures as they are taken, then compare them with the corresponding measurements of the pattern. In most cases it is sufficient to alter the length of a waist lining at the lower part. Some figures, however, are long-waisted from under the arm to the waistline, and short from under the arm to the neck. This is determined by the length of the underarm measure. If the lower part is too long, lay a plait across each piece two and one-half inches above the waistline. (Fig. 187.) The size of the plait depends on the difference between the measure from under the arm to the waistline of the pattern and the corresponding measure of the figure. If the upper part is too long, lay a plait across the front and back, half way between the underarm and the neck. (Fig. 187.)

The lining may be lengthened by cutting it across at either or both of these points and separating the pieces the required space to give them the desired length. (Fig. 188.)

The seams edges should be evened off at the plaits after the plaits are laid. Whatever alteration is made in the length of the lining, corresponding alterations must be made in the pattern of the outside of the waist, taking out or putting in the same amount at the same places.

ADAPTING PATTERNS TO FIGURES WITH EXTRA LARGE OR SMALL BUST—A pattern may be of the correct bust measure and yet require a slight alteration across the bust. This alteration can usually be made at the underarm seam, where an extra allowance, or outlet, is provided for just such cases.

When there are two underarm gores in a pattern, the alterations should be made so that it is equally divided at the two underarm or outlet seams.

Occasionally, however, one finds a figure with what is termed an "extra large" or "extra small" bust, which means that while the bust measure in both cases may be the same as for a figure of average shape, a greater proportion of the measurement is over the front and less at the back in the first case, and less in the front and more at the back in the other.

For an Unusually Large Bust get some stout, inexpensive lining material, as much as the lining pattern calls for. Unbleached muslin will do nicely. Lay your pattern on the material, following the pattern instructions for cutting. Cut it out carefully and mark the working perforations with tailor's tacks. Put the lining together and turn under the hems, following the pattern instructions.

Take a piece of the lining material six inches wide and long enough to reach across the front of your

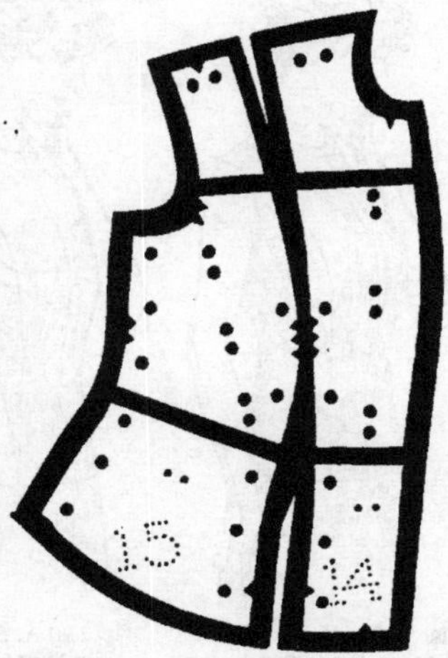

Fig. 188. To Lengthen the Waist Lining

figure to the underarm seams. Place it over your bust and pin it smoothly to your lingerie slip. Put the lining on, pinning the fronts together with the fold edges just meeting and placing the pins about an inch and a half apart. The lining will draw in wrinkles that run from the bust downward toward the underarm seam. (Fig. 189.)

Get some one to cut the lining straight across the figure to the side-front seam (Fig. 189A.), and from the side-front seam upward to three-quarters of an inch below the notches in the armhole edge. (Fig. 189A.)

As soon as the lining is cut it will separate as much as the figure requires (Fig. 189A.) and will drop in place on the abdomen. (Fig. 189A.) Pin the edges of the slash carefully to the piece of lining material underneath. (Fig. 189A.)

Fig. 189. If the Bust is Too Full it Pulls Up the Lining

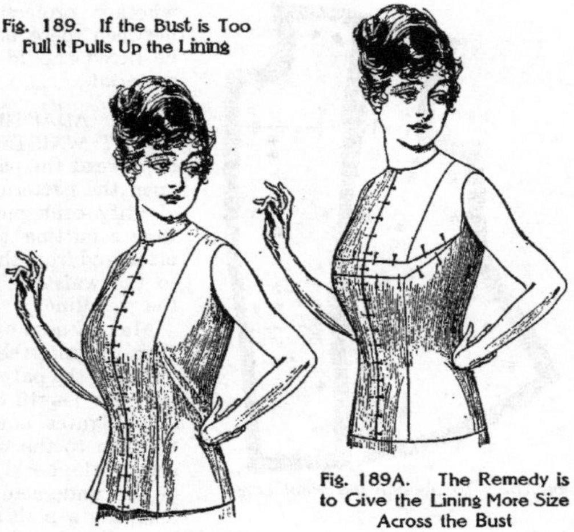

Fig. 189A. The Remedy is to Give the Lining More Size Across the Bust

Take the lining off and baste the edges of the slash to the piece under it. Be sure to baste very carefully.

Try the lining on once more to be sure that it fits perfectly. Then take it off and rip it apart, cutting through the material underneath on a line with the seams.

These lining pieces are not to be used for a pattern or for a lining. Take each piece of this altered lining and the corresponding piece of the pattern and make the same alterations in the pattern, using the lining piece as a guide. Slash the pattern fronts like the lining, separating the pieces of the pattern in the same way and to the same extent, and paste a piece of tissue-paper under the slash.

Never use the altered lining to cut your real lining. The lining material would stretch in handling and would not make an accurate, reliable pattern. Keep the corrected tissue pattern and use it for any waist or dress that calls for a French lining.

The change here suggested and illustrated is for a figure of extreme fulness at the bust. It will not, of course, be necessary to make so great an alteration for figures more nearly the normal shape.

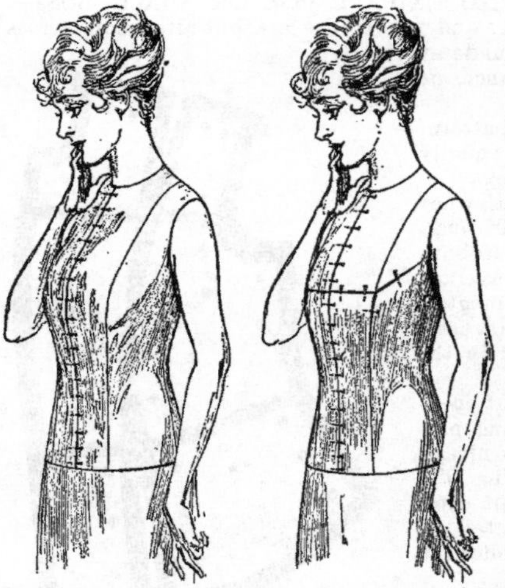

Fig. 190. Here the Bust is Small in Proportion to the Rest of the Figure

Fig. 190 A. Some of the Size Must be Taken Out

FOR A SMALL BUST—Figure 190A shows the same French lining pattern, slashed and adjusted to fit a figure with an extra small bust. This represents an extreme case, where the bust is very small, although the measure taken about the bust is the same as for a figure of average shape. Where the bust is not so small—that is to say, but slightly undersized—such extreme alterations are unnecessary.

Here again you make up your waist lining in unbleached muslin, just as the woman with the large bust would do.

The experimental lining is put on

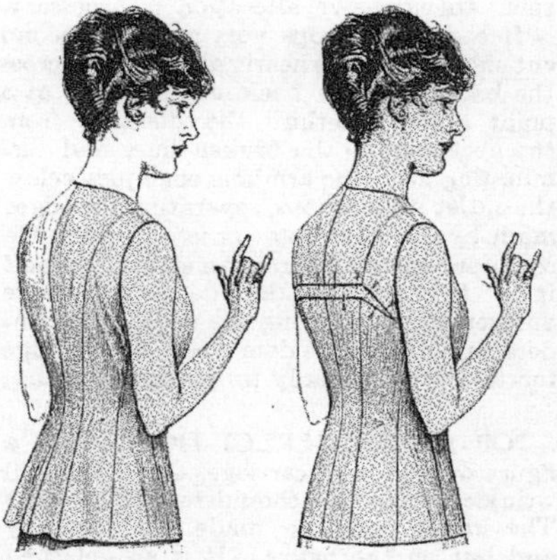

Fig. 191. If the Figure is Round-shouldered

Fig. 192. The Lining Will Require More Size Across the Shoulders

carefully, but it is not necessary to pin a piece of material under it. When the lining is on the figure, the size that is not taken up by the bust will drop in wrinkles below the full part of the figure. (Fig. 190.) The alteration is made at the same point as the alteration for the overfull bust. The lining is again slashed straight across the front to the side-front seams and from the seams upward to within three-quarters of an inch of the notches in the front of the armhole. (Fig. 190 A.) Lap the slashed edges until the lining sets smoothly and comfortably on the figure. Do not try to make it snug or tight. There should be plenty of room so that the lining does not cramp or confine the figure, and so that you can breathe comfortably.

Pin the edges of the slash (Fig. 190 A), remove the lining, baste in the alteration, and try the lining on again. If it fits perfectly, take it off and rip it apart. You will find that the edges of the side-front seams are jagged from the lap laid across the lining. Even them off, following the original seam-line. Correct your paper pattern in the same way. Slash the pieces and lap them as you did in the lining, pasting the edges together.

These alterations for a large or small bust may be made on this kind of a lining—usually called a "French lining"—or on a lining with one or two darts or with a straight or curved edge.

FOR A ROUND-SHOULDERED FIGURE—The lining must again be made up of cheap material so that it can be fitted to the figure and the corrections transferred to the paper pattern.

When your lining is made, have some one pin a strip of the lining material, about four inches wide, smoothly across your back from one arm to the other. Then put your lining on and you'll find that it looks like Figure 191. Wrinkles will run up from under the arm to the side-back seam (Fig. 191), and the lining will stand out across the back at the bottom. (Fig. 191.)

The lining draws in this way because the shoulders pull the lining upward. (Fig. 191.) Have some one cut the lining across the shoulders between the side-back seams (Fig. 192) and from the seams down to within three-eighths of an inch of the underarm seam. (Fig. 192.) The lining will spread apart, separating as much as your figure requires. (Fig. 192.) Have some one pin the cut edges of the lining to the piece beneath it, take off the lining, baste it, and try it on again. Now rip and cut it apart so that you can use the altered pieces to fix the tissue pattern. Slash the pattern just where the lining is slashed, separate the pieces a similar amount, and paste tissue-paper underneath the slash.

If you are not very round-shouldered it will not be necessary to slash the lining as much or separate the pieces as much as shown in Figure 192. It is only for very round-shoulders that

Fig. 193. If a Woman Stands too Erectly, Her Lining Will Wrinkle Across the Shoulders

Fig. 194. The Extra Size Should be Removed

Fig. 195. If a Woman Has Square Shoulders the Lining Will Wrinkle Across the Chest

Fig. 196. The Alteration is Made at the Shoulder Seam

such an extensive alteration is necessary.

If a person stoops very much, a second cut should be made nearly all the way across the back and side back, commencing at a point about one-third the distance from the neck edge to the broken line, and terminating near the armhole edge just below the outlet perforations, separating the edges made by the slash more or less as the figure requires—generally from an eighth to a half inch. In cutting out the side back, preserve an even curve all along the edge. The underarm gore very seldom needs any change for this type of badly proportioned figure.

FOR AN OVER-ERECT FIGURE—On a figure overerect in carriage, the lining will wrinkle across the shoulders. (Fig. 193.) The lining must be made up carefully and put on the figure. It is also slashed across the shoulders from side seam to side seam and downward to within three-eighths of an inch of the underarm seam. (Fig. 194.) The edges of the slash are lapped and pinned. (Fig. 194.) Don't lap them too much or you'll be drawn back more than ever. Baste the slash, try the lining on and then rip it apart. Where it has been lapped there will be slight unevenness at the seam edges that must be trimmed off. Using the lining as a guide, alter the pattern, slashing it, lapping the edges and pasting them securely.

ADAPTING PATTERNS TO SQUARE OR SLOPING SHOULDERS—We have shown how a waist will act and how it should be altered under such conditions. An instance of square shoulders causing crosswise wrinkles at the front is shown in Figure 195. For a case of this kind it is not necessary to make up a lining first in order to alter the paper pattern. The alteration is very slight and can be made on the actual lining.

Cut your lining by the pattern, following the pattern instructions carefully, and baste it together in the usual way. Try it on, pinning the fronts evenly together. You will find that it draws across the chest. (Fig. 195.) It should be taken up at the shoulder seam, taking up as much as necessary near the neck to remove the wrinkles, and gradually sloping off the alteration toward the shoulder. (Fig. 196.) This alteration will make the lining too high around the neck, for the lining has been lifted to the level of the highest part of the shoulder. So the neck edge must be slashed at intervals until it feels comfortable. (Fig. 196.) After you take off the lining, rebaste the shoulder seam and trim off the neck on a line with the slashes. Try the lining on again to be sure the alteration is right, before stitching the shoulder seams.

If there are crosswise wrinkles across the back, the lining can be altered in the same way at the back.

Fig. 197. Sloping Shoulders Make the Lining Wrinkle from Shoulder to Armhole

Fig. 198. The Lining Must be Lifted on the Shoulder

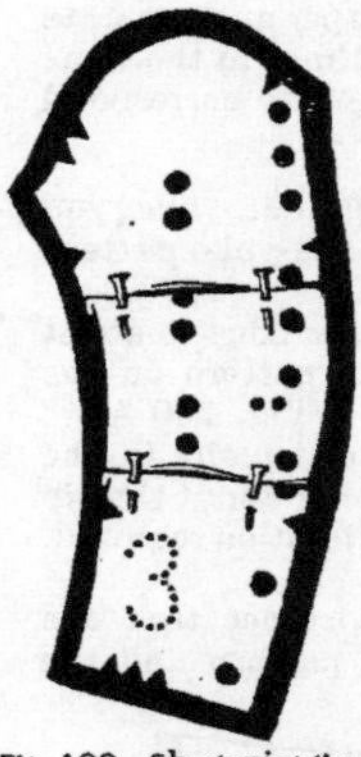

Fig. 199. Shortening the Sleeve Pattern

Shoulders that are more sloping than the average will cause a diagonal wrinkle from the neck to the armhole. (Fig. 197.) This alteration, too, can be made in the actual lining without changing the pattern.

Make up your lining in the usual way and put it on, pinning it carefully. You'll find that it looks like Figure 197, though if your shoulders only slope a little it will not wrinkle as much as it does in the picture. The trouble in your case is that your shoulders droop too much to take up the full size of the lining, so the extra size must be taken out at the shoulder seam. Take up as little as possible near the neck and as much as is necessary out on the shoulder. (Fig. 198.) Lifting the lining at the shoulder will raise the armhole and make it bind. You'll have to slash it a little until it feels just right. Don't slash it too much or your armhole will be too large. (Fig. 198.)

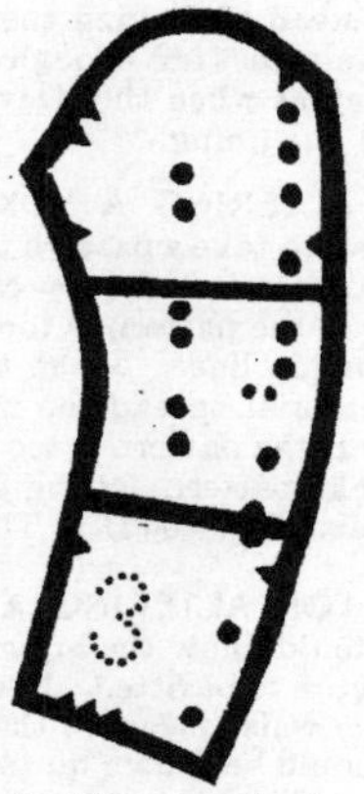

Fig. 200. Lengthening the Sleeve Pattern

Take off your lining, baste the shoulder seams, and cut out the armholes on a line with the slashes. Try it on again to make sure that it is comfortable, and your lining is ready to be stitched.

If there are diagonal wrinkles at the back, they may be handled in the same way as the diagonal wrinkles at the front.

TO LENGTHEN OR SHORTEN SLEEVE PATTERNS, measure along the inside of the arm from the armhole to the bend, and from the bend to the wrist. These two measurements are necessary so that the elbow of the sleeve may be in correct position on the arm, since the upper and lower arm may vary in proportionate length. If all the alterations are made in the upper or lower part of the sleeve, the elbow will be drawn out of place.

If the measure from the armhole to the bend is one inch less than the corresponding part of the pattern, fold a half-inch plait straight across the pattern a little above the elbow. If it is necessary to shorten the lower-arm portion, make a plait half as wide as the amount to be taken out, laying it across the lower part of the sleeve pattern, about three inches below the elbow and parallel with the wrist edge of the sleeve. The plaits across the under-sleeve piece should be made to correspond in size and position with those on the upper piece. The upper-sleeve portion with the plaits pinned in is shown in Figure 199.

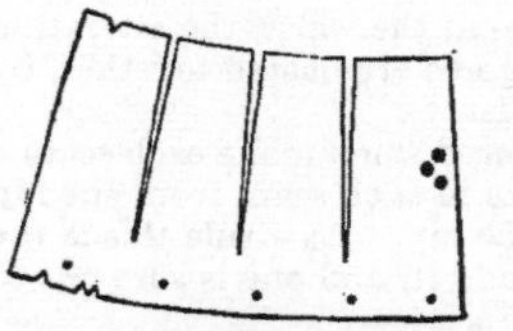

Fig. 200A. Increasing the Waist Size of the Yoke Pattern

When the plaits are folded over, the perforations and the edges of the pattern become uneven. To correct them, lay the altered pattern on a large piece of paper and mark a new outline, running across the edge of the folded part. If the arm is very full, the space between the elbow and the greater width at the top of the sleeve should be filled out, making the edge an even line. But if the arm is not large, the surplus width may be trimmed off to make an even outline from the elbow to the top of the sleeve. Whatever alteration is made at the edges of the seam must be repeated in regard to the large perforations.

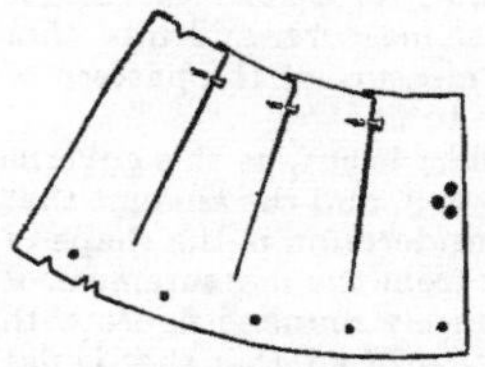

Fig. 200B. Decreasing the Waist Size of the Yoke Pattern

If the sleeve needs lengthening, make the alteration at the same places by cutting across the pattern, instead of making the plaits. Lay the pattern upon another piece of paper and separate the pieces far enough to make it the required length. Correct the outlines in the same way as when the sleeve is shortened. (Fig. 200.) Alter the outside sleeve to correspond to the lining.

ALTERING A YOKE PATTERN—If, in buying a pattern with a circular yoke, you had to take a pattern that was too large or too small for you at the waist, the yoke pattern can be altered very easily. (Figs. 200 A and 200 B on preceding page.)

If the pattern is too small for you, slash the yoke pattern from its upper edge to about the hip line. Make three slashes. (Fig. 200 A.) In pinning the yoke pattern on the material, spread the upper edge until it is the right size for your waist. (Fig. 200 A.)

If the pattern is too large for you at the waist, make three dart-shaped plaits in the yoke pattern, letting the plaits begin at the upper edge and taper to nothing about the hip line. (Fig. 200 B.) The dept of the plaits depends on the amount of the alteration required.

FOR ALTERING A GORED SKIRT PATTERN, it is of greatest importance that one should know the hip measure as well as the waist measure of both the pattern and the figure to be fitted. In taking the waist measure the tape should be drawn quite snugly. The hip measure should be taken seven inches below the waistline, holding the tape easily around the figure. The table of measurements on the envelope should be referred to in order to asoertain if the figure's measures correspond to those of the pattern.

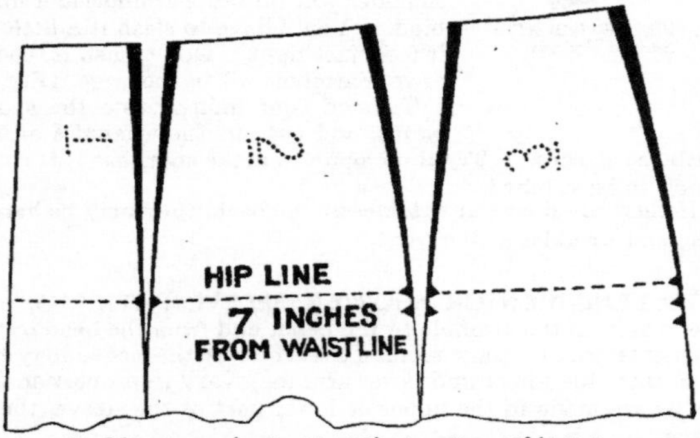

Fig. 201. Increasing the Waist Size in a Gored Skirt Pattern

Order the pattern according to the directions given on the pattern envelope. In some styles a skirt pattern should be ordered by the waist measure, in others by the hip; but in each case the pattern instructions will specify whether it should be bought by the waist or hip.

If a gored skirt is of the correct hip measure, but is too large at the waist, the alteration is quite simple. It can be made in fitting the skirt after the gores are basted together, by making each seam a little deeper from the hip toward the waist.

If the waist is the correct size and the hip is too large in a gored skirt, make each seam a little deeper from the waist toward the hip, continuing to take in each seam from the hip to the lower edge of the skirt the same amount taken in at the hip. As a rule this is the best plan, because it is easier to take in material than to add it, and one is sure not to have a pattern that is too small.

However, if one is proficient in making garments, a gored skirt pattern may be bought by the hip measure, even if too small at the waist, and the waist size may be increased in the following way: The increase must be calculated and planned for before the skirt is cut. We may find, for instance, a figure with 34 inches waist measure, and hips that measure 44. Referring to the "table" we find that the waist measure of the pattern of this hip size is 30 inches—four inches less than the waist we are to fit.

The first consideration is the number of gores in which the skirt is cut, as this governs the number of seams at which allowance may be provided in cutting, and the amount that may be added at each seam. Another and very important consideration is the shape of the figure to be fitted. The same number of inches may result from the measurement of figures that differ entirely in shape. The hip measure of the nicely rounded figure with perfectly proportioned hips and abdomen may be the same as that of another that is flat at the front and back, with abnormal development at the sides; or of still another that has unusual abdominal prominence with extreme flatness at the back.

It will be readily seen that the allowance at the seams must be so distributed that the greater amount will come where the figure has the fullest development. Under ordinary circumstances, it is preferable to make no alteration on either the front or back gores, but this rule can not be followed when the figure is unusually full at the front. In the measurements cited (34 inches waist and 44 inches hip) it is necessary to add 4 inches to the skirt pattern at the waistline, 2 inches on each side.

Figure 201 shows how this amount may be added to a nine-gored skirt pattern. It is a good plan to mark the outline of the pattern on the goods, leaving ample material at each seam which may be let out where the figure requires it, tapering this amount off to nothing at the hipline which is seven and three-eighths inches below the upper edge. A skirt pattern should never be ordered with a hip measure smaller than that of the figure to be fitted.

If a plaited skirt is too large or too small at the waist or hip, the plaits should be made either deeper or shallower to fit the figure.

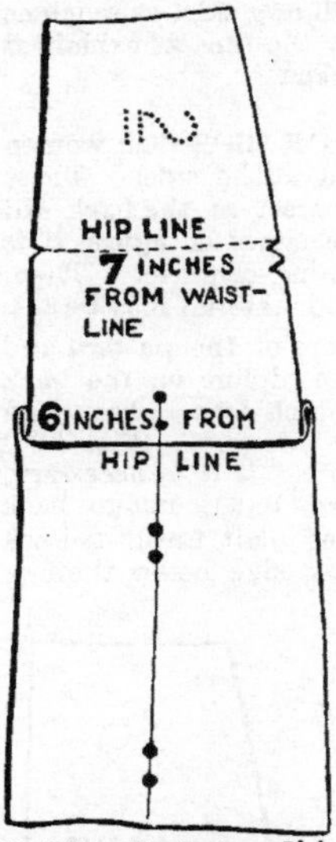

Fig. 202. Shortening a Plain Gored-Skirt Pattern

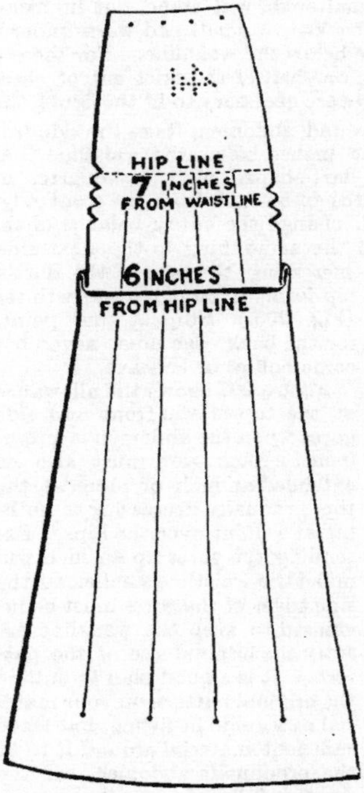

Fig. 203. Shortening a Plaited Gored-Skirt Pattern

LENGTHENING AND SHORTENING GORED SKIRTS—Measure the length of the skirt at the center front from the natural waistline to the floor and compare it with the corresponding measure of the pattern.

To Shorten a gored skirt pattern, lay a plait straight across each gore of the pattern about six inches below the hipline (seven and three-eighth inches below the waistline, the three-eighths of an inch being the seam-allowance at the upper edge). (Fig. 202.) If the gores are cut with one straight edge, measure at the straight edge, or, if both sides of the gores are bias, measure along the line of perforations that indicate a lengthwise thread of the goods. If the figure is full, the slope of the gores at the bias side should be filled out from the folded plait to the hip; but if the figure is slight, this little extension may be taken off.

To Lengthen a gored skirt pattern, cut each gore straight across, six inches below the hipline, and separate the pieces as much as necessary. (Fig. 204.)

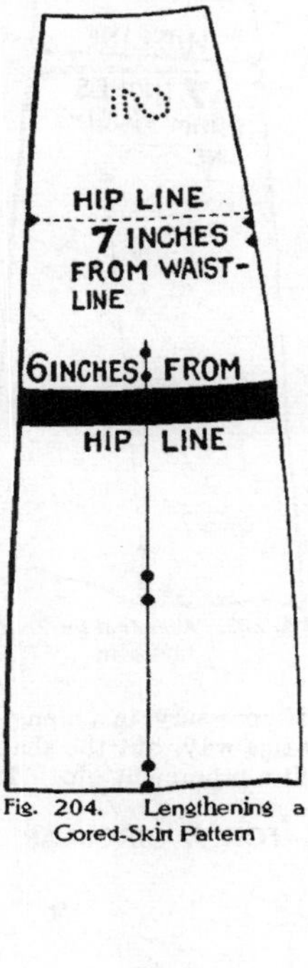

Fig. 204. Lengthening a Gored-Skirt Pattern

To alter the length of a gored *plaited* skirt pattern, follow the same principle as for the plain gored skirt pattern. Then make new lines through the perforations that show the lines for the plaits. Place one end of a yardstick at a perforation near the hipline, and the other end at the corresponding perforation near the bottom, and mark with a pencil. (Fig. 203.)

If, as is rarely the case, it should be necessary to alter the length of a skirt as much as four or five inches, it is best to take half of the amount out below the hips as explained above, and to take the remaining half off at the lower edge of the skirt.

ALTERATIONS FOR A ROUND OR PROMINENT ABDOMEN OR HIPS—On women of this type, the skirt, if unaltered, will stand out in front and at the sides. These women, as a rule, have flat backs. A small pad worn under the corset at the back will fill in the hollow of the figure below the waistline. For these three types of figures it is advisable to experiment with one-half of the skirt cut of cheap lining cambric. Then, after finding just what changes are necessary to fit the figure, the good material may be cut.

For the women with the round abdomen, take the side-front gore of the pattern and mark the hipline on it seven inches below the waistline. At the hipline on the back edge of the gore, take up a dart-shaped plait one-quarter of an inch deep and tapering away to nothing three-eighths of an inch from the front edge of the gore. (Fig. 205.) This quarter of an inch will change the entire balance of the gore. If it is necessary, in a skirt of many gores, do the same thing to the next side gore, but do not go back of the hip. You can keep increasing the size of the dart-shaped plait until the back edge of the gore above the hip forms a straight line with the back edge below the hip. (Fig. 205.) Stop at that point, for the back edge must never become hollow or concave.

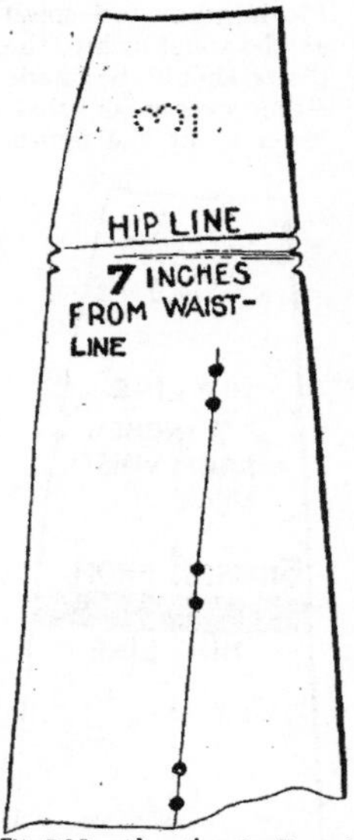

Fig. 205. Alteration for Round Abdomen

Figure 207 shows the allowance at the top of the front and side gores when the abdomen is prominent. Each gore must also be extended an inch or more at the top, gradually decreasing to nothing at a point over the hips. Extending the gores up an inch will make the waistline smaller, so the side edges of the gores must be increased to keep the waistline exactly the original size of the pattern. It is a good plan to outline the original pattern on your material as a guide in fitting, but leave sufficient material around it to fit the prominent abdomen. If the figure is full in front, all garments should have this allowance left at the top of the front when cutting.

For the woman with the prominent hips, select from the pattern the gore with its front edge coming over the fullest part of the hips, pinning the pattern together to find the right one. This gore must be altered in same way as for the round abdomen. (Fig. 206.) If necessary, in a many-gored skirt, the next gore toward the back may be altered in the same way, but the shape of the back gore should never be changed in altering a skirt to fit a prominent hip. These principles apply to any gored skirt pattern.

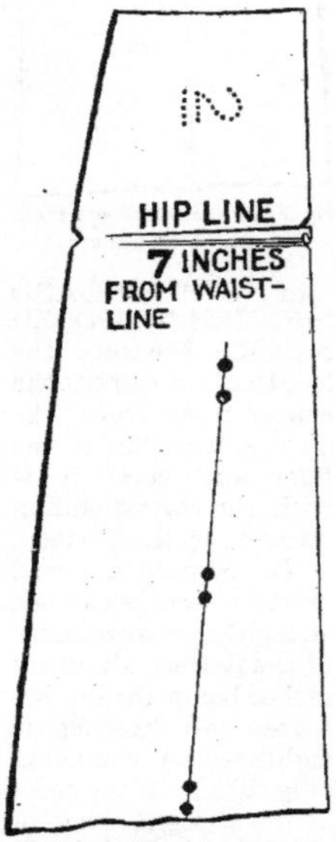

Fig. 206. Alteration on Side Core for Prominent Hip

FOR A CIRCULAR SKIRT PATTERN, it is best to order the pattern by hip measure, as the alterations may easily be made at the waist when the hip measure is correct. A well-cut circular skirt pattern without darts allows from one to two inches extra size, more than the waist measure, on each half of the pattern. This fulness should be eased into the belt over the hips, and the fulness shrunk away after the skirt is finished. When fitting the skirt, mark on the waistline where the fulness should be distributed, and gather this portion to the required size with fine stitches on a strong thread. Dampen the material, or place the wet sponge cloth over it and press it over a tailor's cushion until the cloth has shrunk to the correct size. (Fig. 208.) This must be done very carefully in order not to leave any "bubbles" in the cloth.

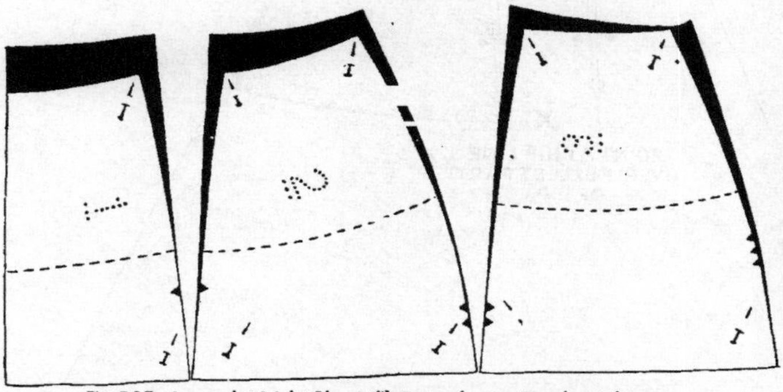

Fig. 207. Increasing Waist Size, With Extension for Prominent Abdomen

If the waist needs to be made very much smaller than the pattern, it may be necessary to make one or two small darts, but if only a small reduction is required, it may often be shrunk in. If the waist size is to be increased, no alteration is necessary. There will simply be less material to ease into the belt. In a circular skirt with darts, the waist size can be made smaller or larger. It can be done by taking in or letting out the darts. If the waist size is to be increased, the darts may be let out. In a circular skirt pattern of the correct hip measure it should not be necessary to make an alteration of more than one inch at the hips on the whole skirt. This alteration may be made at the center back.

To Alter the Length of a circular skirt, it is best to make the change at the lower edge. For a woman having a slightly rounded or decidedly prominent abdomen, an alteration is required to provide for extra length at the top. (Fig. 209.) If this provision is not made in cutting, the skirt will draw up in front and stand out in a very ugly manner.

Fig. 208. Shrinking Out Fulness in Circular Skirt

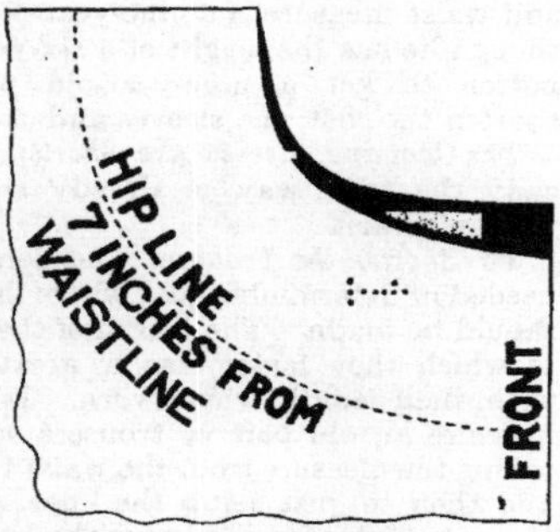

Fig. 209. Extra Length at Top of Circular Skirt

It will be found, in making the alteration, that according to the prominence of the abdomen, from one-half to one and one-half inches will have to be added to the top of the pattern in front, gradually decreasing to nothing at a point over the hips, to make the skirt drop in a straight line from the fullest part of the abdomen to the floor. To do this, it is best to outline the edge of the pattern with chalk or thread, and leave sufficient material to raise the waistline as much as may be necessary. (Fig. 209.) In extreme cases it may be necessary to put a dart at the center front, but usually a slight easing of the skirt into the belt across the front will be sufficient.

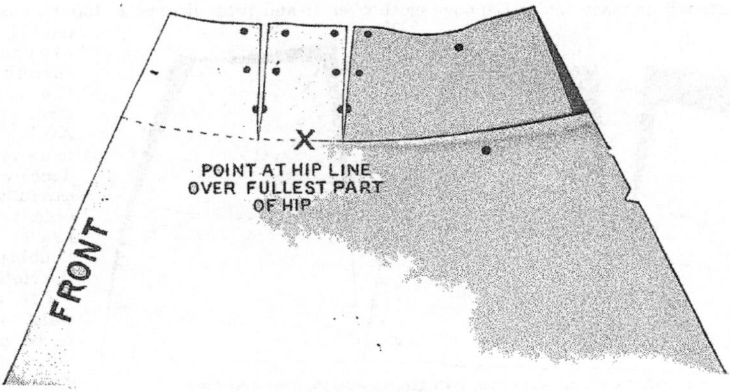

Fig. 210. When the Hips Are Large

FOR A FIGURE WITH PROMINENT HIPS, it is necessary to increase the amount eased in the belt, or increase the size of darts over the fullest part of the hip: Mark the hipline on the pattern seven and three-eighths inches below the waistline. At the hipline on the back edge of the pattern take up a dart-shaped plait about one-half inch deep and tapering away to nothing at a point just over the fullest part of the hip. Slash the pattern from the upper edge, through the darts, to the hipline, to make it lie flat. (Fig. 210.) The darts should be kept the original length.

ALTERING LENGTH OF BOYS' PATTERNS—When a boy of five or six years has the breast and waist measure of a nine-year-old size, even though he has the height of a six-year-old, it is better to get a nine-year-old pattern and shorten the coat, the sleeves and trousers.

The Coat and Sleeves Are Shortened in practically the same way as already shown in the woman's waist.

To Shorten the Trousers considerable care is needed in determining just where the alteration should be made. The length of the underwaist to which they fasten has a great deal to do with their length when worn. It is well to measure an old pair of trousers on the child, taking the measure from the waist to the crotch and then to just below the knee, allowing for the extra fulness to fall over the knee in knickerbockers. Any alteration in length above the crotch should be made across the pattern below the extension for the pocket opening, changing the seam edges as little as possible. In the lower leg part, fold the plait across above the extension piece at the lower part of the leg. (Fig. 211.)

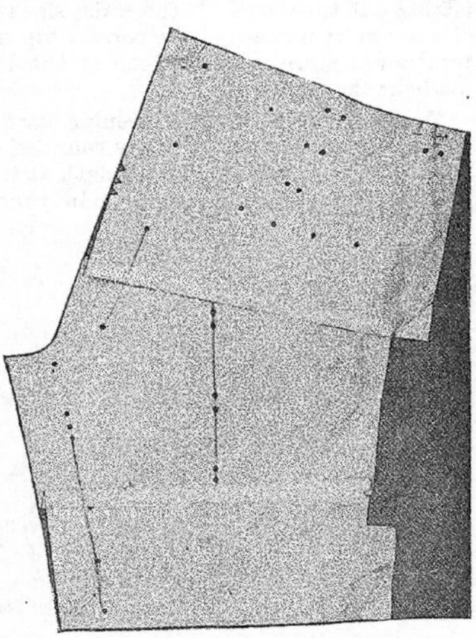

Fig. 211. Shortening the Pattern of Boys' Knickerbockers

CHAPTER XV

UNLINED WAISTS

SEPARATE unlined waists are made from a great variety of materials, sheer batiste, lawn, handkerchief linen, etc., silks of all descriptions and many of the soft woolens.

For Trimming a lingerie waist the combination of two kinds of lace, fine and heavy, or of lace and embroidery, is very effective. Fig. 212 shows a waist made of linen, cut from a perfectly plain pattern, closing in the back. The first step in making this waist is to cut the front and back pieces; baste the seams and fit the waist to the figure. Stitch the shoulder seams. Now open the under-arm seams; lay the waist out flat on the table, and baste or pin the insertion in place, following the design illustrated, repeating it at the back.

Draw the pull-thread in the lace where the curve requires a slight gathering to make it lie flat. At the corners turn the lace sharply, and miter carefully. (Instructions for making mitered corners are given on page 11.) Then sew the edges of the fine and heavy lace together with an overhand stitch. The free edges of the lace are basted to the material and stitched down by machine as close to the edge as possible.

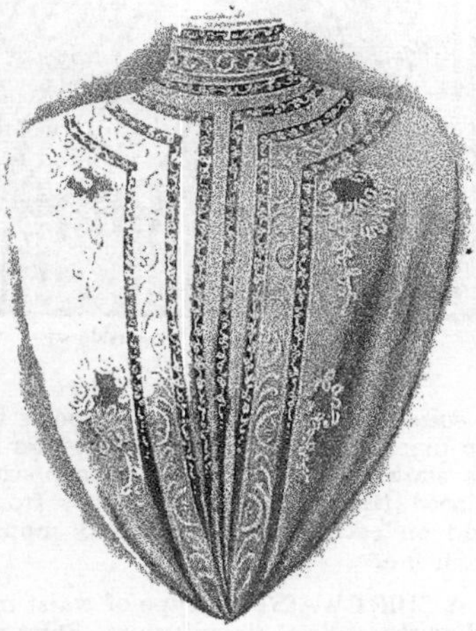

Fig. 212. Ornamentation of Lace and Embroidery Insertion, Medallions and Hand-Embroidery

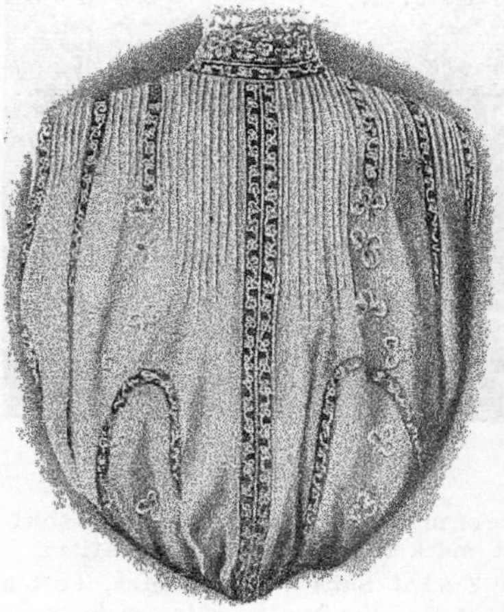

Fig. 213. Tucked Waist with Insertion and Hand Embroidery Trimming

Cut out the material from under the lace, leaving a narrow seam's width at each side. This edge may be turned back and stitched flat by a second row of stitching, leaving a raw edge. Or, it may be overcast closely with the raw edge rolled in to prevent any possible raveling. Fig. 214 on the following page shows a medallion decoration set in in this way. Sometimes, where two finished edges come together, they are lapped and stitched together as illustrated in Fig. 215.

A waist made from a pattern that allows for tucks is shown in Fig. 213. They should be made before the lace is applied. The waist itself is put together like a plain waist.

When all the trimming on the waist has been securely fastened in place, the under-arm

Fig. 214. Finishing the Underside of Medallion Inset

seams are again closed, stitched by machine and finished in the usual manner.

The Collar, which is preferably attached to the waist, may be made of alternate rows of the fine and heavy lace. Cut a fitted collar pattern of stiff paper, turning under a seam at the top and bottom. On this paper collar baste the insertion in place, right side down, drawing the pull-thread sufficiently to give it the proper curve. Overhand the edges together and then remove the collar from the paper.

A narrow seam beading is used to join the collar to the waist. Trim the material away from the upper edge of the beading, and overhand this edge carefully to the lower edge of the collar. Baste the lower edge of the beading to the neck edge of the waist and stitch in a French seam.

To keep the collar from becoming crushed, a suitable number of collar supports should be placed at each side of the center front, as shown in Fig. 216. The supports are placed two and one-half inches from the end on each side, and a third support at each end.

Fig. 215. Medallion and Insertion Set in by Machine

A SHIRT-WAIST is a type of waist modeled on the style of a man's shirt. Shirt-waists are usually made of linen, madras or flannel. A good pattern for the beginner is a perfectly plain design having slight fulness at the waistline. Though a shirt-waist needs careful fitting, not so much skill is required in making it, and it is quite possible to fit oneself.

Always open the pattern, identify each piece and get a clear idea of the construction by reading the instructions carefully before beginning to cut into your material. This care at the beginning will make the work easier and save mistakes and consequent waste of material. In cutting out the shirt-waist, mark all notches and perforations.

Fig. 216. Showing Position of Collar Supports

In Tucked Shirt-Waist Patterns, it often happens that the fronts are too wide to be cut from one width of the goods. In this case it is necessary to piece the material. Take care that the seam comes where it will not show. In Fig. 217 the right front of a shirt-waist is shown pieced in this way. The method of piecing is easily understood.

The pattern should be laid on the material, and the best place to make the joining considered carefully. It will depend on the width of the goods and the style of the shirt-waist. In some cases it may be made at the stitching of the last tuck, but in others this tuck is not stitched to the waist line but terminates at yoke depth; consequently this seam would not be hidden.

In the model illustrated the best place proved to be at the stitching of the first turnback tuck on the right front. According to the pattern instructions, one inch back of the fold edge of the tuck is the stitching line, as the tucks are one inch wide. Mark the stitching line with chalk, allow three-eighths of an inch beyond it toward the front edge for a seam, and cut off the rest of the material.

A piece wide enough to complete the front must be joined at the stitching line, and when the tuck is made, both raw edges of this seam should be turned to one side and included in the tuck so that the seam is completely hidden on both the outside and inside of the waist. A piece sufficiently wide to enlarge the front breadth is sometimes left from the width from which the back is cut. The left front of the waist is turned under for a hem, as directed in the pattern instructions, and stitched.

The Gibson Tuck in a waist necessitates joining the shoulder seam first before basting in the tuck. This leaves the tuck free across the shoulder seam (Fig. 218), and in basting in the sleeves the tucks can simply be turned toward the neck out of the way as illustrated.

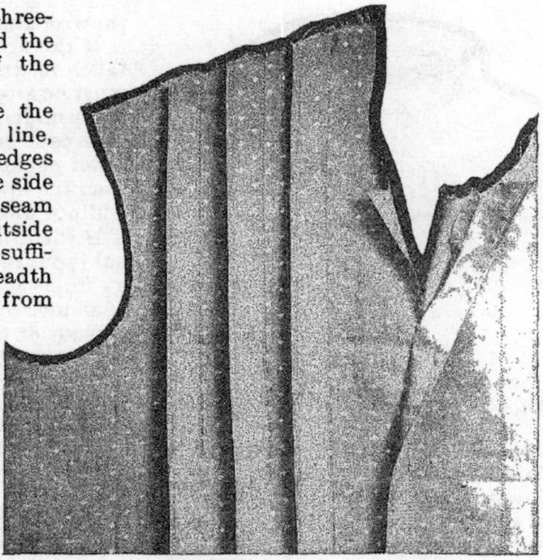

Fig. 217. Hiding the Joining Seam in Front of Tucked Shirt-Waist

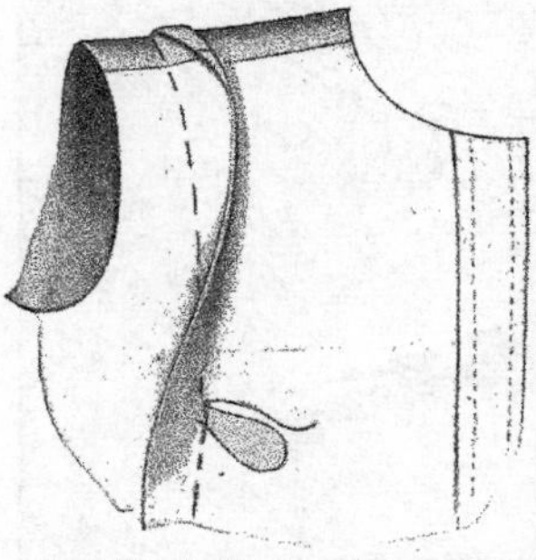

Fig. 218. Basting in a Gibson Tuck

Make the closing for the box plait or turn under the edge for a coat closing, on the right front, and a hem on the left front, as directed.

The direction may be readily understood by referring to Figs. 219 and 220 on the next page. The coat closing is finished by turning both hems toward the wrong side and stitching. (Fig. 222.)

If the waist is to have a blind closing, a fly must be applied to the closing edge. The fly should be made double, folded lengthwise through the center, and a seam turned in at each edge. The fold edges are basted together and then sewed in position. (Fig. 221.)

Stretch the edges of the fronts at the neck and at the shoulder, between the middle of the shoulder and the neck, to make the waist fit into the hollow of the figure around the collar-bone. Baste the shoulder and under-arm seams toward the outside through the lines of perforation with the notches matching. Gather the back and fronts at the waistline perforations and baste to the belt stay unless the fronts are to hang free under the belt. Try on, lapping the fronts.

Any necessary alterations in the shirt-waist should be made at the shoulder and under-arm seams, never at the front. A little adjustment at the shoulder seams will often correct what appears at first to be an ill-fitting shirt-waist. Stitch three-eighths of an inch outside of the basting on the right side of the waist at the shoulder and under-arm seams. Trim off the edges close to the line of stitching; turn the waist to

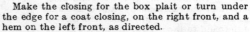

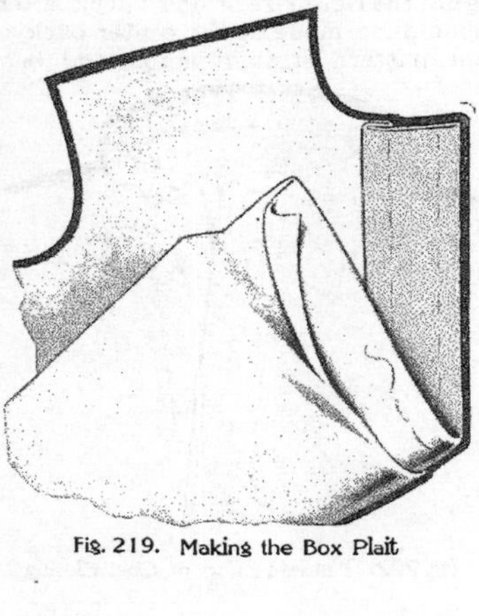

Fig. 219. Making the Box Plait

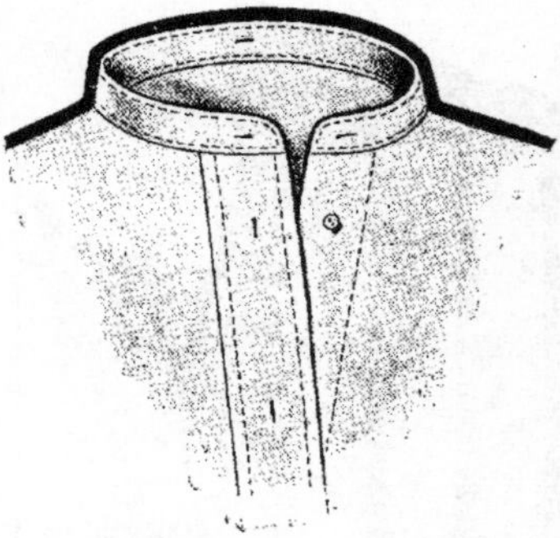

Fig. 220. Finished Effect of Box-Plait Closing

the wrong side, and stitch again in a French seam.

If the under-arm seams have been let out or taken in, the notches in the top of the sleeves must be altered correspondingly. For instance, if the under-arm seam has been let out one inch, raise each notch in the sleeve half an inch. The lower part of the sleeve is purposely cut larger than the lower part of the waist so that the sleeve will not draw on the waist.

If the armhole of the waist is too small, do not cut it out recklessly. Try snipping the material at intervals around the armhole three-eighths of an inch or so. This will allow the armhole to spread on the arm, and will show how much to cut away.

The Neck requires care. It should not be trimmed out too much. The neck-band should fit the neck closely, though not too tightly, or it will be difficult to adjust the collar. Shirt-waists are usually made with a band finishing the neck of the waist and worn with a separate linen collar. In making the band, cut two sections by the collar-band pattern and place them together with the right sides face to face. Baste an even three-eighth-inch seam at the top and ends, turn the band right side out and crease and baste the edges flat. Baste the inside section of the band to the neck of the waist with the seam on the right side. Turn the seam up, turn in the remaining edge of the band fully covering the seam and stitch the outside, continuing this stitching all around the band.

Fig. 221 shows the neck-band sewed to the neck of the waist. It will be seen that the wide lap from right to left requires that the neck-band be longer on the right side than on the left, measuring from the center back. If the band supplied with the pattern is not the right size of one's neck, alterations should be made at the center back, cutting the pattern straight across and basting a piece of paper in the space to make it larger, or lapping it at the center to make it smaller.

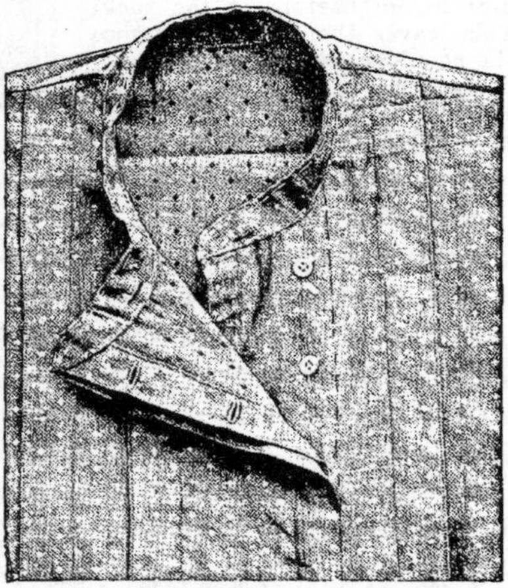

Fig. 221. Fly, Buttons and Neck-Band

The buttonholes which should be worked in the front of the neck-band and at the back, when the waist is worn with a linen collar, are shown in the illustration No. 221.

A back yoke may be applied to the waist as shown in Fig. 223 on next page.

If the fronts are to hang free, baste a tape across the back of the waist, and adjust the fulness over the front under the tape. Many prefer this plan, since it lessens the trouble in making and laundering.

Where the waist is very full in front or is made of heavy material, the front portion is frequently cut away below the waistline where the gathers begin, and the fulness gathered into a band.

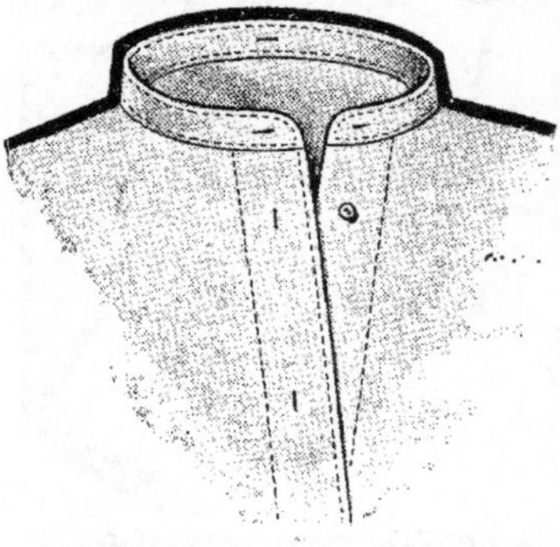

Fig. 222. Finished Effect of Coat Closing

Fig. 223. Method of Applying Yoke

This band is an inch deep, when finished, and is cut a trifle bias in front. Fig. 224.

Be careful not to draw the line of the seam joining the front and back out of place. The material, which is slightly bias under the arm, should be drawn smoothly toward the front as far as it will reach, and pinned at the waistline. The tucks may then be lapped over each other unless the fulness is gathered or laid in overlapping plaits and the waist drawn down or bloused, as preferred.

The tape should be pinned carefully, following the waistline. When the waist is taken off, baste the tape in place. Then take either a strong twill tape or a narrow strip of the material with the ends turned in, and baste to the inside of the waist, following the line of the upper edge of the tape on the outside. Then remove the outside tape and stitch the upper edge of the inside tape to the waist, after disposing of the fulness at the back by making two rows of gathers as far apart as the width of the tape. This method is shown in Fig. 227, on the next page.

Another method of finishing the fronts is to cut across the fronts just above the lower edge of the strip stitched to the inside. (Fig. 225.) The cut must extend only as far as necessary to take out the extra fulness. The uneven upper edge of this piece may be trimmed and turned in and hemmed down to the part from which it was cut, providing sufficient length to hold the waist down. (Fig. 226.) A row of stitching should be placed at the lower edge of the inside band. The band will cover the raw edges of the cut portion at the front. This finish does away with the bulky material below the waistline, which is apt to spoil the set of a close-fitting skirt. The bottom of the waist is finished with a narrow hem.

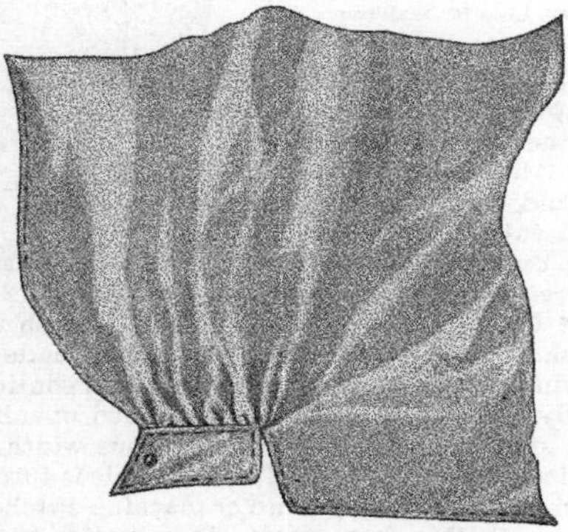

Fig. 224. Fulness below Waistline Dispensed With in Band

The extension below the waist at the sides may have to be slashed to prevent its drawing over the hips. If preferred, a circular peplum such as is given in a corset cover pattern, may be used. The peplum

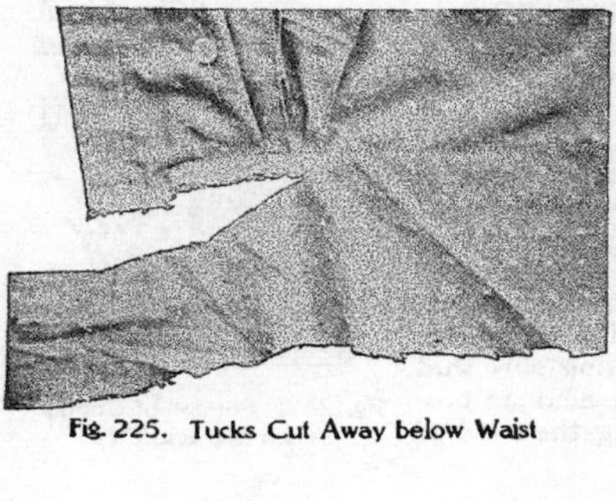

Fig. 225. Tucks Cut Away below Waist

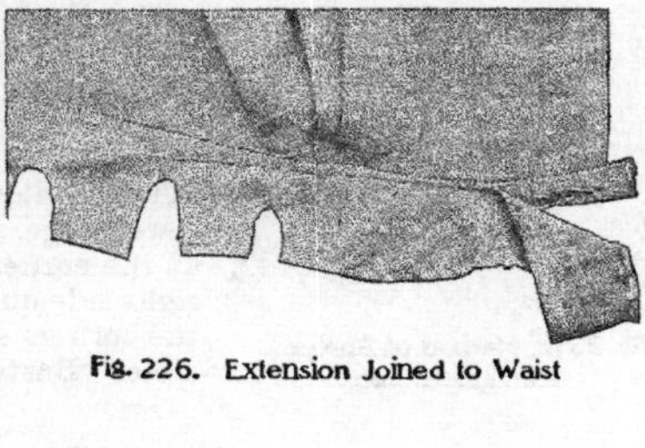

Fig. 226. Extension Joined to Waist

is sewed to the bottom of the waist to hold it down properly. For waists having no fulness at the back, the peplum is used to give the proper spring below the waistline.

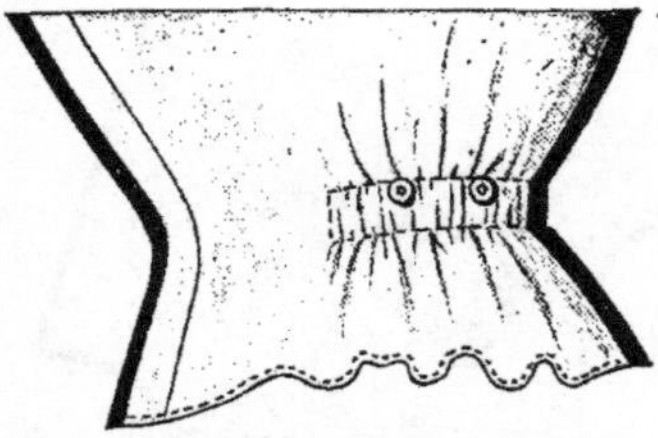

Fig. 227. Gathers and Buttonholed Rings at Back of Waist

Sew buttonholed rings at the back of the waist belt, as shown in Fig. 227. If two are used, each ring should be an inch and one-eighth from the center back. Or, one can be placed at the center of the back with the others two inches apart. Hooks are sewed with the same spacing to the inside of the skirt belt. Do not use hooks any larger than are necessary to fit into the rings. If rings are not procurable, ordinary eyes may be substituted.

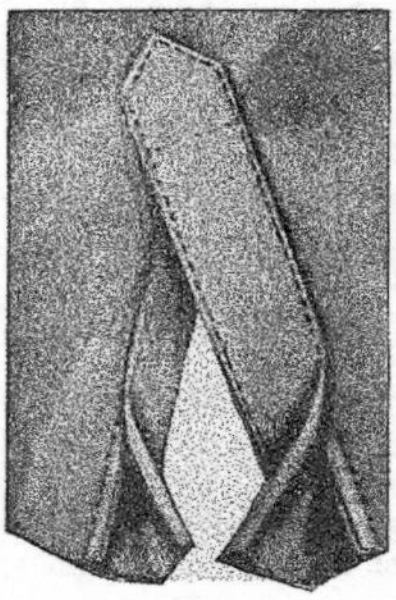

Fig. 228. Method of Applying Laps to Sleeves

For the Slash in the Sleeve sew the underlap piece to the back edge of the slash with the seam toward the right side. Crease the seam on the lap, turn the lap at the perforations; baste down, entirely covering the joining, and stitch. Join the overlap piece to the front edge of the slash in the same manner. (Fig. 228.) Adjust the overlap so that it will conceal the underlap and baste it in place. Stitch all around the overlap, following the shape of the point. At the top of the opening the stitching should cross the lap and catch through the underlap, securely holding the opening in correct position, as shown in Figs. 229 and 230.

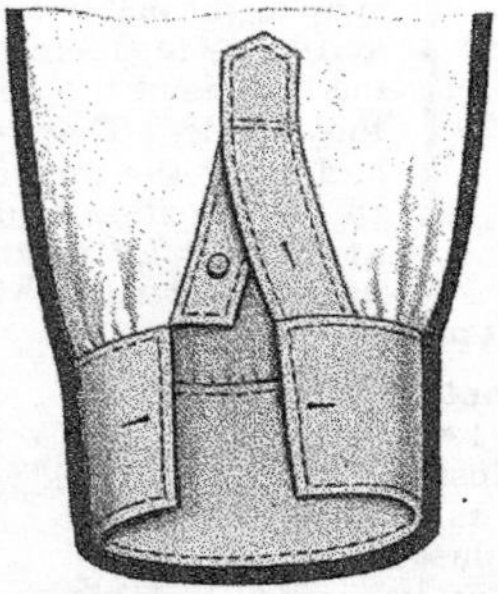

Fig. 229. Finish for Link-Button Closing

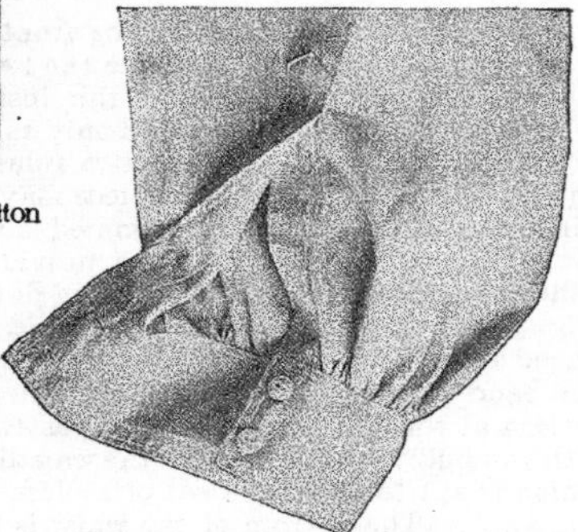

Fig. 230. Finish for Lap Closing

A Continuous Lap is often used to finish the slash at the cuff opening. This lap is made by sewing a straight strip of the material continuously along both edges of the slashed opening, the strip of material being the same width all its length. (Fig. 231.) The other side is turned over and hemmed by hand or machine-stitched, to cover the first seam. This lap is shown in Fig. 232. When the lower edge of the sleeve is gathered this lap is turned under at the front or overlapping edge of the opening and extends on the other side to form an underlap.

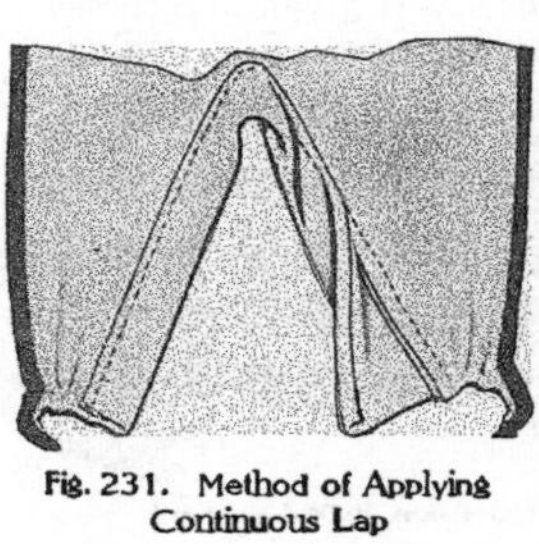

Fig. 231. Method of Applying Continuous Lap

Join the long edges of the sleeve in a French seam and gather the bottom. Cut two sections and an interlining of coarse linen or muslin for each cuff. Baste the interlining to the wrong side of one of the cuff sections. Then baste the second cuff section to the first with the right sides facing each other, stitching along the two ends and lower edge. Trim off the seam at the corners and turn the cuff right side out, making sure that the corners are as neat as possible. Baste along the seamed

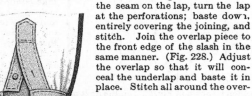

Fig. 232. Position of Continuous Lap and Cuff

edges so that the cuff will be easy to handle in sewing it to the sleeve.

Baste the upper edge of the outside and interlining to the sleeve and overlap, but not to the underlap in a link cuff (Fig. 229), and to the sleeve, overlap and underlap in a lapped cuff. (Fig. 230.) Then stitch, pushing the sleeve fulness well toward the end of the cuff. Turn the seam down and baste. Make a narrow turning on the inside of the cuff and baste in position, covering the seam. Stitch around all the edges of the cuff from the outside. For convenience in handling it is better to turn the sleeve wrong side out before making this stitching.

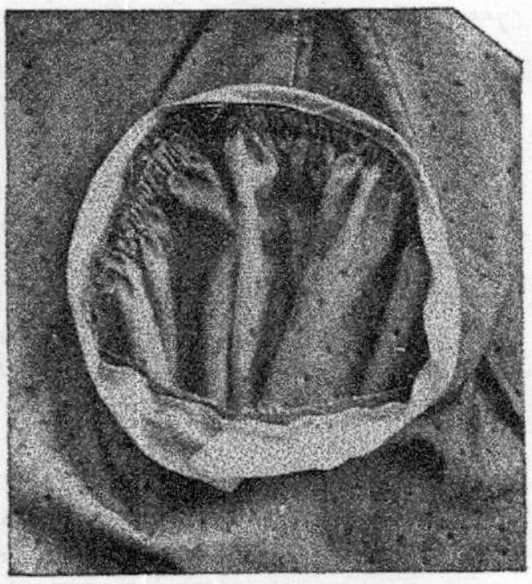
Fig. 233. Binding the Armhole

The notches at the top of the sleeve show where the gathers begin and end and where they are placed on the waist. The fulness should be fairly evenly distributed, but more of it should be pushed to the top of the shoulder than to the front and back. In sewing in the sleeve, hold the sleeve side toward you so that the gathers can be handled easily in basting.

Baste the sleeve to the armhole. If the material is too heavy for a French seam, make the seam toward the inside and cover it with a narrow bias strip of lawn. (Fig. 233.)

The shirt-waist is now ready for the buttonholes. In the box plait they are worked up and down through the center with a bar tack at each end. (Page 13, Fig. 49.) In the neck-band they are worked lengthwise. The buttonhole at the center back is worked one-quarter of an inch above the stitching and has a bar tack at each end. Those at the ends of the band are worked a corresponding distance above the stitching, but with a round front end above the center of the box plait. (Page 14, Fig. 50.) The buttonholes in the cuff are cut one-half inch in from the edge and about in the middle of the cuff. They are worked with one round end and one bar tack.

If a detached collar is desired, cut two sections and an interlining by the collar pattern. Stitch together on the outside edges. Turn, and baste the bottom of the collar and its band with the seam toward the wrong side, and then stitch. Hem the outer edge over to the line of stitching. Stitch around the outside of the collar and work buttonholes corresponding to those on the neck-band of the shirt-waist.

CHAPTER XVI

LINED WAISTS

THE CONSTRUCTION of a lined waist requires the most minute attention to every detail. If great care is given to the work one can feel sure of satisfactory results. For a draped waist the lining is made separately, fitted, and the seams pressed open and boned before the outer material is adjusted.

THE LINING is the foundation of a fitted waist. When cutting the lining, lay the perforations indicating the lengthwise thread of the material parallel to the selvage. If the directions are not followed exactly in this respect the waistline of each section of the pattern will come on the wrong thread, and the lining will stretch out of shape.

Some dressmakers advocate cutting cotton linings crosswise of the material, but they do not cut to advantage this way. The argument is that material used crosswise will stretch very little, if any, and the lining may be strengthened by making it double at the points where the greatest strain will come.

At the seams of the under-arms, the shoulders and the darts, mark the sewing line by tailors' tacks along the line formed by the large perforations. Do this when cutting the lining and while it is double, so that both sides may be marked exactly alike. Mark with a colored thread the perforations that indicate the waistline and also those marking the elbow in the sleeve portion. Baste the seams of the lining together with their notches matched, basting the outlet seams through the perforations and the other seams three-eighths of an inch from the seam edges.

A waist lining should be reenforced for a stout figure in the following way: Before cutting out or closing the dart seams, baste an extra piece of lining from the front of the waist to the second or back dart, and reaching from the top of the dart to the bottom of the lining. (Fig. 239.) Now cut up the center of each dart between the rows of perforations, then bring these perforations together, and, beginning at the top, baste the darts and include the stay pieces in the seams. A waist fastening at the back has the back portions reenforced to a corresponding height.

Baste the under-arm and shoulder seams toward the outside for the first fitting, for it is at these seams that the greatest alterations are usually made. Put the lining on and draw it toward the front, bringing the two raw edges together. Pin them in a seam, placing the first pin at the marks indicating the waistline. Smooth the lining over the figure at both the front and back, and be careful that the waistline of the lining is at the waistline of the figure. Make alterations at the under-arm and shoulder seams and at the front edge if necessary. Draw the lining up well at the shoulder seams, but not enough to draw it from the correct waistline. It may be fitted at these seams a little more snugly at the final fitting.

Sometimes after the shoulders are carefully pinned there will be wrinkles in the front, between the shoulder and the neck. These are caused by the natural hollow of the shoulder. In this case the shoulder seam must be ripped open and the front stretched to the back from the center of the shoulder to the neck. Wrinkles at the back near the neck are often caused by the lining being too long-waisted in back. Or the shoulder seam may have been sloped too much, especially if the person is very square-shouldered. It is always better to rip the bastings and pin the seam over again.

If the waist draws to one side it is because the waistlines have not been pinned together at the line of bastings. The top of the darts must come just below the curve of the bust and they may be raised or lowered if necessary.

If the armholes feel too tight, be very careful not to gouge them out under the arms or around the front, or the waist may be ruined. The best plan is to snip the armholes for about three-eighths of an inch. This will give sufficient spring for the arm, and the sleeve can be stitched in just beyond the end of the snippings. If, however, this does not give sufficient ease to the armhole, pare the edges off a little and snip the seams a trifle deeper. The same caution applies to the neck.

Pin the alterations, and mark carefully along the line of pins with tailors' chalk. Without removing the pins baste through the corrections, keeping a well-shaped line for the seams. Try the lining on again to be sure that the alterations are right. Transfer the alterations to the other side of the waist by using the corrected side as a pattern. Baste the seams again, this time with the seams toward the inside. Stitch the seams just outside the bastings so as not to make the waist any smaller, bearing in mind that the sewing of the seams will tend to tighten them. It also allows the bastings to be drawn easily, for if the seam is stitched directly on top of the bastings, both rows will be so interwoven that it will be almost impossible to pull them out.

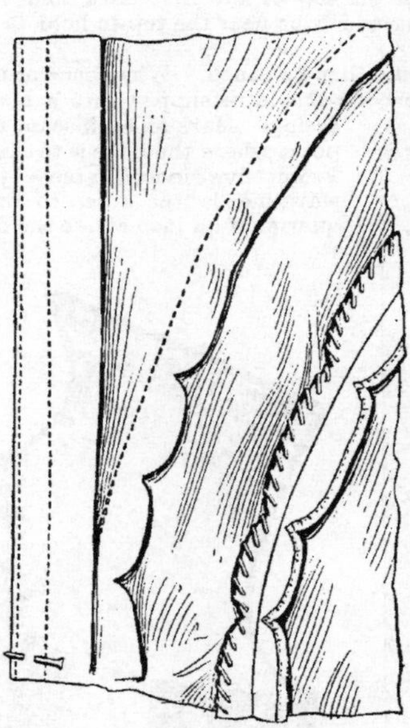
Fig. 234. Notched Seams Before and after Binding

In stitching side-back seams always have the back next the feed of the machine and the side-back next the presser-foot, and hold the parts well up at each end of the presser-foot. Otherwise the side-back seams are liable to pucker or pull when being sewed.

In making seams in which one portion is fulled on to another, place the full portion next the feed, or downward, because if it is placed next the presser-foot, the latter is liable to shove the fulness out of place. Notch the seams at the waistline and two or three times above and below it, enough to allow them to lie flat when pressed. Bind the seams neatly with ribbon seam-binding run on loosely, and press them open. Some dressmakers prefer to overcast the seams, and most of the imported French dresses are finished in that way, but it does not present as neat a finish and takes a great deal of time, as the overcasting must be done closely and carefully.

Many linings, especially those of taffeta, are simply pinked. Fig. 234 shows a seam edge bound, another overcast, and a third notched and ready to bind. It also shows the notching necessary to make the side seam lie flat when it is pressed open.

When no hem is allowed at the closing edge of the lining, it is necessary to face it. Cut two pieces of the lining material in the same outline as the front or back—wherever the opening comes—and two inches wide. Baste one on the outside of each front or back, stitch a seamed edge, and turn the facing over toward the inside. Place a row of stitching one-eighth of an inch inside the edge and another far enough inside the first to allow a whalebone or featherbone to be slipped in.

If a hem is allowed at the closing edge, turn it over toward the inside of the lining and make the two rows of machine-stitching form a casing for the bone. If the waist has a back closing, the hem or closing line is usually indicated by a notch at the neck and another at the bottom of the pattern. Fold a line from one of these notches to the other, keeping the hem an equal width, and with a thread of different color from the lining run a basting along the edge of the fold. Later this will be turned over for the closing.

Make a stay for the hooks and eyes from an extra strip of taffeta or thin lining, two inches wide. Fold lengthwise through the center and place it on the inside of the lining, with its fold at the basting-thread which marks the closing. Turn over both thicknesses and baste very carefully. Then stitch with one row of stitching an eighth of an inch back from the edge, and another row about three-eighths of an inch inside of that. The method is shown in Fig. 234. Pin the fronts together with the waistlines even. Place a tape-measure along the front edge, and with pins mark carefully the position for the hooks and eyes at every inch point, beginning one inch below the neck.

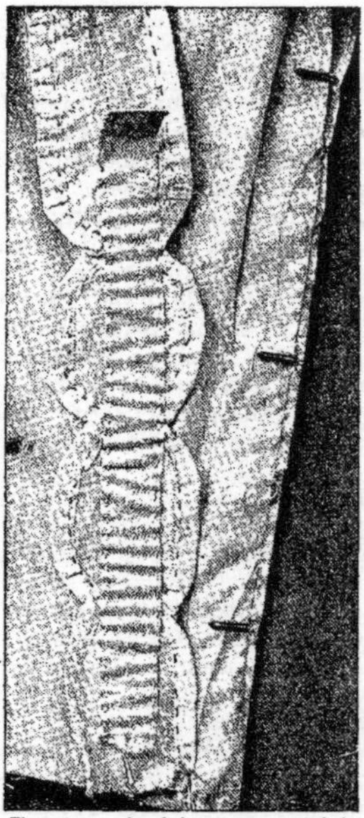

Fig. 235. · Applying Bone Casing

Whalebone can be bought in strips one yard long. About three yards are required to bone a waist. Get a medium-weight quality and let the whalebone soak in tepid water to soften it so the needle can be passed through it. Do not use hot water, as it will make the bone brittle.

Round the ends of the bone and shave them for half an inch to make the ends thinner, using a dull knife or the blade of the scissors. Slip a bone into the casing at each side of the closing, allowing it to reach within an inch of the top of the first dart, and sew through the lining and bone near the top to hold it in place.

The seams should then be boned. Whalebone or the uncovered featherbone should be slipped into a bone-casing. Mark on each seam the point where the bone is to start. From five inches above the waistline is the rule, to one-quarter of an inch above the finished edge of the waist. Procure a piece of single bone-casing or Prussian binding, as it is called. This may be had in several colors, but black or white is to be preferred. Double over one end an inch and over-hand the edges together to make a little pocket. Do not sew this pocket fast to the seam, but begin three-quarters of an inch down from its fold and sew the casing on with a running stitch. (Fig. 235.)

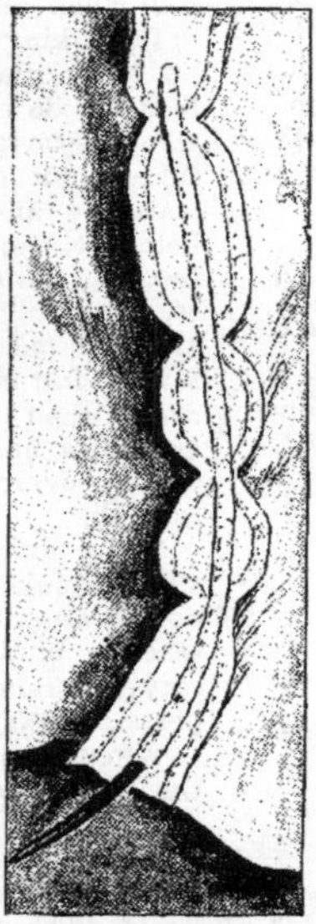

Fig. 236. Whalebone Properly Sprung

Sew both edges, holding the casing somewhat full and keeping it over the middle of the seam.

Run the bone into the pocket at the bottom of each casing and fasten it at the top by sewing through both bone and casing. Sew through again three inches above the waistline. Then push the bone very tight, so it will stretch out the seam and give a curve at the waist (Fig. 236), and sew again there. If the finished edge extends below the waistline, fasten the bone again one-half inch from the bottom. (Fig. 236.) Do not spring the bones in the front so much as at the sides and back. The greatest curve is required at the under-arm seams, less at the front and back.

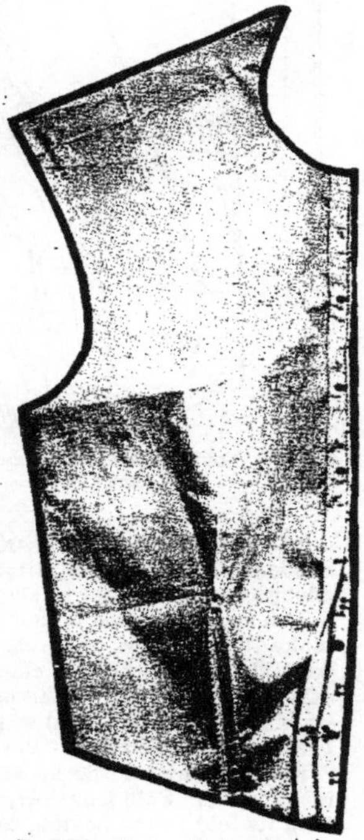

Fig. 237. Hem or Facing Covering Hooks and Eyes

For Covered Featherbone, the method of boning a waist is somewhat different, since it is stitched to the lining by machine, without an applied casing.

The seams of the lining are pressed, bound and marked as for whaleboning. The covering is ripped about half an inch on one end of the featherbone, the bone is cut away, and then the covering is turned over the end, giving it a neat finish. This end is placed over the seam at the mark. Keep the center of the bone over the seam; stitch it in position. Care must be taken to push the bone up and draw the lining down while stitching, as otherwise the lining is likely to be held in on the bone, causing it to wrinkle. Its inexpensiveness and convenience are qualities that have made featherbone very popular with dressmakers. It is obtainable in many different styles, and in twelve and thirty-six yard lengths, so that it can be used without waste. The bone is cut off a trifle shorter than the mark for the length of the waist.

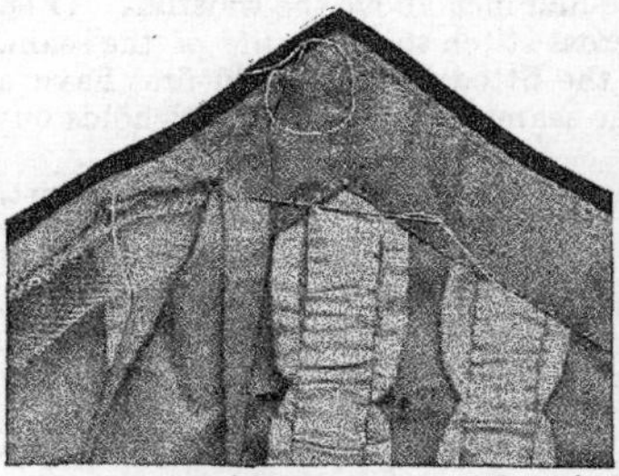

Fig. 238. Facing the Bottom of the Waist

The hooks and eyes, alternating, are sewed on after the bone has been slipped into the casing. (Fig. 237.) Separate the two rings of the hooks at the back to make the hooks lie flatter. Place them well inside the edge; sew through the two rings and also around the end of each hook—this latter sewing a quarter of an inch from the edge. Sew completely *through*, to insure durability, allowing the stitches to go through to the right side. Be careful when sewing the hooks and eyes on the second side of the front to have them exactly correspond in position to those on the opposite side.

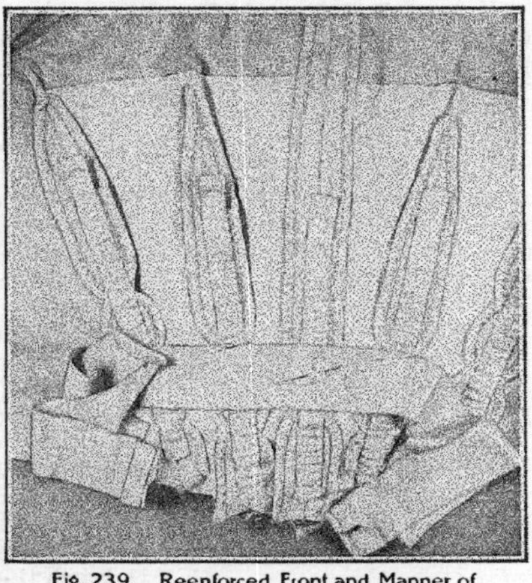

Fig. 239. Reenforced Front and Manner of Attaching Inside Belt

When all the hooks and eyes have been sewed on, turn back a seam at the edge of the facing piece, and hem it over by hand to the row of stitching nearest the edge, thus covering the stitches for the hooks and eyes, as shown in Fig. 237.

Many dressmakers prefer to have all the hooks on one side and the eyes on the other side. If this method is preferred, take care again that the hooks and eyes are sewed on in such a manner that the waist will not gape. The bill of the hook must be one-quarter of an inch back from the edge of the waist and sewed on firmly through the lining at both rings and bill. The eye should extend just far enough beyond the edge to be easily hooked—one-eighth of an inch—and should be sewed firmly at the rings and at the edge of the material. The sewing of the hooks and eyes will give a trifle, even with the greatest care, when the waist is worn.

Hem back over the hooks and eyes in this case also, the hem or facing, bringing it close up under the turned-over part of the hook, and covering the sewing.

Baste an inch-wide bias strip of soft crinoline around the bottom of the waist three-eighths of an inch from its lower edge on the inside. Turn the edge of the waist under a seam's width and catch-stitch it to the crinoline. Cut a bias strip of lining one and a half inches wide. Turn under one edge and hem it down as a facing on the turned-under seam at the bottom of the waist. Turn under its other edge and hem it neatly to the waist, covering the crinoline. (Fig. 238.)

Fig. 240. Hook and Eye on Ends of Belt Tape

Cut a belt of silk or cotton belting sold for this purpose. Make it three inches longer than the waist measure. Turn back an inch and a half at each end, sew a hook on one edge and an eye on the other, and hem the raw edges over them as shown in Fig. 240. Mark the center of the belt and sew it to the center-front seam if the waist opens in the back—or the center-back, if it opens in the front—and to the next seam on each side, with the lower edge of the belt one-half inch above the waistline. (Fig. 239.) Sew across the width of the belt with a long cross-stitch to the inside of the seam. If the material of the waist is thin and transparent, the fitted lining should first have a scant draping of mousseline which serves to cover the seams of the waist and holds out the outside material.

Sew the eyes to the back seams of the lining to correspond to the hooks on the skirt, making the waist belt overlap.

THE OUTER WAIST is easily managed if you have a carefully fitted lining for a foundation. In using material of a width that requires piecing, the place of joining must be determined by the design of the waist. The join must come where it will be least noticeable. This may be the center front, if the waist has much fulness at that point. Or, if there are tucks at the side, extending from shoulder to waist, the seam may be made at the sewing line of one of the tucks.

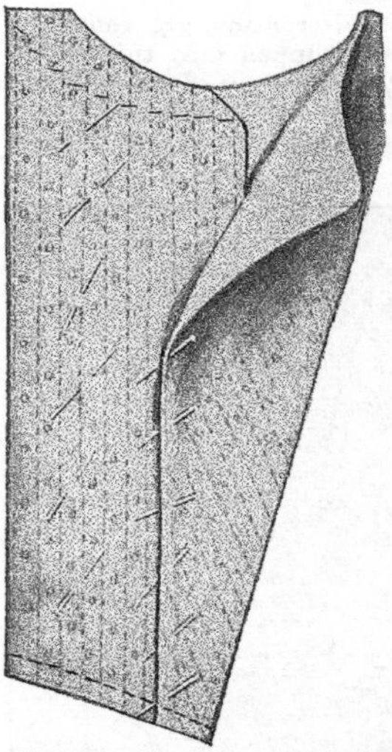

Fig. 241. The Front Waist-Drapery Lapped Across the Back at the Under-Arm

The waist is now ready to be draped, the process being greatly facilitated by the use of the bust form. In the draped waists, whenever they are in style, the outside material usually is not caught in with the lining at any seam except the shoulder seam. However, there are occasions when the material is caught in the under-arm seams as well. In these instances the under-arm seams are not stitched with the other seams of the lining, but are left basted until the entire waist is draped.

The material for the back of the waist, after it is prepared according to the pattern instructions, should be pinned to the lining straight down the center of the back, drawn well down and across toward the sides. Pin it at the shoulder, the armhole and down the under-arm seam, stretching it down that it may lie smooth and flat, and placing the pins near enough together to hold it well in place. Gather the fulness and draw it toward the center of the back.

The front is then draped on the lining according to the lines of perforations and notches at the neck and shoulder. Very elastic material may require to be stretched or drawn a little more tightly than one of firmer texture, and allowance must be made for this fact in matching the perforations that indicate where the outer material is to be tacked to the lining.

When the front drapery is arranged from the shoulder to the bustline, pin carefully about the armhole, then arrange the drapery below the bust; make the rounded part of the bust that lies at the second part of the lining a central point from which to work the drapery in both directions. Draw the front drapery toward the under-arm seams, turn under the raw edge and fit it in a straight, well-shaped line to cover the raw edge of the back drapery. Pin it in place to be sure the line is good. After the other side has been draped and pinned in the same manner remove the waist from the form and baste by slip-stitching. Stitch the seam by machine and press it open. This method is preferred by most people and looks neater when finished than slip-stitching, although the latter may be done closely and used as the final sewing if preferred.

Fig. 241 shows another method of finishing the seam under the arm. The waist is draped as directed, but after pinning the drapery in a good line, baste this folded edge through the front drapery only. Remove the pins, and place a row of machine stitching close to the edge, using silk the same color as the material. Pin the stitched edge in place again, stitching it down well.

Pin the other side in the same manner, remove the waist from the form and stitch by hand, taking the stitches through the row of machine stitching made in the front portion. Try on the waist after draping, because it often happens that boning pushes the waist up so that it needs taking up a little more on the shoulders. If it is correct, stitch the shoulders. Then press them open and finish like the other seams.

If the material is heavy, or there is any likelihood of the lower edge of the waist being bulky, the material is not turned under the bottom of the waist, but is sewed securely to the lining just below the waistline, the material cut away below this line, and the raw edge covered with a piece of seam binding laid on flat and sewed on both its edges as shown in Fig. 242. The girdle covers the line of sewing.

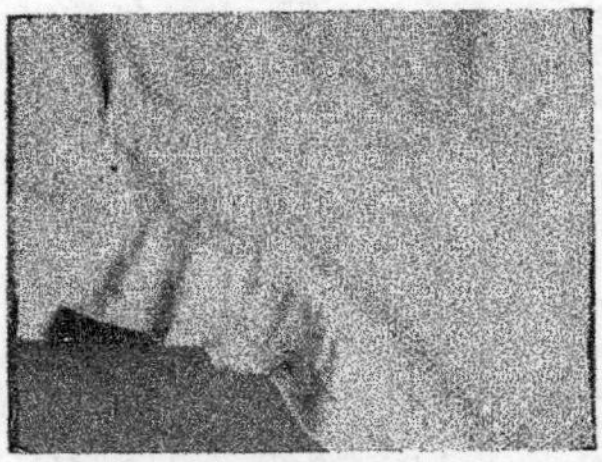
Fig. 242. Waist Drapery Sewed to the Lining

Never bind the armhole of a lined waist, as the lining serves as sufficient stay. When a sleeve of elbow length or an even shorter length is used complete directions for making it will be found in the pattern instructions.

If the collar is to be of woolen or silk like the gown, it should be lined with a piece of soft, light silk. Catch-stitch the collar supports to the silk, taking care to sew through the silk thoroughly. Turn over all the edges of the collar and catch-stitch to the lining. Slip-stitch the lower edge to the neck of the bodice.

If closed at the left side, the entire collar, except the small portion at the back, is stitched firmly to the neck. The neck of the lining at the left side, which is free, is bound with seam binding. For a waist with a front closing, bind the left side of the neck with seam binding, pin the collar around the right side, with the center of the collar at the front edge of the right front, and the right end of the collar at the center-back seam. Sew the collar to the neck, being careful not to catch the stitches through the outside material. Sew four hooks on the left end of the collar (on the inner side) and one to its lower edge about half-way between the center front and back.

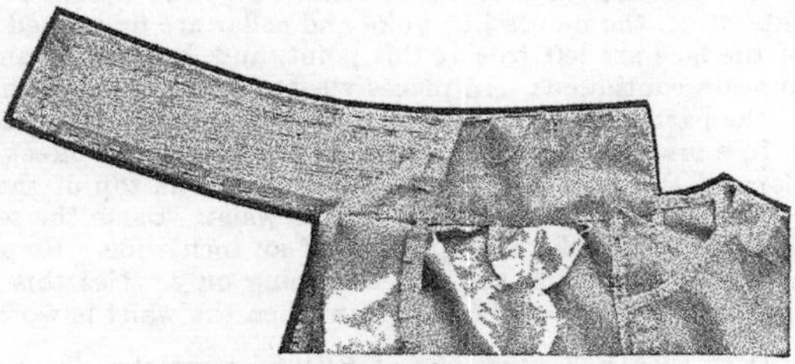
Fig. 243. Collar Applied to Neck

Cut the facing (preferably of silk) the same shape as the collar. Turn in the edges of the facing and hem it to the collar on the left side, and to the neck of the right side of the waist. Work four buttonhole loops at the right of the collar, and one in the left side of the waist at the neck. The collar and facing are shown in Fig. 243. If the collar is made of transparent material, the mousseline de soie should be used instead of the silk and the collar may be held up by collar supports.

For a woman having a very short neck, a high boned collar is an absolute torture. At the same time, some support must be given to the collar or it will look wilted and untidy, and make the neck seem still shorter and stouter. As the ordinary way of placing the supports diagonally at the front does not seem to prevent their poking into the chin, it is a good plan to use two supports about three and one-half inches long, finished. These two supports are then crossed. The same method is used if the collar lining is taffeta silk.

IN A FITTED WAIST MADE WITH A YOKE, the yoke is mounted on the lining before the waist is draped. The yoke line must be marked through the perforations on the pattern to the lining, and then outlined with a colored basting thread as a guide in finishing the lining if it is to be cut from under the yoke. The yoke and collar are cut by the patterns provided for them, and fitted to position on the lining. Usually the yoke is cut in one piece, particularly if it is of lace or embroidery.

If the yoke is in one piece, first cut the yoke of lining material and fit the shoulder seams if necessary. Now place the center front of the yoke lining, if the waist opens at the back, on a lengthwise fold of the yoke material and cut it in one piece. This brings the yoke opening on the bias. If the yoke is of lace, it is better to cut one or two thicknesses of mousseline de soie to soften the effect. The mousseline is stretched over the waist lining first, and hemmed to the lining three-eighths of an inch below the colored thread marking the yoke line. The lining is then cut away, and the edge turned toward the mousseline at the marked line and hemmed down. Stretch the lace over the mousseline, carefully basting all points around the neck, arm's-eye and the yoke line. The lace is then sewed to the lining at the bottom without turning in the edge.

The Lace Collar is also lined with one or two thicknesses of the mousseline. Measure the correct length and height of the collar and cut one of stiff paper. Mark off the seam with pencil. Also mark where supports are to be sewed.

Cut one or two thicknesses of mousseline like the pattern, and baste to the stiff paper. Procure either the bronzebone, which can be bought in the right length, or the narrow silk-covered featherbone. If featherbone, cut the lengths so that the casing may be slipped back three-eighths of an inch and the bone cut off. Draw the covering over the end and turn it back and fasten it. The featherbone is then catch-stitched to the mousseline.

The edge of the bone should be one-eighth of an inch from the top and botton of the collar. Cover the collar with lace, turn the top down three-eighths of an inch to the wrong side and hem, or turn to the right side and cover with applied trimming. The top edge must be slit to keep it from drawing. The lower edge is turned to the under side and basted to the yoke. It should be tried on and any necessary adjustment made around the neck and at the back.

The collar may be slip-stitched from the right side, or the waist may be turned to the wrong side and the collar backstitched to the yoke, taking care not to take the stitches through to the right side. The support is placed at the right end on the line of marking, the edge is turned back one-quarter of an inch beyond the traced line, and hemmed or faced. Sew four hooks on the overlapping end, and eyes or silk loops along the other end in corresponding positions.

The meeting edge of a lace collar and yoke should be appliquéd together. To obtain this effect, the mousseline yoke and collar are first fitted and joined together. The edges of the lace are left free at this point, and, by cutting and weaving together, the pattern appears continuous. In places where the mesh is too thin to disguise the seam, sections of the pattern may be cut from the lace and applied to cover it.

In a low-neck evening gown the bertha or collar effect is put on according to the directions of the pattern. Turn in a seam at the top of the bodice, including the top edge of the bertha, the lining and outside waist. Baste the seam in place, then hem over it a facing of bias silk three-quarters of an inch wide. Be careful when hemming down the lower edge to catch through the lining only. Use this facing as a casing for a narrow ribbon, which should be drawn in when the waist is worn, holding it close to the neck.

THE DRAPING OF THE GIRDLE completes the gown. All kinds of material are used, from the heavier velvets and cloths down to the sheerest chiffons, gauzes and ribbons. The girdle must, of course, harmonize with the trimming of the gown.

If the girdle is of silk or velvet, the material is usually cut on a perfect bias, and the edges hemmed or catch-stitched. Begin by pinning the center of the girdle to the center front of the waist, and draw very firmly toward the back from both sides of the front. It is best to pin a part of the draping on each side of the waist alternately, as sometimes the bias does not stretch evenly on both sides, and it may be found necessary to move the pins at the center front a trifle in order to make the bias draw more naturally. The draping is tacked to the lining wherever it is pinned. The back edges can be finished with a small shirred heading, which is allowed to extend beyond the hooks in order to cover them when the girdle is closed.

When the waist is to be worn inside of the skirt, the girdle is usually separate. Cut pieces of featherbone the desired length for the front, back and sides. Hooks and eyes are sewed firmly to the two featherbones used at the back closing. Cut a piece of belting an inch longer than waist measure, and turn back the ends one-half inch. Sew the featherbones at the back, dropping the bone one-half inch below the belt. The front bone is sewed to the middle of the belt, and the other bones at the sides and back. This foundation is now put on the figure, and the girdle draped over it.

THE SLEEVES are considered by some people as the most difficult part of a costume. Great caution is necessary to keep them exactly alike from the time the sleeves are

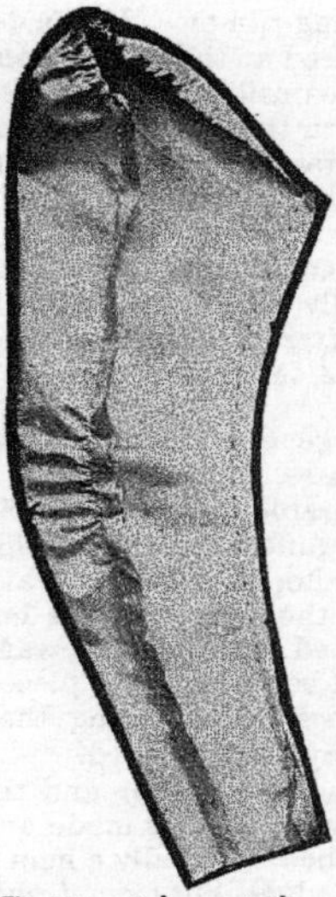

Fig. 244. Fulness at Elbow of Sleeve Lining

cut until they are finished and sewed in the armhole. If not correctly cut and basted, one sleeve may be larger than the other. If they are not stitched in the armhole exactly alike, one may twist while the other hangs without a wrinkle.

The first step before cutting the sleeves is to study the pattern instructions. Measure the sleeve and arm and make alterations in the pattern, if necessary, as instructed in Chapter XIV, "The Use of Butterick Patterns." Be sure that the elbow of the sleeve comes in the right place.

Next, the sleeve must be cut accurately and carefully basted. The seams should be pinned even at both top and bottom, and the extra fulness of the upper back edge gathered in at the elbow. (Fig. 244).

To be very accurate, the pattern should have the outlet seam marked with tailor's tacks. Baste the front seam three-eighths of an inch from the seam edge. The back seam is basted through the line of perforations. A one-seam sleeve should be basted with the upper and lower edges even.

Fig. 245. Correct Location of Front Seam

In joining waist and sleeve seams, short basting stitches are used, as shown in Fig. 244. Never place machine stitching directly on top of a basting. If the seam is stitched just outside the basting there will be no difficulty in removing the latter. Enough emphasis can not be laid on careful basting, for next to cutting, it is the groundwork of dressmaking. If it is poorly done, it is the source of many future difficulties.

If a Fancy Sleeve is to be made, the lining must be fitted first and the material draped or arranged later. In basting the lining, place the under piece of the sleeve upon the upper with the notches of the front seam together, and pin in position. Then baste this seam with small running stitches. Pin the back seam through the outlet perforations from the top to the upper notch, and again from the lower notch to the bottom. The extra material of the upper sleeve portion is gathered into the space between the notches to give room for the elbow. The seam is then basted. The sleeve should always be basted as the pattern directs, and the same width seam will be taken off both upper and under sleeve portion. The outlet seam should be basted on the line of perforations.

Fig. 246. Wrist of Sleeve Prepared for Facing

Adjust the sleeve in the proper position, draw it up well on the arm, so that the elbow is in the correct position, and pin the sleeve in the armhole with notches matched, as directed in the pattern instructions. Distribute the fulness fairly evenly. More of it should come on the top of the arm than at the back or front.

In a sleeve which sets correctly after basting, it will be noticed that the front seam, instead of lying perfectly straight when laid flat on the table, will roll somewhat toward the under side of the sleeve from the center of the seam to the wrist, as shown in Fig. 245. This is quite important, as many workers imagine that the sleeve should set perfectly flat the length of this seam.

Drape the material on the sleeve lining, remove the bastings and press the seams flat.

Clip the front seam, then overcast or bind with a narrow silk binding ribbon. If it is desired to have a firm wrist edge an interlining of soft crinoline is placed at the bottom, one to two inches deep. With the sleeve right side out, roll the crinoline until it can be slipped into the wrist. Place the hand inside and move the fingers about until the crinoline fits the sleeve without either drawing or falling in folds; then baste. The rest of the work is done from the wrong side. Turn the sleeve inside out and turn up the bottom three-eighths of an inch. (Fig. 246.) Catch-stitch it to hold it down, then press. Face the wrist with a bias piece of silk, and slip-stitch or hem it at the upper and lower edges. Any trimming is added and the sleeve fully finished before it is basted in the armhole. After the sleeve has been sewed into the armhole the seam is overcast.

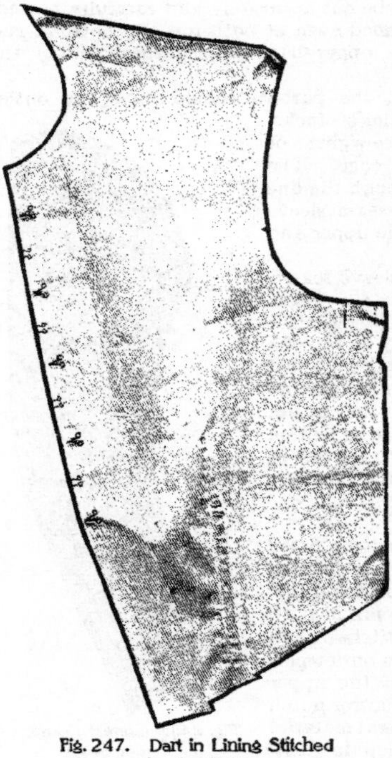

Fig. 247. Dart in Lining Stitched for the Bone

A BLOUSE-WAIST is generally made without a lining. In some cases, for instance in a silk waist, a lining is desirable to save the silk from wear and strain. It differs from the lining used for a closely fitted tailored or draped waist in that it reaches only to the waistline, has but one dart, and, as the curved fitting at the waist and hips is not required, it contains fewer pieces. Consequently, a simpler method of boning than that of the fitted waist may be employed.

The pieces should be basted together and the lining fitted, any necessary alterations made and the under-arm seams stitched. Usually a hem is allowed for at the closing edges, but even if only a seam is provided, the closing line should be marked.

In fitting, bring the closing line of both fronts together, and pin along the tracing, forming a seam toward the outside. Alterations may be made on this seam, if necessary, in which case a new closing line must be marked. If the closing edge is to be faced instead of hemmed, trim the edge, leaving only a seam's width. Cut a straight piece of the lining material two inches wide, and long enough to cover the length of both the front edges. Place the piece with one edge to the edge of the lining on the outside, and stitch a seam. Turn the facing over, making the fold come exactly at the seam, and stitch one-eighth of an inch back from the edge.

The casing for the bone in the front edge is made by a second row of stitching, as shown in Fig. 234. At each of the seams, also, a casing is made in the same way. A bone is run into each casing and tacked in place, as seen in the dart seam in Fig. 247.

The bone in the casing of each closing edge reaches only as high as the bone in the dart seam. If the closing is in the back, the bone may reach a height of five inches.

The under-arm seam of the blouse-waist is usually basted separate from the outer blouse. The shoulder seams may also be stitched separately, if desired, or they may be stitched in the seam with the lining.

TO CLOSE A BLOUSE-WAIST when a lining is used as shown in Fig. 247, pin the two front portions of the blouse together, with the right side lapping over the left, as it should be when finished. Hook the lining at the closing; place the blouse over it with its center line directly over the closing line of the lining. Then pin each side in position and baste together around the neck and armhole edges.

Small hooks are sewed on the right front, and buttonholed loops to correspond are worked on the left. If preferred, the closing of the blouse may be made by means of a fly with buttonholes on the right front and small buttons on the left.

CHAPTER XVII

UNLINED DRESSES

FORMERLY the kind of dresses that were made without linings was strictly limited to those of washable materials, such as muslins, ginghams, lawns, etc. But so popular has the unlined dress become that we are now quite accustomed to seeing organdies, voiles, and even crêpe de Chines made up without linings. They are usually worn over slips, or well-cut corset covers and petticoats.

Before beginning work on the dress, read Chapter XIII, "Cutting Materials, Sponging, Etc.," and Chapter XII, "An Efficient Equipment for Dressmaking."

An unlined dress is really nothing but a blouse or shirt-waist joined to a skirt in what is now called "semi-princess style." The instructions given in the chapters "Unlined Waists" and "Skirts" will cover every point in the construction of the unlined dress, except the matter of the finish at the waistline. In dresses made by a dress pattern the waist and skirt should be joined according to the directions given on the pattern.

Practically any unlined waist can be joined to a skirt in semi-princess style if the openings of the two garments come at the same place at the front, side or back. Of course the designs and materials of the skirt and waist must be suitable.

When a skirt and waist are to be joined together each is made and finished independent of the other. But the belt-stay of the waist is basted to the inside of the blouse, and the belt of the skirt is basted to the skirt, but not stitched.

When the two garments are finished put them on with the skirt over the waist. Adjust the fulness of the waist becomingly and pin the waist and skirt together. Then take them off and baste the two together at the waistline. Try the dress on again to make sure that the waistline is exactly right, and rip the belt-stay from the inside of the blouse before stitching the belt.

IN CLOTH, SILK, CRÊPE DE CHINE DRESSES—in fact, dresses of any material that does not require laundering—stitch the waist and skirt together at the top and bottom of the skirt belt. Cut the bottom of the waist away below the belt and beneath it to remove all unnecessary thickness at the waistline. The belt can be covered with a girdle or sash.

IN LINEN, GINGHAM, PIQUÉ, etc., DRESSES, the skirt belt generally finishes the waistline of the dress. It can be made either of the dress material or of some other wash material of a contrasting color. It should be stitched at the top and bottom after the waist and skirt are basted together. The bottom of the waist can be cut away *below* the belt, but *not* beneath it until the dress has been laundered. Then if the waist shrinks there is an inch or so of material under the belt by which it can be lengthened. After the dress has been laundered two or three times this can be cut away.

IN LINGERIE DRESSES the belt is generally covered with lace or embroidery joined together to the required width. After the skirt and waist are basted together pin the lace belt over the waistline of the dress with its lower edge just *below* the lower edge of the skirt belt. Sew it securely in place, taking care not to stitch through the skirt belt. After the lower edge of the lace is stitched down, rip off the skirt belt and the belt-stay of the blouse and then sew down the upper edge of the lace belt. In this way you get rid of the two unnecessary belts.

The bottom of the waist can be cut away below the belt before the dress is washed. Afterward, if the waist does not shrink, it can be cut away under the belt as well.

Instructions for applying lace and insertions are given in Chapter I, "Sewing Stitches."

The more severe unlined dresses and shirt-waist suits are finished in tailor fashion.

CHAPTER XVIII

MATERNITY DRESSES

GARMENTS for maternity wear are so designed that they may be adjusted comfortably to the changing figure and yet keep the trim appearance of a fitted gown. The clothing should be so skilfully planned and made that no undue pressure will rest upon any part of the body. If corsets are worn they must be very loose, and be laced with rubber lacings at the back and over the abdomen. Dresses and negligees may be made of attractive materials, preferably of soft wool or silk, and in plain, solid colors rather than figured effects. They may be prettily trimmed with lace, embroidery and ribbon.

The great trouble has always been with linings; for when they were once made and fitted there was no way of gradually enlarging them. This difficulty has been overcome by lacing the front seams or the darts. (Fig. 248.) Other necessary changes may be made by moving a few hooks and tapes. The waist lining should be basted and fitted in the usual way, making it fit neatly but not too snugly. Turn back the hem at the front of the lining and stitch it with the usual two rows of stitching, making the first row three-eighths of an inch, and the second three-quarters of an inch, from the edge. Work eyelets near the edge the entire length of the front of both sides, and run a very soft and pliable bone in the casing formed by the two rows of the stitching. Or, place the bone near the edge, as in an ordinary lining, and sew eyes, but not the hooks, along both edges, and lace through them. It would be well to sew a fly or underlap about two inches wide underneath each front, and sew hooks and eyes on their front edges. Lace with a round elastic cord, such as is used for corset lacing.

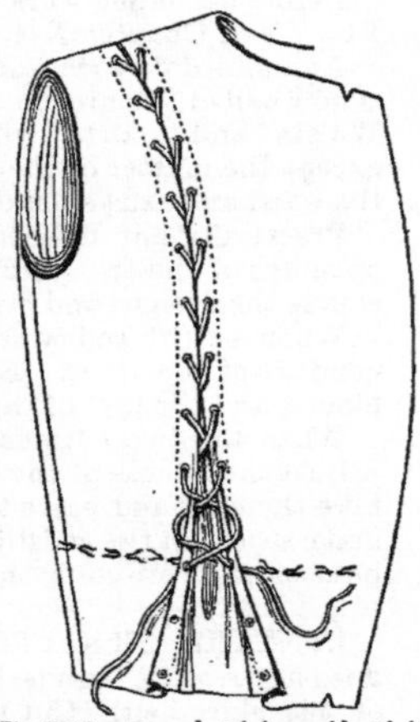

Fig. 248. French Lining with Plait and Lacings

After the lining has been fitted, the under-arm seams should be pressed open and bound. The correct basting line in the side-front and side-back seams should be marked with tailors' tacks or chalk.

Cut four strips of lining on the bias, making each strip three and a half inches wide and a bit longer than the side seams of the front and back. Baste a strip to the under side of the side-front seam with the raw edges together. Baste and stitch them three-eighths of an inch back of the edge. This forms a small plait under each seam. (Fig. 248.) In sewing on the bias strip, one must be particularly careful to ease it over the bust on the outer edges of the side seam. In sewing the strip to the second edge of the side seam—the edge nearer the center front—the bias band should be stretched at the bust to make it easy over the curve of the figure. Baste the second bias strip to the second side seam in the same way as the first. Take out the basting threads in the side seams and sew back three-eighths of an inch from the edges. This gives you a small fold on which to work the eyelets for the lacing of the fronts.

The other two bias strips are used to finish the side-back seams of the lining. They are handled just like the side-front seams and are also laced together instead of being stitched. The edges of the center-back seam are closed in an ordinary seam.

The eyelets should be placed an inch and a quarter apart and a quarter of an inch in from the edge of the fold. (Fig. 248.) They are made with a stiletto and worked with the ordinary buttonhole stitch.

In a lining made with a dart instead of a seam to the shoulder in the front, rip the darts open and mark the seams with a basting thread; then make that thread the edge of a tuck, one-quarter inch deep, running not quite to the top of the dart. Work eyelets or sew eyes just back of the tucks of each edge of the dart seam, and slip a round bone into each tuck.

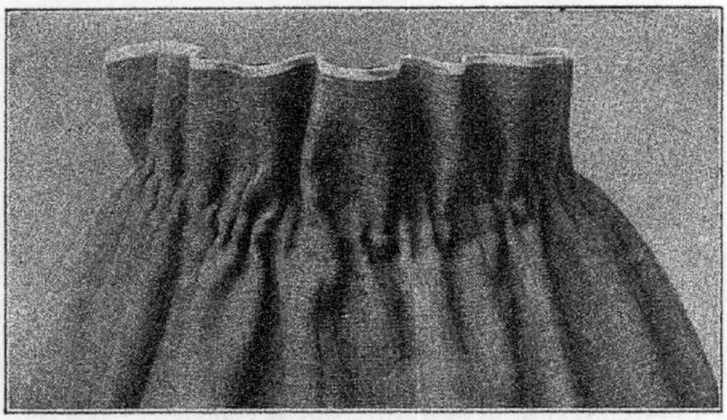

Fig. 249. The Upper Part of Skirt

The shortening in the front, which makes the ordinary skirt undesirable even when the belt is enlarged, is provided against in the maternity skirt by an extension at the top of the pattern as shown in Fig. 249. The crossline perforations indicate where a ribbon casing should be sewed on. A ribbon or tape can be run through it, coming out at a small buttonholed opening in the center front. When fitting this skirt pin a piece of tape around the figure where the belt would naturally come. The tape will show whether the perforations are in the right place for the casing. The part of the skirt which extends above the casing should have its raw edge overcast or bound. As the skirt becomes short across the front and sides, the casing may be moved up toward the top to lengthen it.

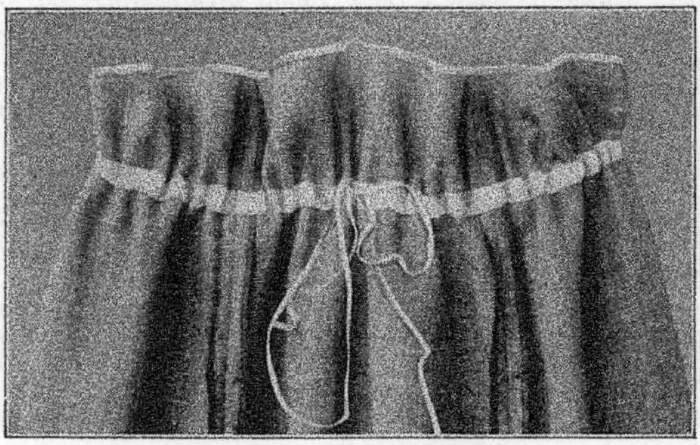

Fig. 250. The Inside Finish of Skirt

For maternity wear women should use rather long, loose or semi-fitted coats that will protect the figure. If a semi-fitted coat is used it should be double-breasted so that the buttons can be moved over as the figure grows larger. In a well-made coat a woman can go about as usual without feeling uncomfortable or conspicuous.

CHAPTER XIX

TAILORED SEAMS

MANY KINDS of seams are used in the making of tailored costumes. It is necessary to keep the cloth extremely smooth at the seams and to make the stitching as even as possible. In making a garment that requires a tailored finish one should not be sparing in the use of bastings and the hot iron. He was a wise and honest tailor who declared "In the flat-iron is our fortune," and the dressmaker who would be successful along the same lines will do well to keep in mind this well-tried maxim.

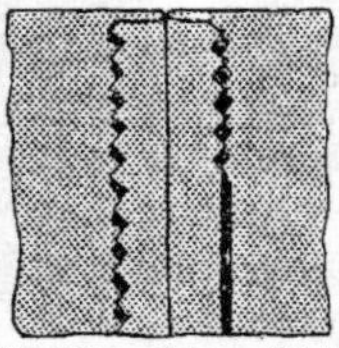

Fig. 251. Edge of Plain Seam Pinked

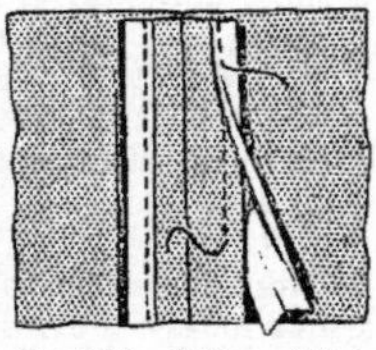

Fig. 252. Edges of Plain Seam Bound

IN PLAIN SEAMS of very closely woven material that does not fray or ravel, the edges of the seams may be simply notched or pinked, and pressed open. (Fig. 251.)

Plain seams of jackets, cloaks and other garments made of heavy material that will fray should be bound with satin, silk or farmers' satin. This is cut in bias strips just a trifle wider than the depth of the seam after it is closed. Stitch the binding on the right side of the seam edge, close to the edge, then baste it flat, covering the edge. Close the seam of the garment with bastings catching through both cloth and bindings. Then stitch.

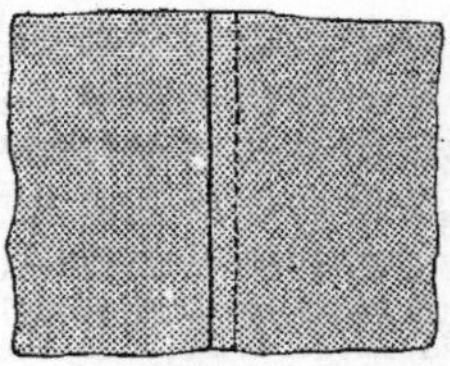

Fig. 253. Stitching on One Side of Seam

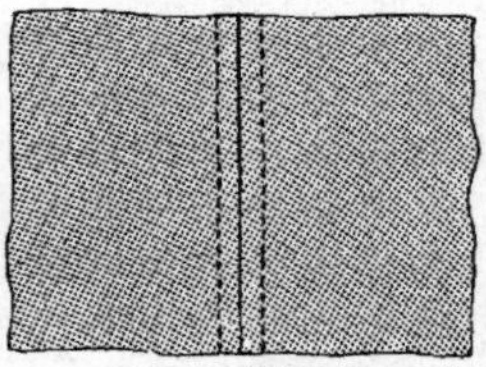

Fig. 254. Stitching on Both Sides of Seam

A better way, requiring more labor, however, is to stitch the seam and press it open. After pressing, the seam will have spread at the edges, especially if it is curved, and the binding can be safely applied without any chance of pulling later.

Baste the strip of binding on the right side of the edges; turn it over the raw seam edge and fell it down on the underside, keeping the turned edges of the binding even on both sides of the seam edge. (Fig. 252.) It is finished with one row of machine stitching close to the edge of the binding.

When Trimming is to be applied over seams, the plain seam is used. It should be finished completely, and pressed before the trimming is added.

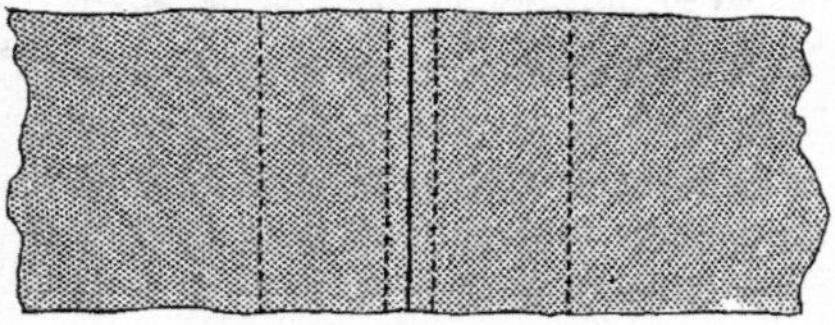

Fig. 255. Broad Seam Stitch

Joined Seams of garments that have the lining cut like the outer pattern and stitched together, are finished by turning in the raw edges of the seams of both cloth and lining toward each other and closing the edge with overhand or running stitches. Where the seam is curved, the edges must be notched every now and then to prevent the garment from pulling at such points.

AN ORDINARY TAILORED SEAM, which makes a good neat finish, is the plain seam pressed with both edges turned to one side, and a row of machine stitching run in neatly along the one side of the seam from the right side of the garment as shown in Fig. 253. Or, if preferred, a row of stitching may be applied to each side of the seam. (Fig. 254.) In the latter case, however, the seam should be pressed open before running in the stitching.

A Broad Seam is a plain wide seam with four rows of ornamental stitching. (Fig. 255.) This seam is mostly used on tailored garments of heavy materials.

A Cord or *Tuck Seam* is a plain seam with both edges turned to one side, and a row of stitching run one-fourth of an inch from the seam, through the three thicknesses of the

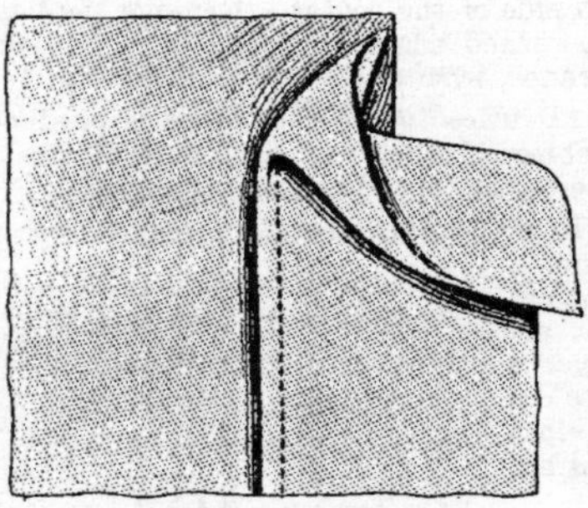

Fig 256. Cord Seam

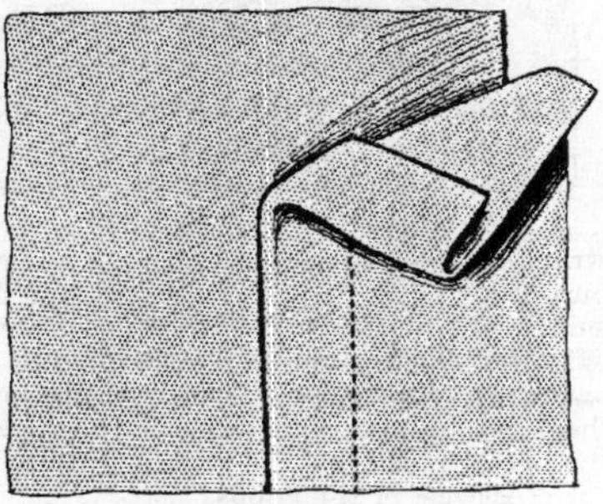

Fig. 257. Welt Seam

goods. This creates a raised or cord-like effect. (Fig. 256.) The undesirable thickness on the under side may be cut away at the inner edge as close to the stitching as possible.

A WELT SEAM is made by first stitching a plain seam with the one edge of the material left very narrow. Then turn back the fold and baste down close along the narrower seam edge. Stitch parallel to the line of bastings, keeping the seam flat. Fig. 257 shows this seam with the machine stitches ripped out at the top to expose the narrow seam edge underneath.

A Double-Stitched Welt Seam has an additional row of stitching set in one-fourth inch or less from the edge. (Fig. 258.)

An Open-Welt Seam is first basted as for a plain seam. The tuck is then basted down

Fig. 258. Double-Stitched Welt

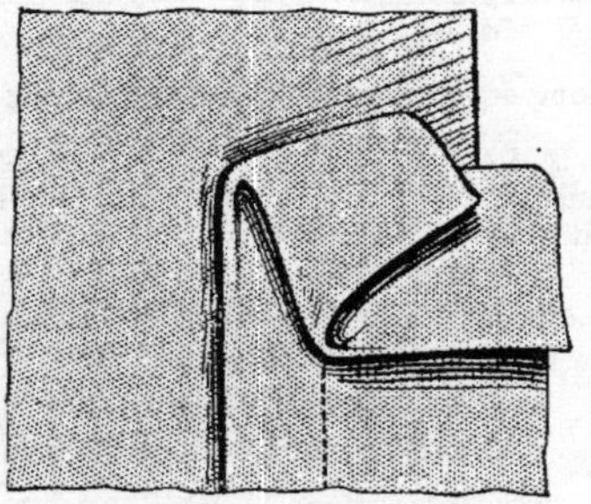

Fig. 259. Open Welt

flat, with the stitches directly over the line of bastings in the seam. With one row of machine stitching the tuck-like fold and the seam are made secure. (Fig. 259.)

The raw edges on the underside of an open-welt seam may be bound with velveteen or with narrow grosgrain ribbon, which can be bought for the purpose. Baste the binding over the double seam edges, and stitch through all the thicknesses as near the edge of the binding as possible. (Fig. 260, on next page.)

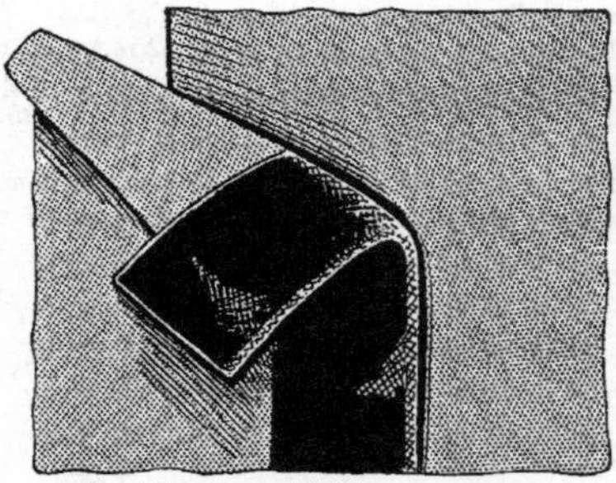

Fig. 260 Open Welt Seam, Bound

A SLOT SEAM is made by basting the seam as for a plain seam. The basting stitches should be short enough to keep the seam firm while it is being pressed open. Then baste an understrip of the material a trifle narrower than the combined width of the seam edges, directly under the basted seam. (Fig. 262.) From the right side, stitch three-eighths of an inch on each side of the center. Remove the bastings. The turned edges, now free, give the slot appearance, whence the name. (Fig. 261.)

A Double-Stitched Slot Seam is produced by stitching another row each side of the center close to the turned edges. (Fig. 261.)

STRAP SEAMS are plain seams over which straps of the material are stitched for ornamental purposes. The strips for these straps may be cut lengthwise of the material from pieces that are left after cutting out the garment, but experience has taught that when silk is used it is better to cut them on the bias, and when the material is cloth the better result will be obtained if the straps are cut crosswise of the goods.

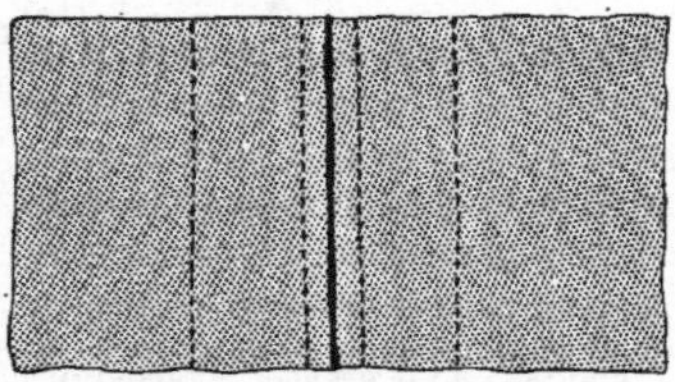

Fig. 261. Double-Stitched Slot Seam

For a finished strap that is five-eighths of an inch wide, the strips are cut one and one-fourth inches wide. Join the two raw edges with loose overhand stitches as shown in Fig. 10, page 4; spread out the strap with the line of joining directly on the center, and press.

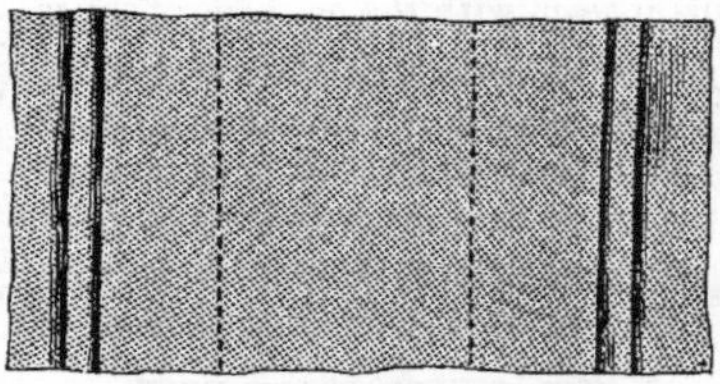

Fig. 262. Reverse Side of Slot Seam

When making strap seams it is desirable to graduate the thickness at the seam as much as possible. For this reason, cut the seams either wide enough so the edges on the underside will extend beyond the edges of the strap, or, cut them narrower so the edges of the strap will extend beyond the seam edges.

Baste the straps carefully over the seams, with a line of bastings run along each edge. (Fig. 263.) When it is necessary to piece the straps for long seams, avoid having the joining seam in a prominent place on the garment.

A LAPPED or IMITATION STRAP SEAM is the most practical finish for unlined garments. The edges at the seams are lapped and the raw edges turned in with a row of stitches finishing it alike on the right and wrong sides. (Fig. 264.)

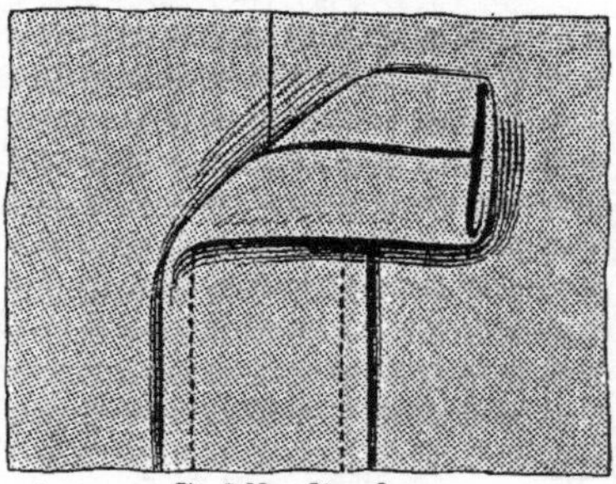

Fig 263. Strap Seam

Fig. 264. Imitation Strap Seam

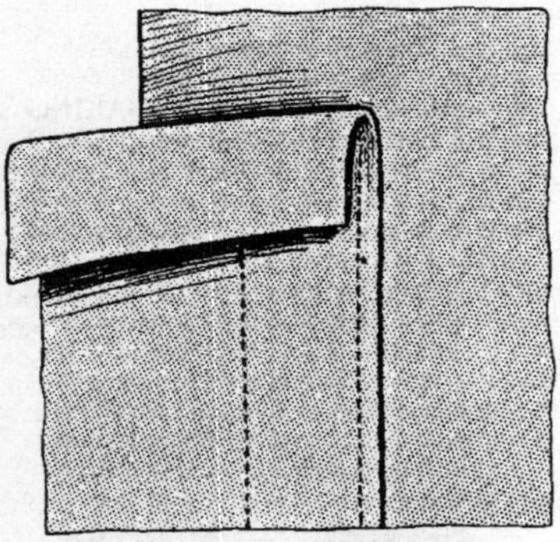
Fig. 265. Raw-Edge Lapped Seam

A Raw-Edge Lapped Seam is used in making garments of heavy, closely woven material that will not fray or ravel. The seam edges must be cut very accurately and smoothly. Baste the edges evenly, lapping them the full allowance, and stitch as near the edge of the upper lap as possible. A second row of stitching five-eighths of an inch from the first gives it a neat and tailored finish. The seam on the under side should be trimmed off evenly. (Fig. 265.)

One should be very careful in deciding on the style of seam used on a tailored garment. Tweeds, homespuns, friezes, and all other rather loosely woven woolen materials should be finished with bound seams. In linens, pongees and crashes one should use the cord, bound or lapped seam. Broadcloth, meltons, kerseys, covert, and other heavy driving cloths can be pinked, as they are so closely woven that they will not ravel. To have a good tailored look the machine-stitchings on any seam must not be too fine. The thread and needle should be of medium thickness and the stitch should correspond in size.

CHAPTER XX

POCKETS

A PHASE OF DRESSMAKING that is generally regarded as tedious and difficult is the work involved in putting pockets neatly into a garment. The difficulty, however, is one that can easily be overcome by the simple remedy of "knowing how."

The various styles of pockets used on tailored and boys' suits which require some technical knowledge will be treated in this chapter.

A PATCH POCKET is, as its name implies, simply a patch sewed on three of its sides to the outside of the garment. Patch pockets vary in size and shape according to the style of the garment and the position they occupy. The upper edge that is left open may be simply hemmed or faced, and trimmed in any way that the character of the garment may suggest. In all cases the essential feature of a patch pocket is neatness.

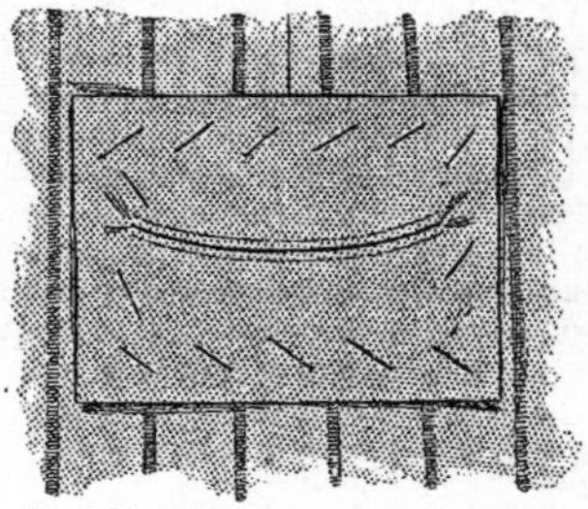

Fig. 266. Facing of the Slash Pocket

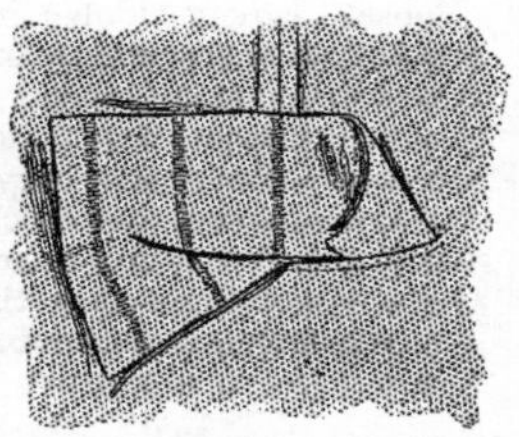

Fig. 267. Pushing Facing Through to Wrong Side

A SLASH POCKET is one that is made on the inside of the garment and has a slit opening through to the outside. Mark the line for the opening with tailors' tacks. Run a line of bastings in colored thread through the perforations to mark the line still more sharply, letting the bastings show on both sides of the material.

Cut a piece of the suit material for a facing. It should be about three inches wide and an inch longer than the pocket opening. Baste it face down to the right side of the garment so that its center comes exactly over the pocket opening and the facing itself extends half an inch beyond each end of the opening. (Fig. 266.) From the wrong side of the garment run another row of colored bastings along the line for the pocket opening so that the second row will show through on the pocket facing.

From the right side place a row of machine stitching on each side of the pocket line and about an eighth of an

Fig. 268. Pocket Slipped Under the Facing

Fig. 269. Pocket Turned up and Stitched

Fig. 270. Inside View of a Slash Pocket

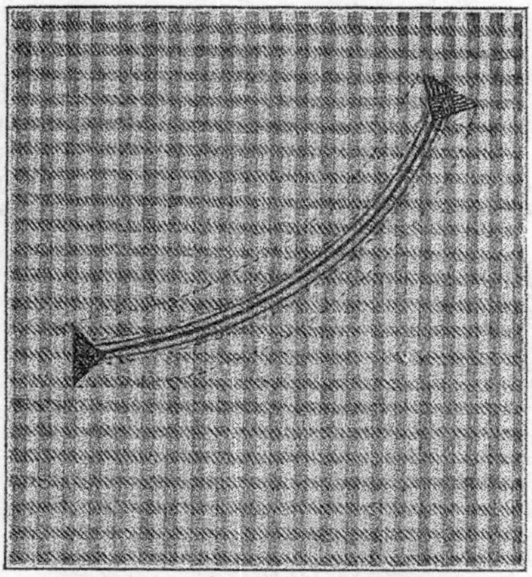

Fig. 271. Outside View of a Slash Pocket

inch from it. (Fig. 266.) Tie the ends of the threads firmly so that the stitching can not pull out, and then cut through the pocket line with a sharp knife, cutting through both the facing and the garment material. Push the facing through the slit. (Fig. 267.)

Rebaste the facing from the outside, letting it form a head or cording an eighth of an inch deep at the edges of the pocket. It should be stitched on the upper edge of the pocket hole from the right side. The pocket edges should be cross-stitched together to hold them in shape until the rest of the work on the garment is finished. Turn down the upper edge of the pocket facing as close to the stitching as possible, and press it flat to the wrong side of the garment. (Fig. 269.)

Cut from strong cotton or light-weight canvas a pocket piece about twelve and a half inches long and two inches wider than the pocket opening. Shape one end of the pocket like the curved pocket opening and insert it between the lower pocket facing and the garment, close to the opening. (Fig. 268.) Baste it in place from the wrong side, turn the garment portion over to the right side, and stitch through both facing and pocket. This row of stitching should be set close to the pocket opening. Turn under the lower edge of the pocket facing and stitch it to the pocket (Fig. 268), but be careful not to stitch through the garment.

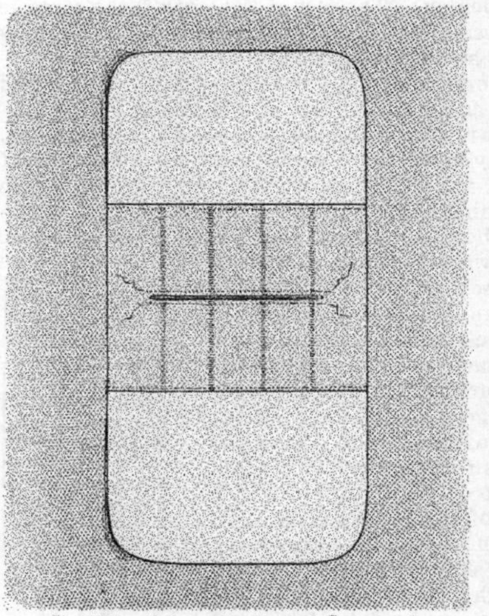

Fig. 272. When the Pocket Opening is Perfectly Straight

Now turn up the pocket about four and a half inches from the opening and baste it in place with its upper edge toward the top of the garment. From the right side, stitch through the garment and the pocket along the upper edge of the pocket opening. Turn under the edge of the upper part of the facing and hem it to the pocket. The easiest way to do it is from the right side, pushing the pocket and facing through the slit so that you can get at it easily.

The sides of the pocket are closed with a single row of machine stitching about three-eighths of an inch from the edges. (Fig. 269.)

A Perfectly Straight Opening has a facing of material applied as directed above. (Figs. 266-267.) Two pocket pieces are cut of pocketing or drill, the lower four and a half inches long, the upper piece five inches long. Both pieces should be an inch wider than the opening. They are slipped under the facings, basted and stitched from the right side. Strengthen the ends of the opening with a bar tack.

The raw edges of the facings are turned under and stitched to the pocket pieces. The upper pocket piece is then turned down over the lower and basted and stitched to it around its three open sides. The raw edges may be bound or overcast.

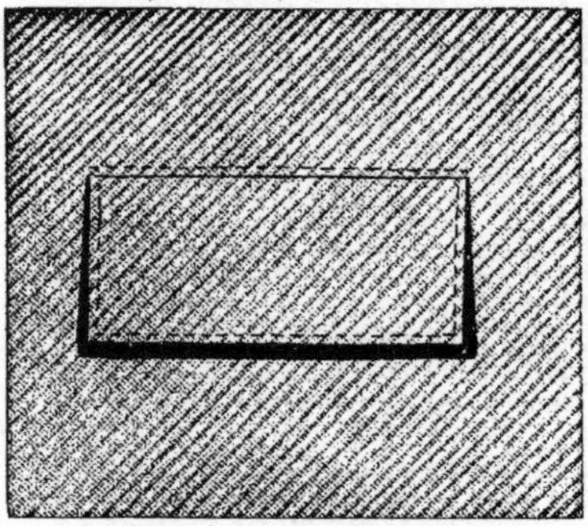

Fig. 273. In and Out Lap on Pocket

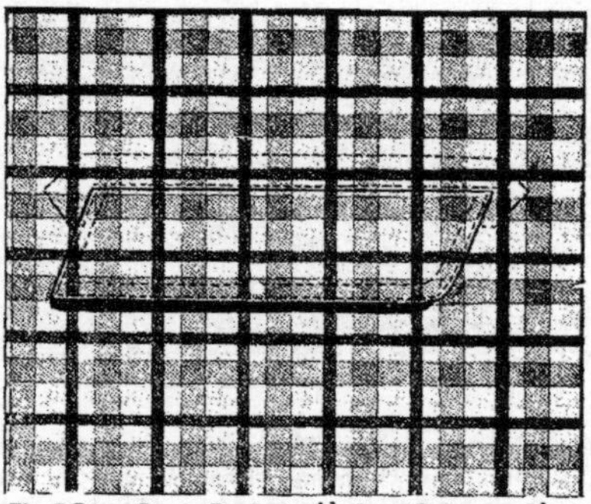

Fig. 274. Open Pocket with Lap Cut on a Slant

IN A POCKET WITH AN IN-AND-OUT LAP the latter is finished completely before the pocket is begun. Cut the piece for the lap from the cloth, being careful to have the grain or stripe of the goods match when the lap is laid on the jacket in the position it will have when the pocket is completed. Turn in and baste a seam on three sides. Run two rows of even stitching around the edge from the right side, the first row one-eighth of an inch from the edge. Then add a lining of silk, slip-stitching it on by hand.

Now lay the finished lap face down on the goods, with its raw edge down, and even with the line of bastings that indicate the pocket opening. The rest of the work is the same as for the pocket described above. In this case, however, that section of the facing strip which is supplemented by the lap is cut away. (Fig. 273.)

AN OPEN POCKET is made similar to the one having an in-and-out lap. The lap is made straight or on a slant, not quite so wide as for a loose lap, and is joined to the garment at the lower edge of the slit in an upright position, and is attached to it at each side.

SIDE POCKETS OF TROUSERS are usually made in a seam. Cut a square piece of silesia or stout lining material the size desired, and, doubling it over, notch the edges to indicate the pocket opening. Make corresponding notches in the seam edges of the trousers. Face the back edge of the pocket on both the right and wrong sides with bias facings of the cloth one inch and a quarter wide and long enough to extend from the top of the pocket to an inch below the notch in the opening. (Fig. 275.) Lay the front edge of the pocket edge to edge with the front edge of the trousers on their wrong side and baste it to them. In the same seam baste a bias facing of the cloth to the front of the trousers on the right side. This facing should be the same length and width as the facings on the back edge of the pocket. Stitch the pocket, trousers and facing together in a narrow seam. Turn the facing over onto the pocket and run a row of stitching close to the fold to hold it in place. Turn under the back edge of the facing and stitch it to the pocket. Trim off the lower corners of the pocket (Fig. 275), and crease the edge for a seam toward the inside. The seam of the pocket may then be closed. Baste it first, and close it with one stitching. The back edge of the pocket is caught to the front at the notches with bar stay-tacks. The upper edges are held by the waist band.

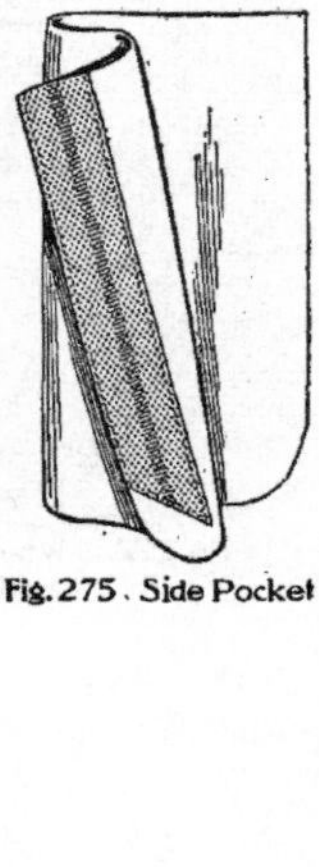

Fig. 275. Side Pocket

CHAPTER XXI

SKIRTS

THE PRESENT STYLE of making skirts without linings has considerably simplified the work of the dressmaker. These unlined skirts, however, unless made of very heavy material, call for well-fitting underskirts as a foundation, and on them largely depends the fit of the overskirt.

THE FOUNDATION SKIRT may or may not be joined in the same belt with the overskirt, as preferred. In either case, both the overskirt and the foundation are made and finished separately, with the exception of the inside belt. The foundation skirt is made first. China silk, India silk, taffeta, and satin are good materials for this purpose, though for wearing qualities some of the lining materials, mixtures of silk and cotton, or the better grades of percalines, sateens, etc., are preferred.

Get a good pattern, and make a careful study of the figure which is to be fitted. Many women have a slight hollow below the waistline in the back—an ugly defect, but one which can easily be overcome. It is frequently found in connection with a round or prominent abdomen.

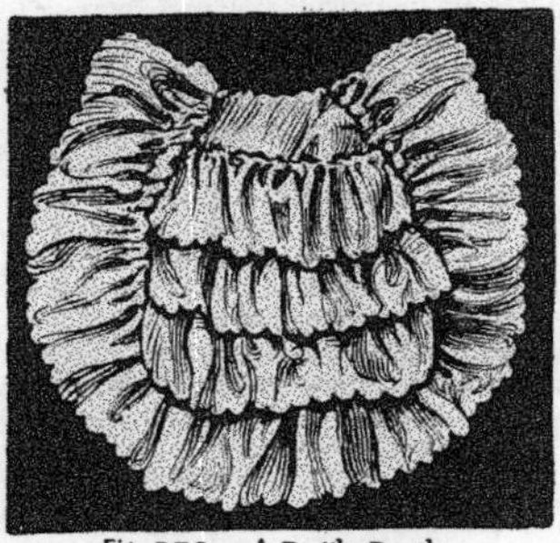

Fig. 276. A Ruffle Bustle

A Small Light Bustle that will not interfere with the wearer's comfort adds much to the set of the skirt on such a figure. It can be made of the same material as the foundation skirt. Cut a piece of the lining material the size and shape desired for a foundation, and hem or pink the edges. Make ruffles four inches wide, and treat their edges in the same way. Sew several rows of these ruffles across the foundation piece, and one all around the edge except at the top. (Fig. 276.) The completed bustle may be attached inside the skirt, or it may be hung around the waist under the corset by means of a narrow tape sewed at each side.

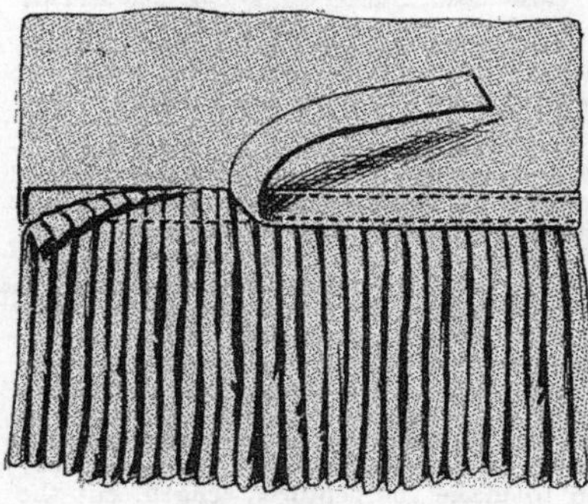

Fig. 277. Plaiting Stitched on Foundation Skirt

If the figure to be fitted is abnormally short or tall, stout or thin, or out of proportion in any way, instructions for adjusting the pattern to the figure will be found in Chapter XIV, "The Use of Butterick Patterns." Separate patterns are used for the foundation and skirt except in the case of tunics, overskirts, etc.

Cut the gores for the foundation skirt; baste them together according to the pattern instructions and try it on. If the skirt is to end in a full plaiting at the lower edge, measure the width of the finished plaiting and deduct this width from each gore in cutting, allowing, of course, three-eighths of an inch on each for a seam.

For the Plaiting, cut strips crosswise of

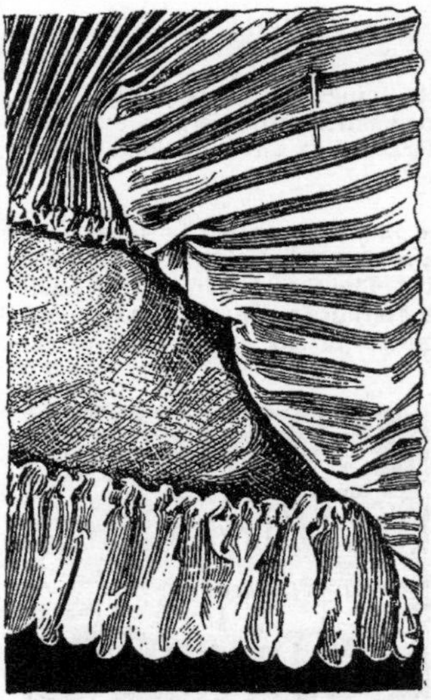

Fig. 278. Plaited Flounce and Dust Ruffle

the material. The combined length of these strips should measure at least twice the width of the skirt at its lower edge. Stitch them together, and make a narrow hem along one edge. Then plait the entire piece. If a side-plaiting is used, run in a row of stitching along the upper edge to keep the plaits flat. When an accordion plaiting is used, the upper edge may be pressed flat, and a gathering thread run in to keep the fulness of the plaits perfectly even.

Lay the plaiting right side up along the lower edge of the skirt on the wrong side. Baste the raw edges of skirt and plaiting evenly together. Then on the right side of the skirt stitch a narrow bias fold or strip over these raw edges as shown in Fig. 277. This makes a neat finish on both the right and wrong sides of the garment.

If the foundation skirt is to be full length, the plaiting or flounce may be set on above the hem. The skirt in this case must, of course, be tried on and the even length secured all around the lower edge (see Fig. 301B), and the hem or facing finished before the flounce is added.

When the skirt is ready for the flounce, plaiting or ruffle, mark a line parallel to the lower edge of the skirt a distance above it to equal the width of the finished plaiting. Then lay the flounce face down over the skirt, with the raw edge over this line and the hem of the flounce toward the belt of the skirt. Baste a narrow seam along the mark, and stitch. Turn the flounce over and stitch again three-eighths of an inch from the turned edge, keeping the plaits even and flat.

Fig. 279. Simple Ruche for Edge of Chiffon Accordion Plaiting

If preferred, the flounce may also be hemmed at the top, and stitched to the skirt with a narrow heading.

If the plaited flounce is of chiffon, a dust ruffle of the silk is generally used under it. The lower edge of this ruffle is simply pinked, and the upper edge is finished with a very narrow hem. The ruffle is stitched on with a narrow heading. (Fig. 278.)

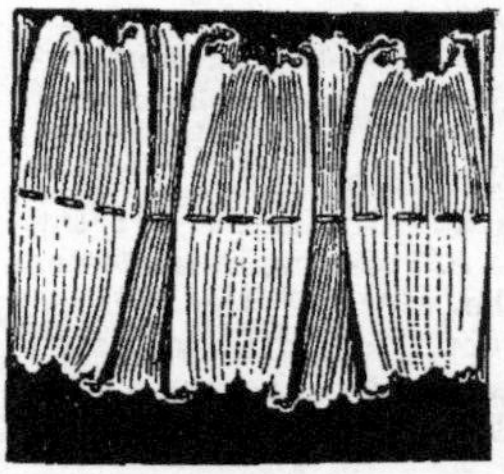

Fig. 280. Box-Plaited Ruche

Another good method for giving the graceful flare or fulness at the lower edge of a foundation skirt is by adding several tiny ruffles or ruchings to the plaited flounce or ruffle. These are cut bias, if made of taffeta, and simply pinked at both edges and gathered or plaited through the middle. (Fig. 280.)

A Simple Ruche of chiffon for the edge of a flounce is made by doubling a strip of the chiffon over on the center line with the upper raw edge turned under and the gathering thread run in along this line. (Fig. 279.) After joining as many strips of the chiffon to make the required length, cut the selvages off, as the stiffness will prevent the chiffon from falling into a soft, graceful ruche.

A Three-Tuck Ruche is used when more fulness is desired than is given by a simple ruche. This is made by cutting the chiffon strips about seven inches wide. After joining the strips as before, hold them in thirds, bringing the two raw edges together three-eighths of an inch from the folds. Run a gathering thread through all the layers of chiffon at one time. (Fig. 281.)

A Puff Ruffle is sometimes used over a silk plaiting or ruffle. This is made of strips of

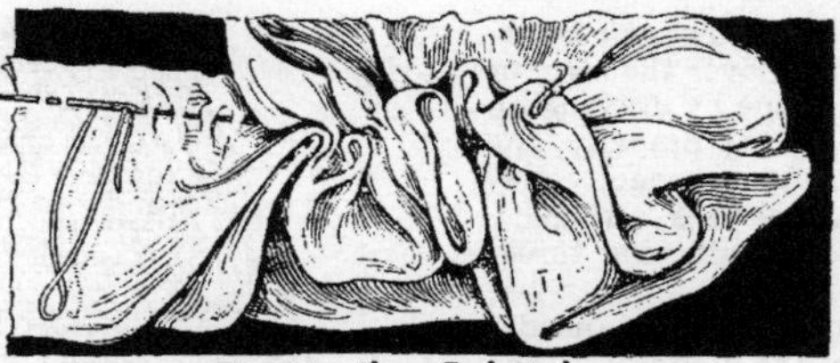
Fig. 281. Three-Tuck Ruche

chiffon double the width of the ruffle desired, plus the two inches required for the heading at the top. Fold the chiffon double, bringing the two raw edges together on a line one inch below the edge that will be the upper edge of the ruffle. Turn under the upper raw edge and run in the gathering thread, using small stitches. Baste and then sew the puff ruffle to the skirt above the silk flounce. (Fig. 282.)

A Circular Flounce may be used as a finish at the bottom of the foundation skirt if desired. This may be cut from any good circular pattern. The lower edge is turned up in an inch hem, and the upper edge joined to the skirt in a French seam. The flounce may be trimmed with tiny ruchings or ruffles, as may be preferred.

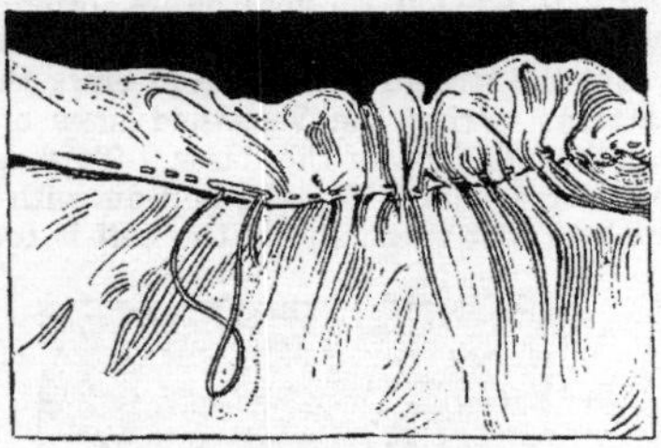
Fig. 282. Puff Ruffle

A Dust Ruffle is sometimes sewed on the inside of an outside skirt when it is desired to give it a graceful flare at the lower edge without making it necessary to wear additional underskirts. The dust ruffle is also used on foundation skirts when one is desired. It is usually four inches wide, pinked at both edges, and sewed to the skirt by hand with invisible stitches. The ruffle is held down at intervals by French tacks. They are made by taking a small stitch in the skirt and one in the ruffle, leaving a half-inch or more of thread between. Pass the needle back and forth once more, putting it into the same place, and then work several loose buttonhole-stitches back over the three strands of the silk thread. (Fig. 283.)

Foundation skirts vary in style and shape according to the prevailing fashions in outside skirts. These instructions are intended, therefore, to be of general use in making either drop skirts, petticoats or foundation skirts for evening dresses, etc.

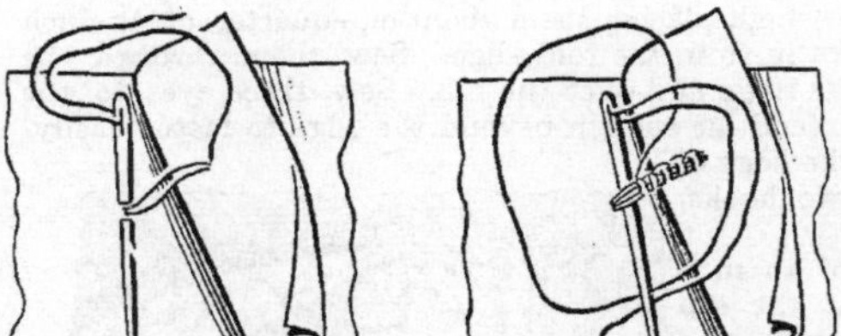
Fig. 283. Method of Making French Tack

THE DRESS SKIRT is, of course, made and finished according to the material used and the style of pattern chosen. Directions for putting the skirt together will be found in the pattern instructions. If the figure to be fitted is out of proportion in any particular, read Chapter XIV, "The Use of Butterick Patterns," before cutting out the skirt. The first step is to lay out the pattern on the material, following, of course, the perforations indicating the right grain of the material, and being careful to keep the nap or figure running the proper direction. (Read Chapter XIII, "Cutting Materials, Sponging, etc.")

Before basting, lay the gores together, with the more bias edge on top (Fig. 284), and smooth the two gores out by running the hand lightly down and across with the weave of the fabric, being careful neither to pull nor stretch the bias edges. Beginning at the top, pin the edges together at intervals, and then baste along the sewing line with small even stitches until well over the hips, where the strain will come in fitting. Below this point the basting stitches may be longer.

Try on the skirt, and make alterations wherever necessary. Be careful not to fit it too tightly over the hips, or it will tend to make the skirt lose its shape by drawing up and wrinkling when one is sitting. To set properly, the center line of the front of a skirt must stand exactly perpendicular. Draw the skirt up well at the back, and mark the line for the belt with tailor's tacks, allowing three-eighths of an inch for the seam.

Stitch the seams and press. The finish of the seams depends on the weight and texture of the material. (See Chapter XIX, "Tailored Seams.")

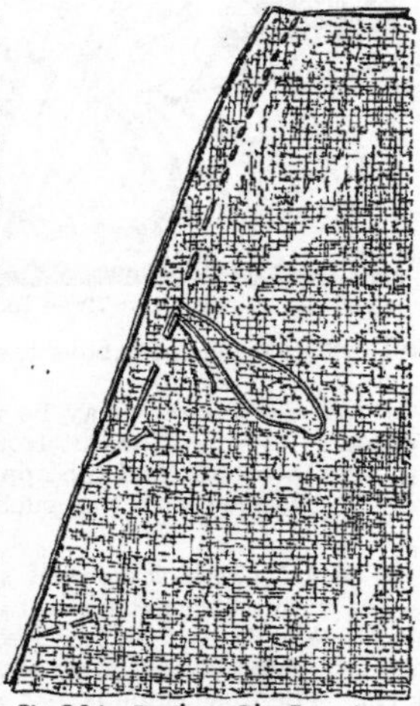

Fig. 284. Basting a Bias Edge to a Straight One

The Inside Belt—For your inside belt use silk or cotton belting of the width recommended on the pattern envelope. You can get it at any notion counter. Cotton answers, but get it in a good quality or it will be too limp to hold the weight of the skirt. It is of the utmost importance to make the belt by the pattern, for if it does not fit correctly it will slip on your figure, bringing the skirt in the wrong place, in which case it will not fit at the hips.

Get the straight belting, and mark the darts by the belt pattern. Bring the V-shaped lines of dart perforations together, and baste the darts. Turn each end under one inch for a hem. Try the belt on with the fold edges of the hem just meeting. If the belt is too large or too small turn in or let out the hems. If it is too large at the top, do not make the darts deeper. Let the darts out a trifle, and take the extra length off the ends of the hems. When the belt fits snugly, but not tightly, stitch the darts and the fold edges of the hems. Turn under the raw edge of the hem and stitch the fold to the belt. Turn the darts flat against the belt and stitch them. Mark the center of the belt with cross-stitching, and sew the loops to the sides, to hang the skirt up by. Fasten your belt with good-sized hooks and eyes, number 8 are the best. For a belt of average width, sew three hooks to the right end of belt, placing them about one-quarter of an inch in from the fold edge. Sew them through the rings and over the bill. Sew three eyes to the left end of the belt, letting them extend far enough beyond the edge to fasten easily. Sew them through the rings and at the edge of the belt. Some women use only two hooks, and their belts bulge at the center.

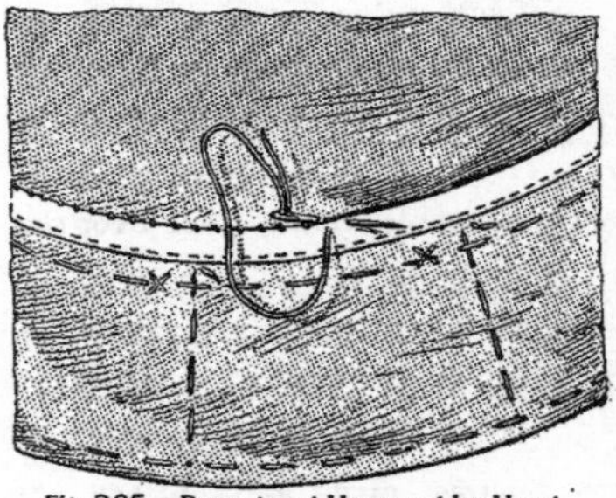

Fig. 285. Bound and Hemmed by Hand

The hooks should be one-eighth of an inch back from the edge, and the eye at the top touching the seam of the facing and skirt.

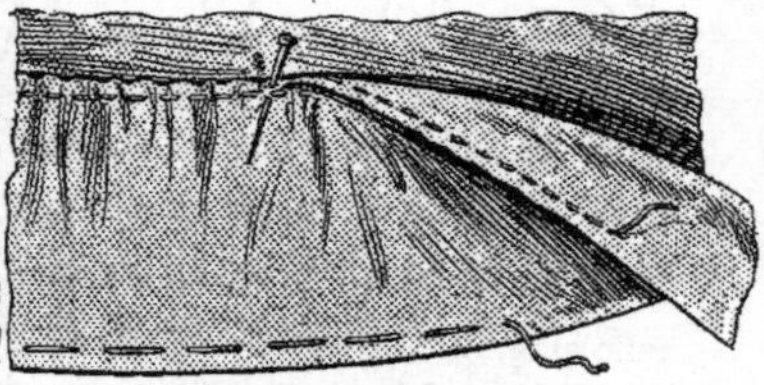

Fig. 286. Hem Gathered at Top

A Hem two or three inches deep is the usual finish of the lower edge of skirts. The extra length required for the hem must be allowed for when cutting. The patterns usually allow only three-eighths inch for seaming. If the material is of soft texture, the hem is simply turned under, its edge turned in and sewed down by hand in blind stitches, or finished with a row or two of machine-stitching. The lower edge of the skirt measures more than the line of sewing, so it must be fulled or laid in tiny plaits here and there, to make the hem lie flat. (Fig. 286.) If the skirt is of heavy material the upper edge of the hem or facing may be bound with a bias strip of lining material instead of turning in the edge of the cloth. The stitching should be made through the binding. (Fig. 285.)

A False Hem or *Facing* is sometimes preferred for the finish of the lower edge, especially if there is a wide sweep at the bottom. The facing is cut in bias strips, or shaped to fit the lower edge of the skirt. The strips are pieced together and the seams pressed open. Then baste and stitch the facing with a narrow seam, to the lower edge of the skirt on the right side. Turn over to the wrong side and baste down flatly along the edge. Then baste again along the upper edge of the facing, turning in a narrow seam. (Fig. 287.)

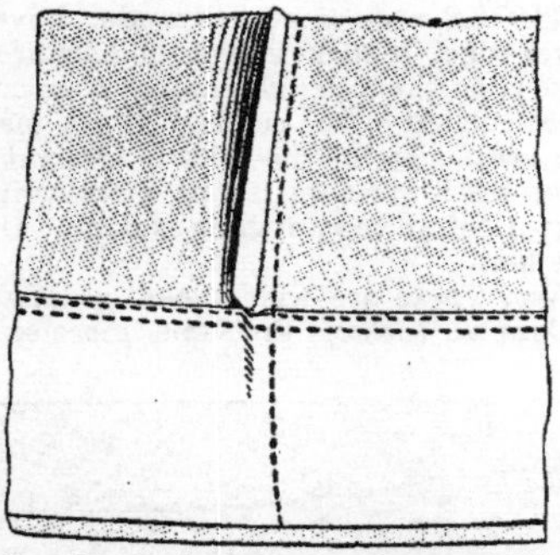

Fig. 287. Facing Hemmed to Bottom of Skirt

Velveteen or *Skirt Braid* may be added to protect the lower edge of the skirt, if desired. The velveteen strip is first stitched by hand, on the inner side of the skirt very near the edge, then turned up, leaving a narrow fold extending below the edge, and again sewed to the inner hem or facing, as shown in Fig. 288. The skirt braid should be shrunken —wet thoroughly and pressed dry—before it is used. It is sewed flat to the under side of the skirt, its lower edge one-eighth of an inch below the bottom of the skirt. Sew it with a running stitch, just above the lower edge of the skirt. The upper edge of the braid is hemmed down. In other words it is sewed with two rows of stitching—running stitches near its lower edge and hemming stitching at its upper edge.

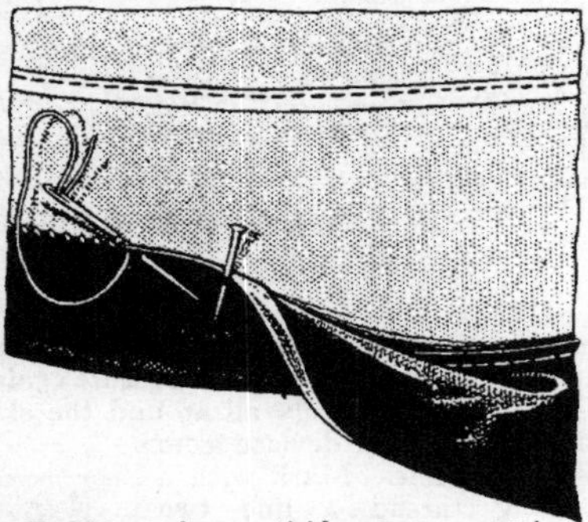

Fig. 288. Velveteen Finish on Bottom of Skirt

An Interlining may be used in the hem or facing if it is desirable to add weight at the lower edge of the skirt. The material used for the purpose may be strips of lining, or, according to the texture of the skirt material, any substantial material such as heavy flannel or broadcloth. These materials are used where body is required in the garment. Since it is simply a question of giving weight to the skirt edge, especially in the case of soft silks, etc., the interlining for the hem may be made of light-weight cotton flannel.

The interlining is cut in strips as wide as the hem or facing, omitting the seam edges at both sides. Baste it to the skirt along its lower edge, if the skirt is to have a facing. For a hem that is to have an interlining, mark the skirt all around a distance above the lower edge to equal the width of the hem. Then the strip for the interlining is basted along this line. The hem is then turned up, and with the narrow seam turned in at the top, one row of stitching catches through both the hem edge and the upper edge of the interlining.

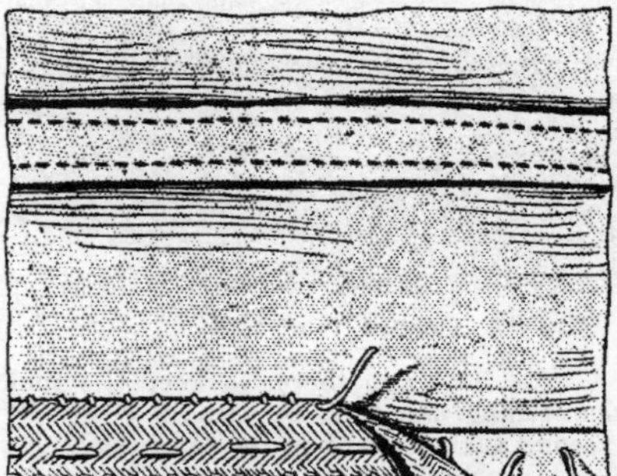

Fig. 289. Braid Finish

When it is not desirable to finish a hem with machine stitching, and it must be done by hand, do it with blind or slip stitches. When this is the case, the interlining must first be securely stitched on the inner side of the facing, or the turned-up portion of the hem, with the seam edge turned over the upper edge of the interlining.

TUCKS are sometimes made above the hem for trimming or adding weight to the lower edge. If tucks above the hem are desired they should be basted in before the lower edge is finished. If the pattern does not allow for the tucks, the additional length must be calculated in the cutting. They may be of any width and of any number desired. If the lower edge of the skirt is straight the tucking is simple. The greatest difficulty is when the lower edge is very circular in outline, for then the tucks must be marked and basted before the stitching is done. Usually the skirt is fitted and finished at the waist-line first.

Nun Tucks are wide tucks, usually two inches or more in depth. The method for making all tucks is the same, more or less, but the wider the tuck the greater the difficulty in keeping the lines and the distances between the tucks even when the bottom of the skirt is circular at its lower edge.

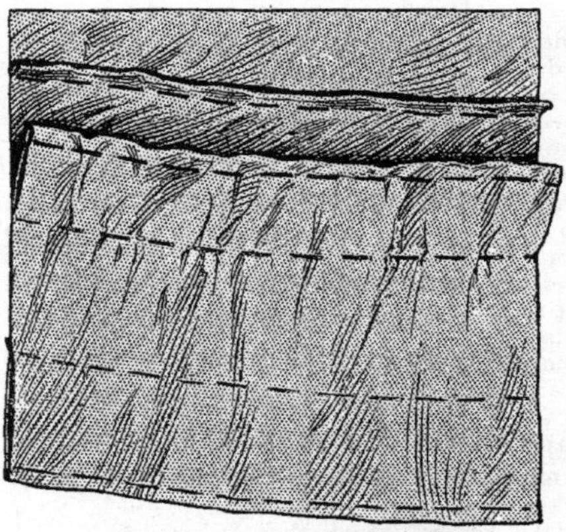

Fig. 290. Preparing "Nun" Tucks

The number and width of the tucks must be decided before the skirt is cut, and the additional length allowed in each gore. For instance, when two tucks two inches wide are desired, you must add eight extra inches in the length, and two inches more if a hem is to be used also.

After the gores of the skirt have been joined, and the belt finished, the length of the skirt is made perfectly even at its lower edge. The easiest way to get an even line is to try the skirt on the figure, standing on a footstool or some elevation that will permit the entire skirt length, including the allowance for the tucks, to hang straight.

The hem is then pinned up and basted. From the sewing line of the hem measure the distance desired between the tucks (the hem is counted as a tuck in this instance), and from this point measure again to a line two inches above, for a two-inch tuck.

Baste a fold evenly all around the skirt at this point, being careful not to twist at the fold edge nor deviate from the exact line. Mark with a basting thread a line two inches above and also one two inches below this fold edge all around the skirt. Then having the skirt on the lap board or sewing-table, with its lower edge toward you, baste in the tuck by bringing these two lines together. It will be seen that the lower line is a trifle wider than the upper one, and this is just wherein the difficulty of making tucks lies. (Fig. 290.) As you proceed, the lower basting thread must be drawn up a trifle here and there, to keep the tuck perfectly flat on its upper surface. The final stitching can then be put in, either by hand or machine sewing. (Fig. 291.) For the second tuck proceed in the same way.

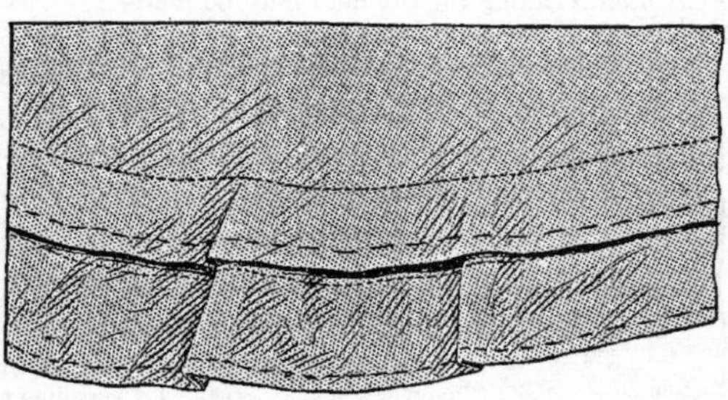

Fig. 291. Finished "Nun" Tucks

PLAITED SKIRTS are more or less worn at all times, though some years they are more popular than others. Different arrangements of plaits are worn each season, but there are certain general instructions that apply equally well to the different styles of plaited skirts.

The first step, of course, is to read the pattern instructions carefully, and to get a clear idea of the particular style of the skirt that is being made.

In cases where the skirts are composed of seven, nine or more gores it is not so difficult to handle them successfully, since alterations may be made at the seams. But in skirts where few gores are employed, particular attention must be paid to the correct position of the lines, in order to keep the plaits perfectly even. Furthermore, the skirt must be joined to the belt and the material between the plaits properly disposed, so that the plaits themselves will have a uniform appearance.

Before cutting the material read the pattern instructions, examine the pattern and identify the pieces, observing the notches and perforations according to the directions. No fixed rule can be given for laying out material for cutting. It is frequently necessary to open out double-width material, cutting each part separately. Be careful in this case to observe the right and left side of the garment. In cutting a skirt, make a lengthwise fold in the material for the center of the front gore. Never start cutting with the widest part of your pattern toward the solid part of your material. Lay out your pattern carefully and place it on the material economically before starting to cut. If the material is narrow, it will be necessary to piece the lower part of this gore at each side; but this need not be done until after the rest of the skirt is cut, as some of the pieces cut from the side gores will probably be large enough for this purpose.

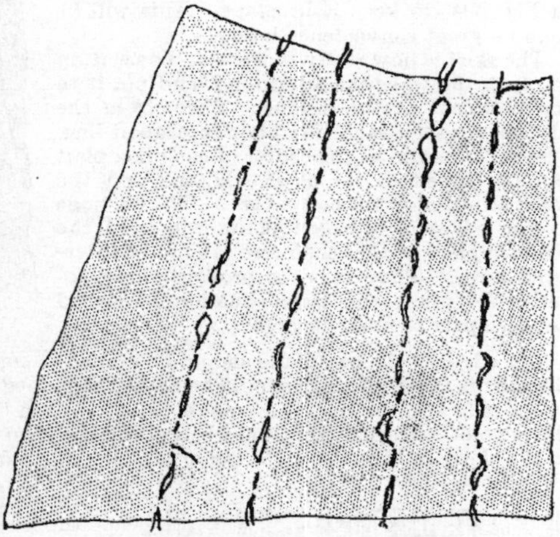

Fig. 292. A Gore Marked for the Plaits

Single-width material should be laid out straight for all breadths except the front. It may be folded *across* at half its length, or cut in two and reversed (if it has a nap) and cut double. After all the breadths are cut, and before removing the pattern, mark all perforations except the ones that indicate the cutting or grain line, with tailors' tacks. (See Chapter IV, Fig. 71.) In a plaited skirt remove the pattern and place a yard-stick on the cloth with its edge even with the tailors' tacks, and draw a continuous line with chalk. Mark this line with tailors' tacks. (Fig. 292.)

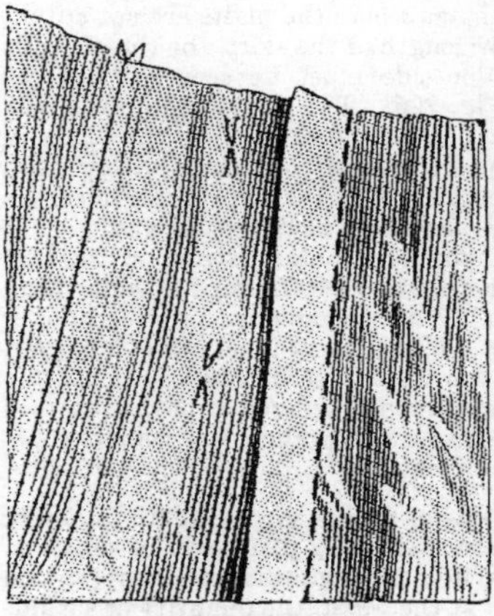

Fig. 293. Basting the Plaits in Tucks

The long threads should be cut, the pieces separated, and the breadths joined at the seams. In sewing a bias edge be careful not to stretch it. Basting the seams is shown in Fig. 284 on page 110.

For a Box-Plaited Skirt, after all the seams are joined (except the back seam, which is not basted until the plaits are all laid), begin at the front breadth and bring the two lines of markings at each side of the center front together and baste. This forms a large tuck. (Fig. 293.) The next two rows of markings are then basted together to form a second tuck. Continue in this way around each side of the skirt. Each seam corresponds to a row of markings, and is to be basted to the line formed at the perforations on the breadth toward the front. After the plaits are basted into tucks, each one is flattened to form a box plait, bringing the seam in the center on the wrong side. The method of forming the plaits is shown in Fig. 293.

Be careful to get the box plaits even, without any draw, especially where the edges come bias. As each one is flattened, it should be basted a quarter of an inch from the fold edge, as shown in Fig. 294, to keep it in shape. This will be found a great convenience later.

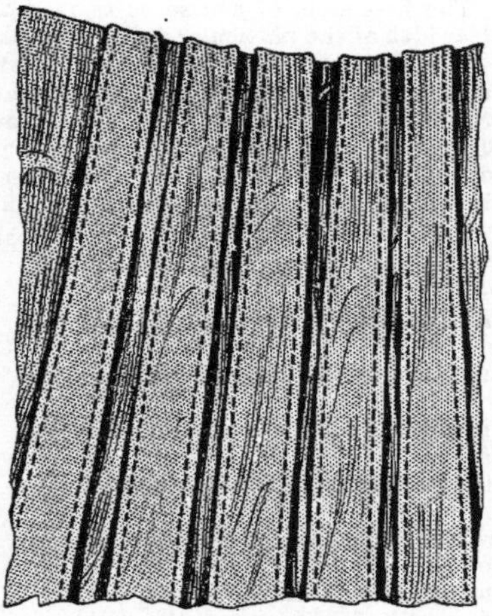

Fig. 294. The Box Plaits Basted in Place.

The skirt is now ready to try on. Draw it up to reach the waistline all around, and pin it to the petticoat at the hipline. Then, from the hip up, arrange each box plait in a good line. The basted seam at the center of each box plait can be ripped as far as the hipline and the waist adjusted to the correct size. The bastings at the edges of the box plaits will hold the plaits in place so that their size can not be interfered with. They may be brought closer together to make the waist smaller or spread farther apart to make it larger.

The edges of the box plaits should be pinned in correct position at the fitting, and when the skirt is taken off, they should be basted as pinned. The skirt can then be turned to the wrong side and the ripped seams rebasted. When this has been done, mark on the skirt the edge of each plait that has been altered. Then remove the bastings that hold them to the skirt, so that the under seam may be stitched.

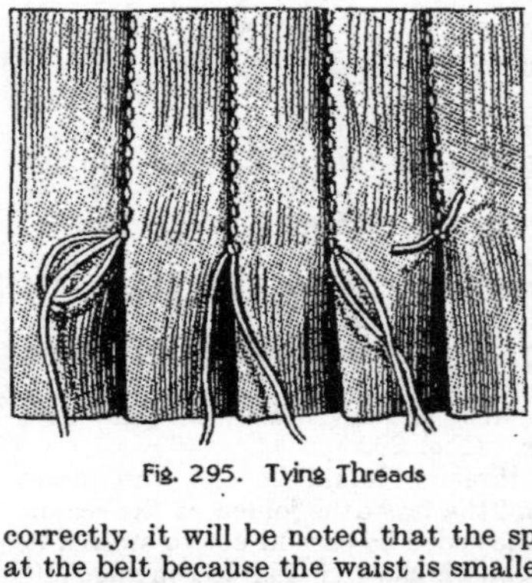

Fig. 295. Tying Threads

The plaits should be basted to the skirt again at the line of markings made after the fitting. The bastings should run down as far as they are to be stitched. It would be advisable to rip the basting of the back seam, as the skirt can be more easily handled under the machine if it is opened out flat. Stitch the plaits down through both plait and skirt to the desired depth. In cases where the plaits are not stitched the entire length of the skirt, the thread-ends on the under side must be securely tied, as shown in Fig. 295. Then baste and stitch the back seam, put on the belt, press the plaits in place to the bottom of the skirt, and try it on again to secure the correct length. Finish the hem, placket and belt in the usual way.

When a box-plaited skirt is put on the belt correctly, it will be noted that the space between the plaits over the hips is wider than at the belt because the waist is smaller than the hips. Where seams are provided under the plaits, the superfluous material may be taken out. Where there is no seam, however, the fulness which occurs must be disposed of under the plaits. If this fulness is not too great, the material may be held a trifle easy, or, one might say, puckered or pushed toward the line of stitching. To present a thoroughly well-made appearance, this fulness must be hidden; and on that account the plaits are very convenient.

Notwithstanding the fact that it is possible to dispose of all the surplus material under one plait, it should not be done, since it would throw the other plaits out of position. There must be an equal space between the plaits. Where the figure is out of proportion in any way, either very large around the hips or small at the waist, the quantity of surplus material is increased. While a small amount may be managed as directed, and after careful pressing be unnoticeable, a larger quantity would be too bulky, and had best be treated differently.

When the plaits are laid the full length of the skirt. and the skirt is being fitted, side plaits or darts should be used to adjust the extra material to a small waist. Fig. 296 shows the method of placing the darts. If a dart is used it is sewed in a position that will come well under the plait so that there will be no likelihood of its being seen. Even if folded over, the upper edges of the box plait should not be disturbed, for this would disarrange the size and width on the outside. The material near the stitching is folded over one-eighth or one-quarter of an inch to form a dart-like tuck, and these new lines are joined or folded in such a way that they taper gradually into the line of the original plait just above the full part of the hips, as seen in the illustration. It should then be pressed flat, and the extra fold will not be objectionable. Treat the extra fulness in this manner where it is necessary, and keep the spaces an equal width.

Fig. 296. Arrangement of Dart under Plait

A Skirt Made with Side Plaits or Kilts is shown in Fig. 297. The manner of preparing the skirt and marking the perforations that indicate the plaits is the same as that already described. At each line of markings that represents the fold of a plait, the plait should be folded with the markings as an edge, and the doubled goods should be basted one-quarter of an inch back of the edge. This will hold all the plaits in the correct line, no matter what alteration may be necessary in fitting. Many plaited models have one row of stitching placed just back of the fold edge, and through the two thicknesses only, in the same way as the basting just described. This row of stitching answers a double purpose. It is ornamental and at the same time holds the edge of the plait in shape, and is especially desirable for wash goods or a thin woolen material that is likely to twist on a bias edge. The second row of stitching is placed a little distance back of the first and is taken through both plait and skirt. Stitch it to the desired depth and leave the ends of the thread two or three inches long at the end of the stitching, so that they may be drawn through to the wrong side and tied securely. (See Fig. 295 on page 114).

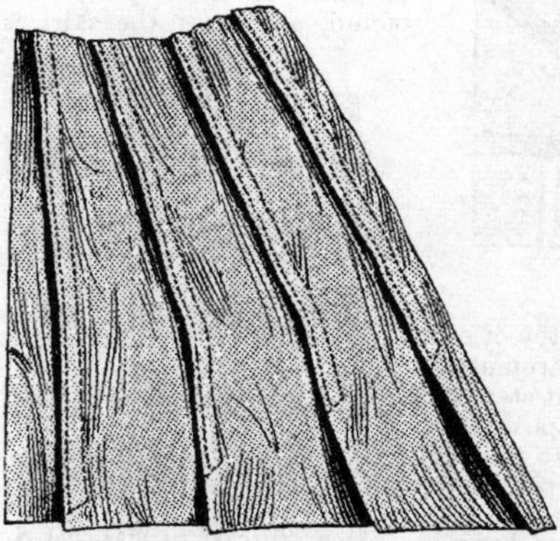
Fig. 297. Side Plaits with Two Rows of Stitching

When a plaited skirt is made of heavy material or is lapped very much at the waist in fitting, it may be made less bulky by cutting away the surplus material after the plaits are stitched. The under-lapping goods is cut away to within an inch or so of where the stitching finishes. From that point it is cut across the top of the plait. The raw edges left in this way are bound with a bias strip of lining, that will finish across the top of each plait except where the seams that join the breadths form the inner fold of a plait, when the binding will continue down the raw edges of that seam to the bottom of the skirt. (Fig. 298 on the next page.)

As each figure has some trifling peculiarity, careful study should be given the instructions on the pattern and judgment used as to the best means of alteration or adjustment. It must always be remembered, however, that the tucks or plaits must be evenly arranged and that the space between them must be the same, as this is quite an important point in making a plaited skirt.

When a plaited skirt is made of washable material, the laundering is not difficult if one goes about it in the right way. The lower part of the skirt should not be pressed out flat, but each plait as it is pressed at the stitched upper portion should be laid in position all the way to the bottom of the skirt, smoothed and arranged with the hand and pressed into position. Afterward the iron may be run under the plait to smooth the part underneath. This is the same method that is employed in pressing a similar skirt made of cloth. In laundering or pressing a skirt the value of shrinking the material before cutting and of observing the "grain" of the weave is realized.

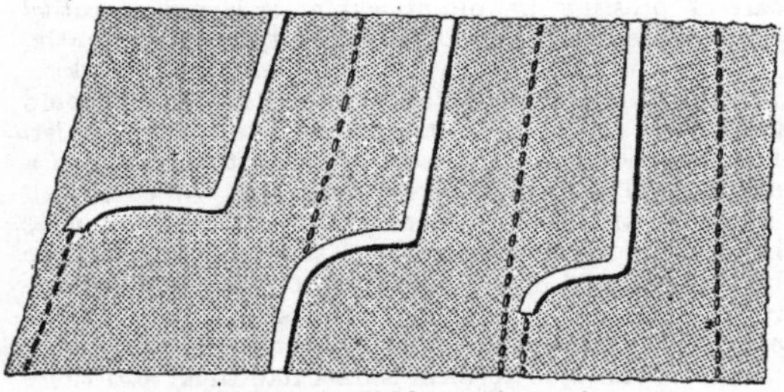

Fig. 298. Inside Finish of a Kilted Skirt

Gored skirts that have a side plait or an inverted box plait let into the seams some distance up from the bottom, are sometimes troublesome because of a tendency of these plaits to show below the bottom edge of the skirt since there is nothing to which they may be attached. This trouble may be avoided in the manner shown in Fig. 299.

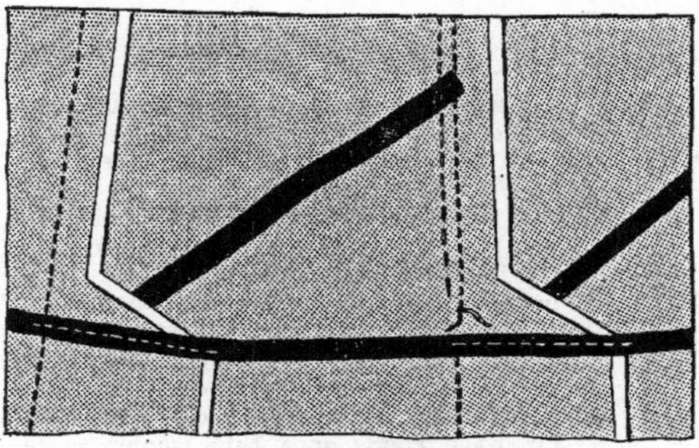

Fig. 299. Supporting Inlaid Plaids

The seam edge and the edge of each of these plaits are bound, and after the skirt is finished a tape or strap of lining is sewed to the top of each plait and is carried from one to the other all around the skirt. The tape will generally be found sufficient stay, but in a woolen skirt of heavy cloth an additional tape or strap may run diagonally from the top of each plait to the next seam and be securely sewed there to the wrong side of the skirt. This stay also is shown in the illustration.

Flare Skirts are many-gored skirts that do not hang in plaits below the hips, and are made to stand out from the feet at the lower edge. These need special treatment in finishing, to preserve the flare and make them hang in just the right way. The proper finish of the seams on the inside can be seen in Fig. 300. After the seams have been basted and stitched, it is advisable to try on the skirt and pin a tape around the figure to determine the hip depth to which the flat seam shall extend. At the same time the length of the skirt should be determined by pinning it up around the bottom or by marking it with chalk. Mark the line for the bottom of the skirt with a basting thread and also mark the skirt with a thread along the edge of the tape. At the hipline clip both raw edges of each seam at the inside of the skirt in order to divide the flat-finished hip part from the rippled part. Make this clip or cut extend the full width of the seam edges, running in as far as

Fig. 300. Inside Finish of a Many-Gored Flare Skirt

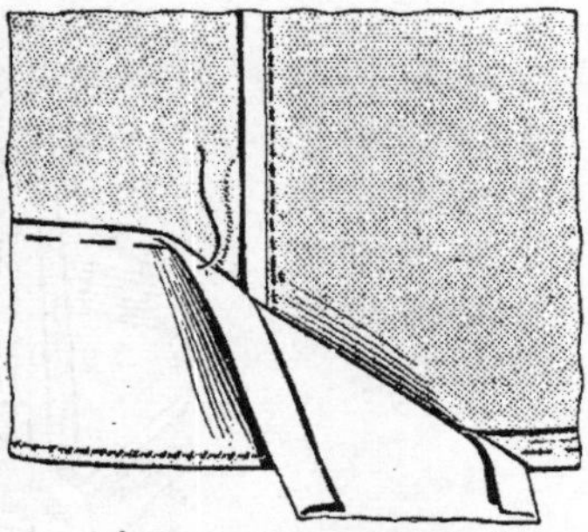

Fig. 301 Seam Stitched Across Facing to Hold Flare Effect

the stitching of the seam. The seam above the clip is to be pressed open, clipping or notching it wherever necessary to make it lie flat. It may be finished with a row of machine-stitching at each side of the seam and quite close to it, or both edges of the seam may be turned the same way, a row of stitching on the outside holding them in lap-seam effect.

Mark the hem or facing depth at the bottom of the skirt—it is usually about three inches deep. Clip the seam in at this point; press this lower part of the seam open in order to hem or face the skirt properly. The part of the seam which has not been pressed open should be bound as shown in Fig. 301, using a narrow bias strip of lining material for the purpose. This portion of the seam is not to be pressed to either one side or the other, but stands out straight from the inside of the skirt, and gives a fluted effect to the breadths. Baste a bias facing in place, hem the lower edge to the turned-over edge of the skirt. The upper edge may be hemmed by hand or may have one or two rows of machine-stitching to correspond with the stitching on the upper part of the seams. The skirt should then be folded at each seam and placed in the machine in the same way as when the breadths were first stitched together, and a row of stitching, as shown in Fig. 301, made along the bound part of the seam close to the first row and extending across the facing forming that into a small seam.

HANGING A CIRCULAR SKIRT. A circular skirt is cut on the bias and a bias will always stretch more or less. One should let, in fact encourage, the skirt to stretch as much as possible, before the bottom is finished so that it will stretch very little, if at all, after it is hung.

A skirt stretches because its own weight and the weight of the hem or facing drags down the bias grain. If you hang the skirt up for two or three days properly weighted you will exhaust its powers of stretching. In your piece bag you will find plenty of useless material that can be used to weigh the skirt. Cut strips three or four inches wide and enough of them to make four or five thicknesses. Pin them to the lower part of your skirt. (Fig. 301 A.) Pin the two halves of your skirt together at the top and pin loops of material to the skirt to hang it up by. (Fig. 301 A.) Slip the loops over hooks placed just far enough apart to hold the skirt band out even. Let the skirt hang for two or three days with the weight of the strips stretching it as much as it will. Then you can turn up the bottom without fear of its sagging.

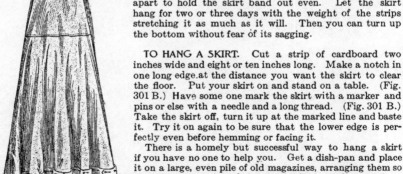

Fig. 301 A. Hanging a Circular Skirt to Prevent Sagging.

TO HANG A SKIRT. Cut a strip of cardboard two inches wide and eight or ten inches long. Make a notch in one long edge at the distance you want the skirt to clear the floor. Put your skirt on and stand on a table. (Fig. 301 B.) Have some one mark the skirt with a marker and pins or else with a needle and a long thread. (Fig. 301 B.) Take the skirt off, turn it up at the marked line and baste it. Try it on again to be sure that the lower edge is perfectly even before hemming or facing it.

There is a homely but successful way to hang a skirt if you have no one to help you. Get a dish-pan and place it on a large, even pile of old magazines, arranging them so that the upper edge of the pan is the same distance from the floor that you want the lower edge of your skirt to be. Fasten a piece of soft chalk to a long stick. Stand in the dishpan with your skirt over the pan. With the stick

Fig. 301 B. Getting an Even Line at the Bottom of the Skirt

and chalk tap your skirt against the rim of the pan. You can easily mark an even line in this way. Take the skirt off, turn it up at the chalk marks and baste it. Try it on again to be sure that it is even at the bottom. This is an easy method for the woman who has no one to help her with her dressmaking.

CHAPTER XXII

COATS AND JACKETS

FITTED COATS, outlining the figure, require more care and attention in the making than fancy coats, though the latter, when finished, may look much more elaborate. The first important step is to have the cloth thoroughly shrunken, according to Chapter XIII, "Cutting Materials, Sponging, Etc."

Measure the length of the back from the collar seam to the waistline, and the length of the arm from the armhole to the wrist, and alter the pattern, if necessary, according to the directions given with it. When the cloth is ready, lay the pattern on it to the best advantage. Be careful, if there is a nap, to place the pieces so they will all run the same way of the goods. Otherwise, the pieces with the nap running in the opposite direction will shade; that is, some will look darker than others. In cloth the nap should always run toward the bottom of the garment. In velvet, but not in panne velvet, it should run upward. In panne velvet it should run downward. Be sure to follow carefully the directions accompanying the pattern, in regard to the grain of the goods; otherwise the garment will draw and stretch. (See Chapter XIII.)

When using full-width cloth—that is, fifty-two or fifty-four inches wide—many coats may be cut economically with the cloth folded lengthwise through the center, as it is folded when bought. For a long coat, however, it is sometimes necessary to open the cloth to its full width. Lay it out smoothly, with the wrong side up, and arrange the pattern upon it.

Pin the pattern carefully to the material and cut it out with sharp scissors, following the outline most exactly. After you have cut the first half, lay it face down on your material, with the pattern still pinned to it, and cut the second half. Be sure that the nap runs the same way in both halves and that you do not cut two halves for the same side—a common mistake of the amateur. Clip all the notches, and mark all the perforations, except the ones that indicate the grain line, with tailors' tacks. (See Chapter IV, "Practical and Ornamental Stitches.")

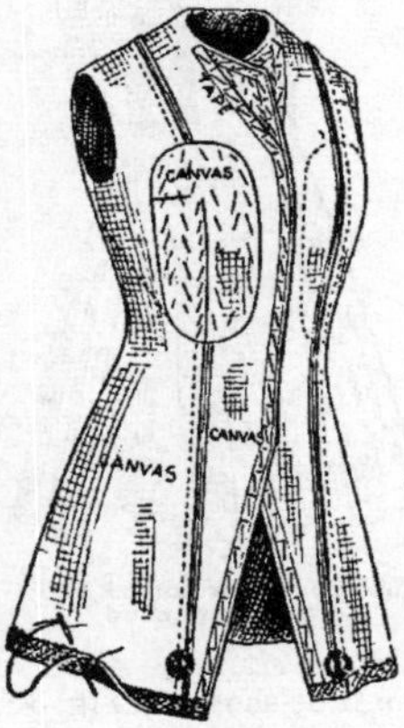

Fig. 302. Canvas and Tape in Place

THE FRONT of a cloth coat must be interlined with a soft, pliable canvas, cotton serge, or cambric, which should be shrunken before it is used. For a coat that is cut with a seam to the shoulder, the canvas is cut by the pattern of the front and side front. The canvas in the side front may stop three inches below the armhole on the under-arm seam and slope to the waistline on the side seam as shown by the dotted line in Fig. 302, or it may be used throughout the entire front. In a linen coat use butchers' linen instead of the canvas. In a silk coat use a lining material about the weight of a cotton serge, sateen or cambric, in the fronts, and a light-weight lining canvas or soft crinoline for the collar, sleeve caps and wrist. These interlinings should be shrunken before they are used.

Baste the canvas to the wrong side of the coat. (Fig. 302.) Then baste the seams of the coat and canvas together according to the notches, lapping the canvas edges flatly over each other and catch-stitching them together after the cloth seams are pressed. Try the coat on and make alterations if any are necessary before stitching the seams.

To give the coat more body over the bust, an extra piece of thin canvas not quite as heavy as used in the fronts should be applied to each front as shown in Fig. 302. Do not make a seam in the canvas to make it fit the bust, but slash it and lap the edges to make it fit smoothly in the coat. This canvas should be attached to the other canvas in the fronts by padding stitches. Fig. 305 shows how these stitches are made.

In a coat that is made with a dart instead of a seam to the shoulder in front, the canvas must be cut with the pattern of the front as a guide. The canvas should be about six inches wide along the front edges of the coat. At the waistline it should slope outward and upward to the under-arm seam, where it should stop three inches below the armhole.

Fur and fur-cloth coats are generally without seams in front. If the coat is made of fur cloth, the entire coat should be lined with cambric before the canvas is put in. (Fig. 304.) This cambric reenforces and strengthens the rather loose weave of the fur-cloth. It is also used in fur coats if the pelts are tender and perishable.

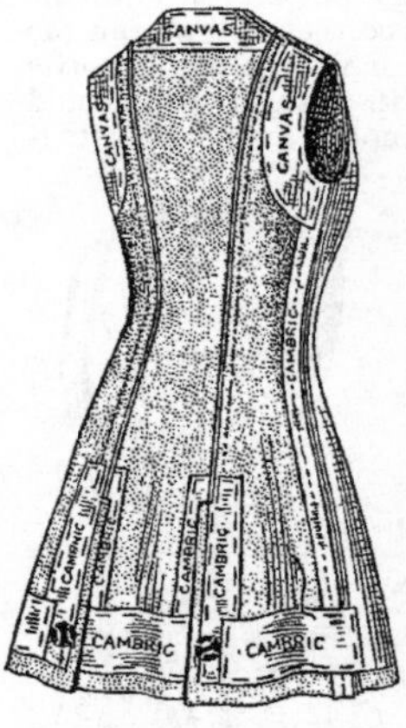

Fig. 303. How Cambric and Canvas Are Used

If the coat is made with a dart, the darts in the coat and in the canvas should be closed separately. Take up the dart in the coat in the usual way, but lap the edges of the dart in the canvas and tack them together. (Fig. 304.)

When the garment is an Eton or any other short jacket, the interlining in the front is cut to the waistline and to the extreme front edge, whether the jacket is single or double breasted.

Baste a piece of canvas or other interlining the shape of the neck and shoulders of the back, and about two inches deep, across the neck at the back, and similar pieces around the armholes of the back and underarm, to meet the interlining of the fronts as shown in Fig. 303. This stays the coat and prevents the breaking around the armhole. The side seams, the vents at the back and the bottom of the coat are reenforced with cambric. (Fig. 303.) Stitch all the seams of the coat. If they are to be finished with stitching or lapped seams, press them before completing the finish. (Chapter XIX.)

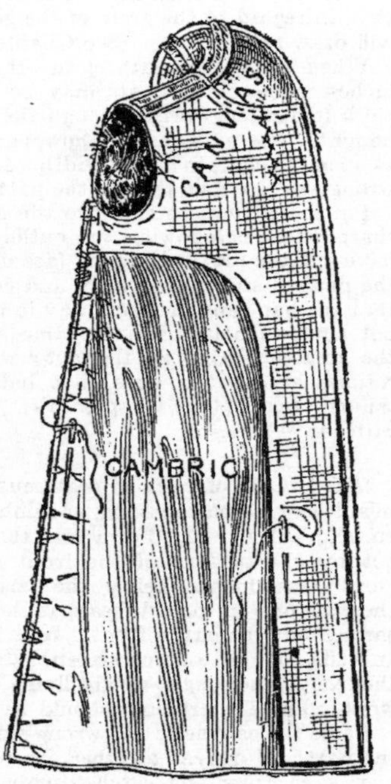

Fig. 304. Canvas and Cambric in the Front of Fur-Cloth Coat

FOR THE STRICTLY TAILORED COLLAR cut an interlining of tailor's canvas. Use the collar pattern as a guide, but cut the canvas three-eighths of an inch smaller at all edges than the pattern. The canvas should be shrunken before it is used. The "stand" of the collar—the part next the neck that stands up when the coat is worn—is marked by perforations. It is a crescent-shaped section which should be covered with parallel rows of machine stitching about a quarter of an inch apart. (Fig. 306.)

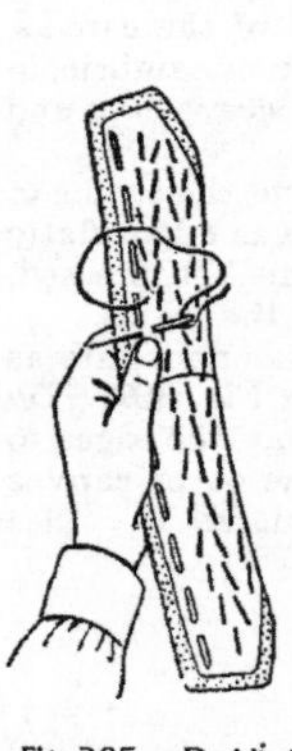

Fig. 305. Padding Stitches in Collar

The canvas and cloth in the turnover part of the collar, and in the lapel or revers on

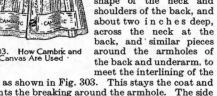

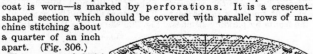

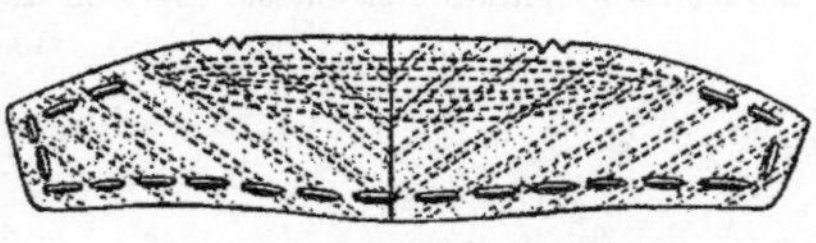

Fig. 306. Stitching on the Stand of the Collar

the front, must be held firmly by many small stitches called "padding stitches." These stitches are about half an inch long on the canvas side and just barely caught through on the right side. Hold the collar or lapel firmly over the hand, the canvas side uppermost, and, in stitching, roll and shape the section in the direction in which it is to lie. (Fig. 305.) The stitch should be started at the line of the fold of the lapel or collar and worked in successive rows to the edge. The edges should be turned under, caught to the canvas and pressed.

Baste the collar, canvas side up, flat on the coat, according to the notches in the collar and in the neck. (Fig. 307.) Stretch the neck edge of the collar between the notches so that it will set smoothly on the coat. The upper or turnover part of the collar must lie flat, joining the turned-over lapels at the top of the fronts, to form the notched collar.

Fig. 307. Stretch the Collar Between Notches

When the coat has advanced thus far, try it on. Fold over the lapel corners at the top of the fronts and see that the collar is the correct size and fits properly. If it does not, it may be shaped by shrinking, stretching and pressing. The front edges of the coat should lie close to the figure at the bust, and a well-fitted coat should hold itself in shape to the figure at this point, even when unbuttoned. If the coat is inclined to flare away at the front line, pin one or two small dart-like tucks about one-quarter of an inch wide at the coat's edge and running out to nothing about two inches inside the edge, to shape in the edge and take out the stretched appearance. Mark these tucks with chalk, remove the pins and slash in the canvas at each chalk mark. Lap the canvas the same space that the tucks were made, cut away one edge to meet the other, lay a piece of cambric over the slash and sew the cambric to hold it to shape. The cloth will still have the fulness that has been taken out of the canvas, and must be gathered on a thread, dampened and shrunk out with the iron.

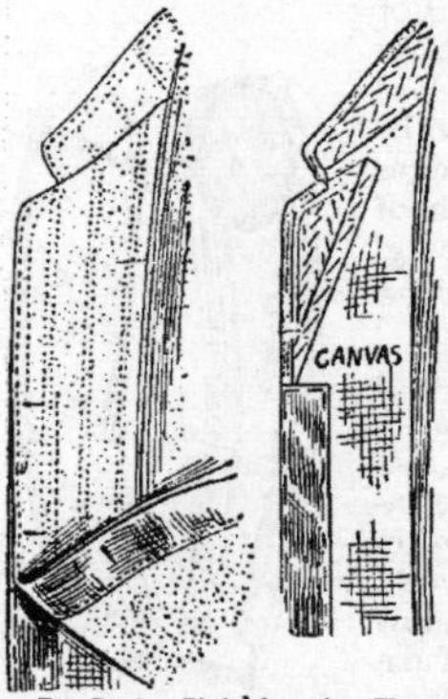

Fig. 308. Finishing the Fly

Narrow linen tape, well shrunken, should be sewed to the canvas toward the inside of the coat at the crease of the lapel, drawing it taut to prevent stretching. (Fig . 302.) The edges of the lapel and the front coat edges should also be taped, drawing the tape snug at these edges to give them a good shape. Press the fronts carefully.

An additional Interlining, if required for warmth, should be made of outing flannel or the regular silk-and-wool interlining that comes for the purpose. Cut it with the pattern of the coat as a guide, letting it extend an inch or two below the waistline. (Figs. 309 and 310, on page 122.) Slash the interlining at intervals along the bottom so that it will not bind the coat. Do not put the interlining together with ordinary seams, but tack it inside the coat, letting one seam edge of the interlining overlap the one next to it.

From the cloth, cut facings for the collar and fronts. The front facings must be cut to the shape of the front after the edges have been altered and taped. Lay the cloth on the fronts and over the lapel corners; pin it carefully in place, holding the front and lapel in to their proper shape; then cut it to the required width. It need extend only about three inches inside of the line that marks the center of the front. The collar facing, if of cloth, must be cut on the width or crosswise of the material and must not have a seam in the center of the back.

Fit the collar facing to the canvas collar and join it to the front facings, matching the notches on the collar and the front facings. Press the seams open and baste to the canvas collar and to the front of the coat, turning in the edges of both coat and facing. This finish is for visible closing, when the buttonholes are to be worked through both the outside and the cloth facing.

A SINGLE-BREASTED COAT PATTERN allows a lap which is ample for the buttonholes on each front edge beyond the perforations that mark the center of the front. It may be finished with visible buttons and buttonholes or with a fly which conceals the fastenings. (Fig. 308.)

For a Fly Facing, leave the facing of the right side of the front separate from the coat below the lapel, as it will form the fly for the invisible buttonholes. Turn the edge of the cloth under on this right side. From the crease of the turned-over lapel to the bottom of the coat stitch on the upper or finished side of the coat one or more rows of stitching as a finish about a quarter of an inch from the edge. Then face this side with a piece of the silk lining. (Fig. 308, page 121.)

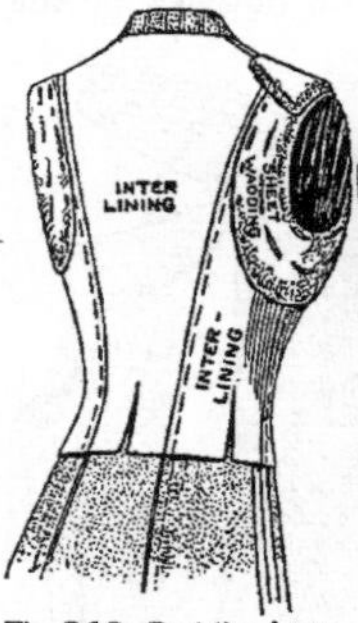

Fig. 309. Pad the Lower Shoulder

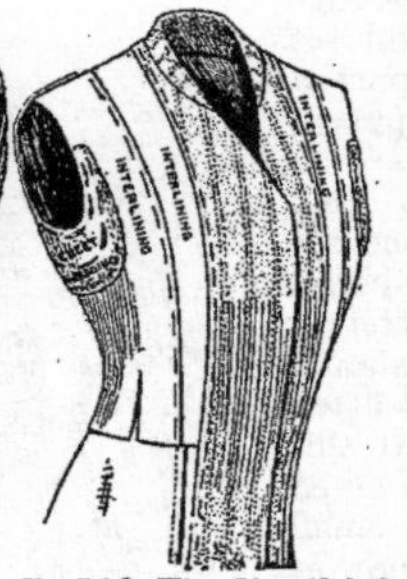

Fig. 310. The Sheet Wadding and Interlining

The cloth facing for the right side must itself be faced upon the side toward the coat with a piece of the same lining (Fig. 308), and should be stitched a quarter inch in from the front edge Baste the cloth underfacing to the inside of the right-hand side of the coat, and at the center line stitch with one row of stitching through both coat and facing to hold them firmly together. Buttonholes are then worked in the facing at equal distances apart. The front edge of the facing should be tacked to the coat midway between the buttonholes. Now continue the row of stitching at the edge from the place where it began at the top of the right side around the turned-over lapels, around the collar and down the left side.

COLLAR FACINGS of velvet are sometimes used, but instead of being applied directly over the canvas the edges of the velvet are turned under and catch-stitched to the cloth collar. If a velvet collar facing is used instead of one of the same cloth, it should be made of a seamless bias strip of velvet. Do not stitch the edges of the collar, but only the cloth turned-over lapels. One-eighth of a yard of velvet cut on the bias is usually enough for a collar facing. All pressing and shaping of the collar must be done before putting on the velvet facing.

The shawl-collar facing is sometimes cut in one with the front facing. The collar proper is cut and joined as just described—stitched to the body of the coat and pressed. The two facing sections are joined at the back, and the seam pressed open. The facing is pinned in position with wrong sides together. The outer edge of the facing is turned in even with the fold edge of the coat. Baste the free edges of the facing in place, being careful to allow sufficient ease for the roll. The edges are basted and stitched. Turn up the bottom edge of the coat over a narrow strip of bias cambric, and catch the coat edge to it. (Fig. 302, page 119.)

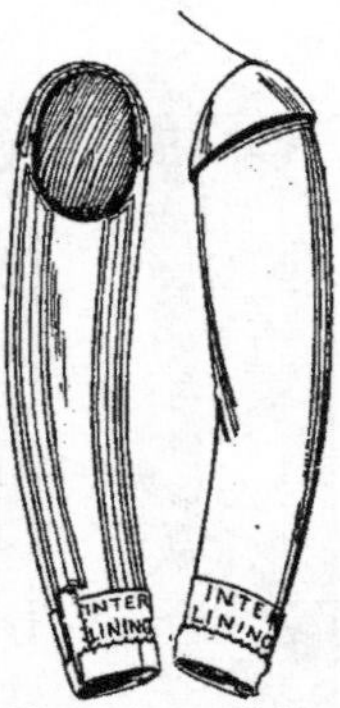

Fig. 311. Interlining and Cap

If Padding Is Needed, a few layers of sheet wadding decreasing toward the edges may be basted around the armhole from the front of the shoulder to the back, deepening under the arm, and made thick or thin as the figure may require. (Figs. 309 and 310.) If you wish to make the shoulders look more square, place a triangular piece of wadding on the shoulder with the point at about the middle of the shoulder seam and the wider part at the armhole, making the wadding thick enough to give the required squareness to the shoulders. If the shoulders are uneven, fit the upper one and pad the lower one with a triangular piece of wadding. (Fig. 309.)

Baste the Seams of the Sleeves and try them on. If they need any alteration in size around the arm, make it at the seam marked by outlet perforations. A bias strip of canvas, or whatever is used in the fronts, three inches deep should be basted into the wrist just above the turning line of the hem part, and the cloth turned over and catch-stitched to it. (Fig. 311.)

If a vent or opening is provided at the outer seam of the sleeve, the extension on the upper part is turned under for a hem: and the lower part, neatly faced with the lining, forms an underlap. This opening may be closed by buttons used as a decoration or by buttons and buttonholes. Finish the edge with one or two rows of machine-stitching to match the stitching on the edges of the coat. If stitching at cuff depth is desired, it must be made before closing the outside seam.

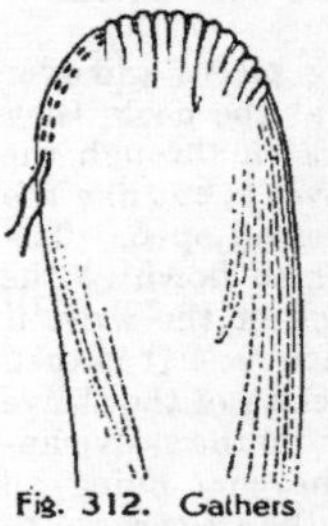
Fig. 312. Gathers

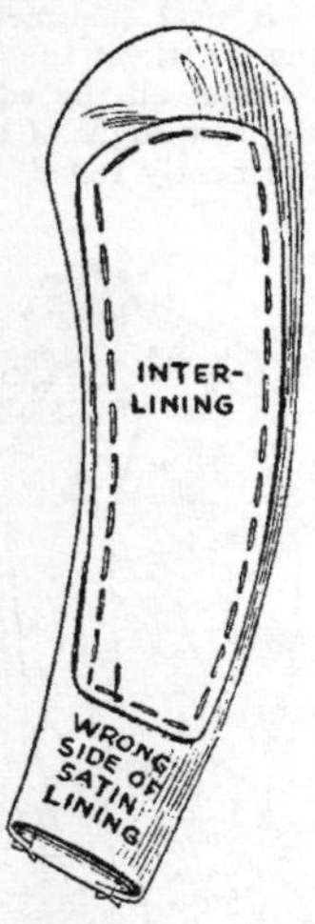

Fig. 313. The Inter-lining

Cut a piece of cambric in the same outline as the top of the sleeve and about three inches deep, and baste it in position to the inside of the sleeve. (Fig. 311.) Gage the top of the sleeve with two rows of gatherings, as shown in Fig. 312. This is done by taking up a short stitch on the upper side and a longer stitch on the under side. All the stitches of the second row should be directly underneath those of the first row. Baste the sleeves into the armholes, try the coat on to see if the sleeve sets right, and then stitch it.

In some sleeves the fulness at the top is taken out by small darts. These are marked with tailor's tacks, as directed on the pattern, stitched, cut and pressed open. Often, if the fulness is slight, it can be shrunken out entirely. It is first gathered with one row of very fine gatherings and then placed over the small end of a tailor's padded cushion. (Illustrated on page 61.) A damp cloth is laid over the sleeves and they are pressed with a hot iron until dry. (Figs. 314 and 315.)

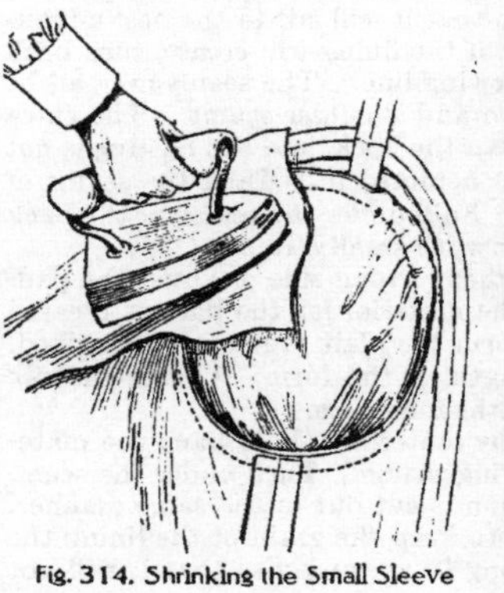
Fig. 314. Shrinking the Small Sleeve

Work the Buttonholes, the top one just at the lowest corner of the turned-over lapel, and sew the buttons at the left side to correspond, sewing through coat and canvas, but not through the facing.

Flat lead weights about the size of a quarter are tacked in the bottom of the coat to weight it properly. They should be covered with the lining satin so that they will not wear through the lining.

THE LINING is the final step of coat-making; the outside must be entirely finished, the pockets put in, and all the ornamental stitching done before beginning on the lining. Silk or satin is unquestionably the only satisfactory lining for a coat. One of the several silk substitutes may be used for lining a gown, but only the greatest necessity for economy excuses its use as coat-lining. White satin of a good firm quality is attractive, but satin matching the shade of the cloth is more serviceable.

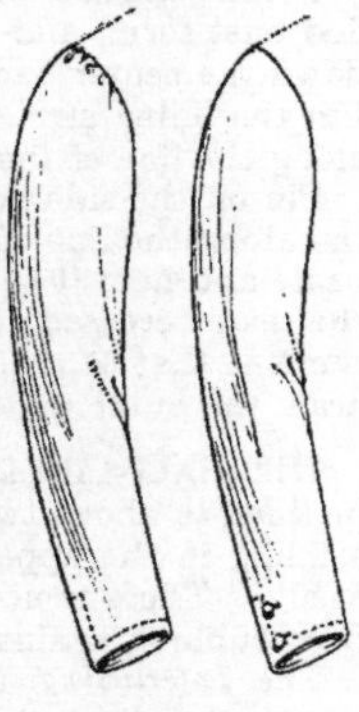
Fig. 315.
Before Shrinking
After Shrinking

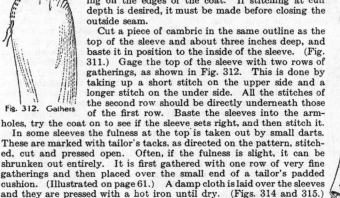

Cut the lining from the same pattern as the cloth, allowing for any alterations which have been made in fitting.

Cut the lining of the fronts to extend to the front facings only, and cut the back pieces each one-half an inch wider than the pattern to allow for a small plait in the center back. Leave good seams, as the lining must be quite easy in width as well as length. (Fig. 316.) If it is tight it will draw the outside of the coat and make wrinkles.

Baste a small plait at the center back to avoid any possibility of tightness. With the back piece of the lining basted in the coat, the two outer edges will be raw. Catch these raw edges flat with a loose basting-stitch to the inside seams of the coat over which they lie. Now take the next piece of the lining and baste it through the center to the corresponding piece of the coat, then turn under the edge toward the back and baste it down like a hem over the raw edge of the back piece, notching the edges of both seams at the waistline and immediately above and below it, so they will fit the curves of the coat.

Repeat this method with each piece of the lining. Turn it up at the bottom, allowing a little of the cloth to show.

After all the edges are turned under, and basted over the preceding pieces and over the raw edges of the facings in front, and over the edges of the collar at the neck, they are neatly felled down to the cloth. (Fig. 316.) Be careful not to catch through the cloth to the outside. The lining of the sleeves is cut like the outside, and the seams are stitched and pressed open. The lining is slipped inside the sleeve and hemmed down at the hand and on the small opening at the back of the wrist if there is an opening allowed in the sleeve pattern. It is then drawn up in place, and basted through the cloth of the sleeve about five inches from the top. Then draw up the sleeve lining, turn in the raw edge, and baste it to the coat lining all around the armhole and fell it in place. If the sleeves are to be interlined, the interlining should be tacked to the sleeve lining. It is used on the upper part of the sleeve only, and should stop three inches below the upper edge and three inches above the wrist edge. (Fig. 313, on page 123.)

Fig. 316. Inside of Completed Coat

Occasionally one has to line a coat for which there is no pattern. If the coat has had one lining and it is only a matter of replacing it by a fresh one, rip the old lining apart and press each portion open. Fold the new material with the two cut ends together, and, taking one-half of the old lining, lay it carefully on the material so that it will cut to the best advantage. Mark the seams, or, if the lining will crease, turn back the seams and crease the sewing line. The seams may all be stitched save the under-arm and shoulder seams. The extra half-inch plait is basted down the back, and the basting is not removed until the lining is hemmed in. Tack the seams of the lining to those of the coat, with long loose stitches. Fold under the seams of the back at the underarm and the shoulder, and hem them down with small stitches.

If the coat has had no previous lining, place the garment wrong side out over the padded bust form, and fit a piece of silk to the front. The material for the back is creased down the center back and basted in one-half inch to form the plait previously described. Pin the lining straight across the back the entire length of the form. Crease the silk along the line of the seam, and cut, allowing three-eighths-inch seams.

Pin on the side portion, keeping the same grain of the material. Fold back the material along the line of the sewing, and cut it away, allowing seams. Turn under the seam, baste and hem it to the back portion. The next portion is cut out in the same manner, the seams creased and hemmed. Care must be taken to keep the grain of the lining the same as that of the garment, and also to baste the lining in very easy so that it will not draw the outer material and cause it to wrinkle.

THE HALF-LINED COAT. Top coats, storm coats, motor coats, etc., should only be lined to about twenty-five or twenty-six inches from the neck. (Fig. 316A.) You need a lining in the upper part to cover the interlining and to make the coat slip on and off easily. There is no real need for a lining in the lower part, and it wears out so quickly, from rubbing against your skirt, that it is really better not to use it.

The Interlining. The interlining is used in all coats, *not* for the sake of additional warmth, but in order to give the material sufficient body so that it will not break and look poor and flimsy when the coat is on the figure. The best interlinings are soft French canvas, cotton serge or cambric. The interlining should be cut according to the directions given in the "Illustrated Instructions."

After the interlining is cut it is laid on the wrong side of the coat, with the edges and notches of the coat and interlining even. The interlining is then pinned and basted in place.

The Seam Edges. When a coat is lined to the waist only, the seam edges in the lower part of the coat must be finished neatly. Heavy materials like wool velvet and

Fig. 316A The half-lined coat

army cloth are really self-finished, for they are so closely woven that they will not fray and can be left raw quite satisfactorily.

Tweed, cheviot, mixtures, etc., *will* fray and must be bound. The seams should be bound with ribbon seam-binding, the color of the coat. Seam-binding comes in different widths and you can get it wide enough for even a heavy coating. Put the seam-binding on by hand with an easy running stitch, sewing it neatly and evenly. (Fig. 252, chapter XIX.) The seam-binding should run up well above the line of the lower edge of the lining.

The Lining. The coat lining should be cut with the coat pattern as a guide, following the directions given in the Illustrated Instructions. The lining must be cut slightly wider than the pattern. A lining must be loose and very easy. If it draws at all, it will wear out almost at once. In a half-lined coat the lining comes only to about twenty-six inches from the neck. Put the lining in according to the directions given in the Illustrated Instructions in the pattern.

AN UNLINED COAT. An unlined coat needs interlining. The interlining for the front of the coat should be cut and put in according to the pattern instructions. The interlining in the front of the coat should be covered with a facing of the coat material. The part of the interlining left exposed back of the facing should be covered neatly with a lining.

In cloth or linen the raw edges of the interlining and facing of the side fronts should be bound together. In silk they may both be turned under three-eighths of an inch, facing each other, and stitched. In either case, these edges should be left loose from the coat; they should lie against it, but should not be caught or stitched to it.

A yoke-shaped piece of lining material must be used in the back of the coat. It should be six inches deep at the center, and run straight across the shoulders. Turn under its lower edge three-eighths of an inch, and stitch it in a narrow hem. Then baste it to the back of the coat at the shoulders and neck, leaving its lower edge free.

The shoulder edges of the back yoke should be turned under, and then basted and felled carefully over the shoulder edges of the front lining.

In silk the coat should be finished with French seams. In a coat of cloth the seams may be pressed open and the edges bound separately with silk seam-binding or they may be bound together, turned to one side, and stitched down flat to the coat. If they are pressed open, they need not be stitched again unless you prefer to stitch them on both sides of the seam. In heavy wash materials the seams can be handled in the same way, using a cotton seam-binding instead of silk. Be sure the binding is shrunken. It should be the same color as the coat. Or, on a linen, cotton rep, etc., you can use the flat stitched seam.

The lower edge of the coat should be turned under according to the instructions on the pattern, weighted with lead weights at the seams, and its raw edge either hemmed or bound.

A RUSSIAN BLOUSE JACKET is not difficult to make. Follow the same directions for laying the pattern on the material and marking the perforations that are given on page 130. Face the jacket opening, and insert the pocket as directed by the pattern instructions. Baste the body portions together, try on, and stitch. The seams should be pressed open and the edges bound. Or, if lapped seams are preferred, the seams should be cut wider and finished according to the method described in Chapter XIX, "Tailored Seams." Finish the front and lower edges of the jacket according to the pattern directions.

The deep collar on the jacket should be lined with a piece of lining material of the same shade. The collar should be turned under a seam's width at its edge and finished with one or more rows of stitching or braid around it. The lining is also turned under a seam's width, and hemmed to the underside of the collar, covering the stitching. The neck portion of the collar is joined to the neck according to the notches, with the seam toward the outside of the jacket or blouse. The collar lining is then turned under at its neck edge and hemmed to the neck of the blouse, concealing the seam.

Bind the seams of the sleeves in the same manner as the seams of the jacket, and face the wrist with a cuff, according to the directions of the pattern. Baste the sleeves in the armhole, try the coat on, and if the sleeves set properly stitch them in by machine and bind the raw edges.

The coat is fastened with buttons and buttonholes either in a visible or blind closing. If a blind closing is desired, a double strip of lining is cut for the fly and stitched one-fourth inch from the outer edge, and again along the inner edge, through all thicknesses. It is tacked along the outer edge of the coat midway between the buttonholes. If a visible closing is used, the buttonholes should be carefully worked, using the eyelet buttonhole. Directions for working eyelet buttonholes, as well as the correct manner of sewing on the buttons, will be found in Chapter II, "Buttonholes."

A belt either of the material or of leather is slipped through straps of the coat material which are fastened at each under-arm seam. When a cloth belt is used it should be stitched at its edges to correspond with the stitching on the jacket.

There are many variations of the Russian blouse jacket, but the methods of finishing them vary so little from this model that the worker will have no trouble with them whatsoever.

FOR A NORFOLK JACKET, cut the material carefully as directed and mark the perforations for seams, box plaits, pocket opening, etc.

Bring the thread lines marking the box plaits together, baste and stitch. This makes a large tuck, which is flattened to form a box plait by bringing the seam exactly under the center. As each one is flattened it should be basted one-quarter of an inch from each fold edge. Press well. The box plaits at the front must match those of the back on the shoulders.

If the box plait is applied, cut the plait by the pattern. It is better to stitch the plaits separately and slip-stitch them to the jacket. Interline the belt with canvas, and hem a lining to the turned-over cloth. When the jacket is made with a seam running to the shoulder in both the front and back portions, the simulated box plait is applied afterward over these seams, covering them.

Insert a pocket in each side of the jacket in the manner described on page 106, Fig. 273, in the chapter "Pockets." Face the fronts with canvas from the shoulders as shown on page 132. Join the back of the jacket to the side and front pieces, and press the seams open. In the upper corner of the front that is to turn over as a continuation of the collar, the canvas and cloth should be held together with the "padding stitch." In Fig. 323 is shown an inside view of the front with the canvas and pocket in place.

The collar is cut from the cloth, and a canvas interlining for it is cut a seam's width smaller at all edges than the collar itself. The space from the perforations that mark the turning line of the collar to the neck edge should be stitched with several rows of machine stitching. The remainder of the collar is to be filled with padding stitches, as shown in Fig. 305. The cloth edges of the collar are turned over the canvas and catch-stitched to it. The collar is then hemmed by hand to the outside of the jacket, the end of the collar and the turned-over corner at the top of the jacket fronts forming a notch collar. The canvas should be trimmed away a seam's width from this corner and down the front of the jacket. Cut a facing for the collar and a front facing like the front, extending back an inch beyond the turned-over corner at the top.

Lay the front facing face down on the outside of the jacket fronts and stitch a seam around the corner and down the front of the jacket; turn it over and baste near the edge. Baste the collar-facing to the collar, turn under the edges and slip-stitch to the collar and to the front facing where it joins it at the top. Stitch one or two rows around the edge of the collar and down the fronts. Turn up the bottom of the jacket according to the pattern directions.

Cut the back lining like the cloth back, but allow a half-inch plait down the center of the lining. Cut the lining of the front and side pieces in one, laying a dart-like plait from the shoulders, running out to nothing about five inches down. Full directions for lining a coat will be found on pages 123 and 124.

CHAPTER XXIII

BOYS' SUITS

THE MAKING of a boy's suit is not at all a difficult matter if one goes about it in the right way. There are a few tedious details of finish, the proper carrying out of which determines the success of the suit. A hot iron is a necessary requisite to good work, and its frequent use will help much toward the progress of the suit. Follow the pattern directions closely and there will be no trouble.

Before Cutting have the cloth shrunk and pressed. Then lay the entire pattern out on the material to the best advantage, as explained in the pattern instructions. With tailors' chalk trace the seams along the perforations that indicate the sewing line of the outlet seams. With tailors' tacks, one long and two short stitches (see Chapter IV), mark these seams through the two thicknesses of the cloth. Cut the stitches and separate the pieces.

The various sections of the suit should have the pockets in place before they are joined. Mark the positions of the pockets as indicated by the perforations.

THE TROUSERS will be our first consideration. As the initial step, baste and stitch the darts in the back portions of the trousers, and press them open. In the right-back portion make a pocket, instructions for which will be found on page 104, Chapter XX, "Pockets."

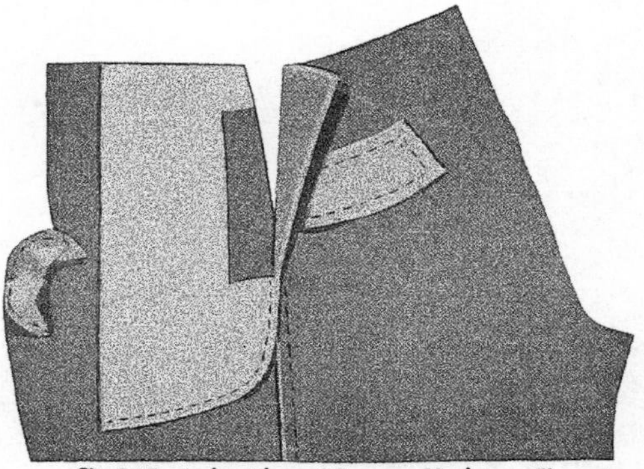

Fig. 317. Inside View of Trousers Having no Fly

The Fly is next put into the front portion. Baste a facing, cut from the fly-piece pattern, to the outside of the front edge of the left-front portion, with the notches even. Stitch a narrow seam from the top to the notch. Turn the facing to the wrong side, and baste it flat, with the cloth at the seam edge entirely covering the lining.

Now lay together, face to face, two fly pieces, one of cloth and one of lining, and stitch a seam on the notched edge from the top to the notch. Turn it to the right side, baste flat and press.

It is more convenient to make the buttonholes in the fly now, than after it is stitched in place. They are worked from the cloth side, the first one coming just below the waistband. Then baste the fly into position, its edge a trifle back of the edge on the left front of the trousers. Stitch one-quarter inch back of the buttonholes, through the four thicknesses of goods, down from the waistband, ending in a curved line on the lower edge. (Fig. 318.) Tack the fly between the buttonholes to the facing. Overcast the raw edges on the inside.

The underlapping fly piece for the buttons on the right front of the trousers should be faced with lining; the seam sewed at the unnotched edge. The notched edge of the cloth piece is then basted and stitched to the edge of the right front of the trousers. This seam is then pressed open. Turn under the lining, clipping the edge to make it lie flat, and baste it to the cloth seam. From the right side stitch neatly an even line down close to the bastings and across the free edge at the bottom.

Small trousers buttons are sewed on in position corresponding to the buttonholes on the opposite fly.

For the Smaller Boys, when buttons and buttonholes are impracticable, the small facing provided for in the pattern is attached to the right side of both of the fronts, turned in and stitched down. (Fig. 317, page 128.) The front seam is then closed from the notch above to the waistline.

The Side Pockets should be put in next. Complete instructions for making them will be found on page 106, Chapter XX, "Pockets."

Trousers Having no Fly Closing have the waistband divided into a front and back waistband, leaving an opening at each side of the trousers. In this case the extension on the side of the back pieces of the trousers is faced, thus forming the underlap for the opening. The loose edge of the pocket piece is then faced on both sides with the cloth, and two rows of stitching, a quarter of an inch apart close to the edge, give it a firm finish. Now the upper edges of the pocket are basted to the upper edge of the trouser's front. (Fig. 317, page 128.)

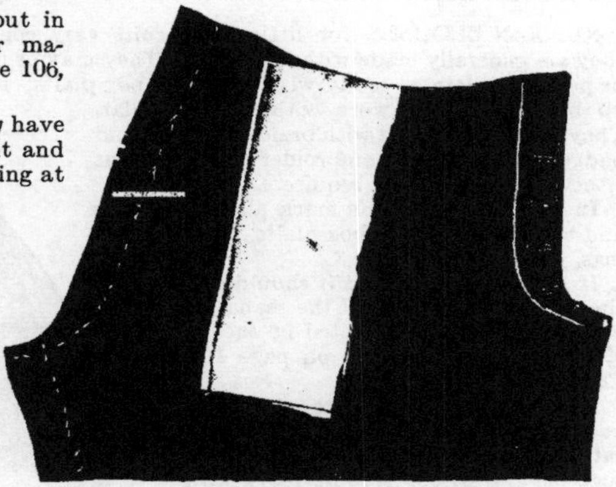

Fig. 318. Inside View of Pocket with Buttonhole Fly

Make a bar, overcast or buttonholed, between the two rows of stitching, catching through the cloth, and both sides of the pocket at the top and at the bottom of the opening.

The pocket may now be closed. Round off one or both of the corners, and, turning in the seam with the raw edges toward the inside of the pocket, stitch securely.

The Outside Seam of the trousers is closed next. In knickerbockers, it is stitched in a seam all the way down. The lower edge of the leg is gathered in a casing with an elastic. In trousers finished with a band the extension allowed at the lower part for an opening at the side is turned under for a facing on the upper side, and faced and used as an extension on the under side. The band can be fastened with a buckle or with a button and buttonhole. After stitching the seam, turn the raw edges toward the front. From the outside, run a line of stitching one-eighth of an inch from the seam.

Fig. 319. Outside View of Fly and Pocket

Now stitch and press open the inside seam of each leg. The two leg portions may then be joined, beginning the seam down the back at the waist, and extending it to the notches in the lower edge of the fly pieces, including in the seam the seams of the fly pieces below the notches. Press this seam open and baste over it, flat on the inside, a piece of tape or a bias strip. Stitch from the outside a row on each side of the seam. Turn the end of the tape over and hem neatly down at the end of the fly stitching. On the outside, at the end of the fly opening, make a strong stay-stitch or bar, to keep it from tearing out.

The Top Edge of the trousers is turned over a seam, and a strip of lining stitched to it, then basted down in a faced hem. A band, with the buttonholes worked in it with stout thread or twist, is basted over this faced hem, and from the right side stitched through both facing and band at the lower edge and the ends. A strong tack thread should catch the band and the facing between the buttonholes.

The Lower Edge of each trousers leg is hemmed up by hand with invisible stitches.

RUSSIAN BLOUSES for little boys' suits vary considerably in detail of style, but they are generally made without lining. They may or may not have a pocket; they may be perfectly plain or made with tucks or box plaits; with sailor collar or with a stand-up band, or to be worn with a linen collar. They may be trimmed with braid, chevrons and badges, with hand embroidery, or without either, as the case may require.

In cutting observe and mark all perforations and notches for seams, box plaits, pocket openings, etc. See Chapter X.

If a pocket is desired it should be put into the left-front piece before the seams are closed. Proceed as directed in the instructions for the pocket on page 104, Chapter XX, "Pockets."

Bind the raw edges of the front and back pieces at the seams with lining satin or seam-binding. Baste the pieces together and stitch. If preferred, a seam requiring no binding may be made by allowing a wider seam when cutting and arranging a lap seam, as explained in Chapter XIX, "Tailored Seams" Then press it flat and from the right side stitch an even row down on each side of the seam.

The Front is closed by means of buttons and buttonholes whether in fly, the single lap, or double-breasted style. In case of a fly make a strip of lining, doubled, in which the buttonholes are worked. This strip is then basted to the overlapping front, one-fourth inch from the outer edge of the blouse, and stitched from the outside through all the thicknesses, on the line of the inner edge of the fly. Tack the fly between the buttonholes. With a visible closing, the eyelet buttonholes are used. See Chapter II. The lower edge of the blouse is hemmed.

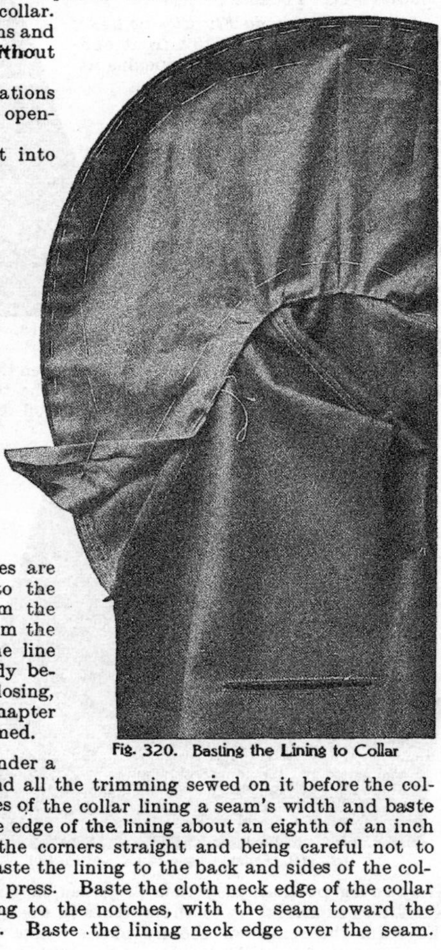

Fig. 320. Basting the Lining to Collar

The Sailor Collar should be turned under a seam's width around the outside edge, and all the trimming sewed on it before the collar is lined. Turn under the outside edges of the collar lining a seam's width and baste it to the wrong side of the collar with the edge of the lining about an eighth of an inch within the edge of the collar, keeping the corners straight and being careful not to stretch or pull the edge of the cloth. Baste the lining to the back and sides of the collar, then stitch, turn to the right side and press. Baste the cloth neck edge of the collar to the neck edge of the blouse, according to the notches, with the seam toward the under or outside of the blouse and stitch. Baste the lining neck edge over the seam. Hem it down by hand. Fig. 320.

The Sleeves may have a cuff or not, according to the pattern. The seams are stitched and finished like the seams of the blouse. Baste the sleeves into the armhole and try the blouse on before stitching by machine. Bind the raw edges at the armhole with a bias strip of the lining or with seam-binding. For illustrations see Chapters X, "Children's Clothes," and XI, "Sailor or Naval Suits."

A Belt, either of leather or of the blouse material, is worn with the Russian blouse suit. It is slipped through cloth straps which are fastened, according to the perforations, at each under-arm seam. When a belt of the material is used it should be stitched flat, to correspond to the stitching on the collar.

A NORFOLK JACKET is somewhat more like a coat, in that it is lined and has a more strictly tailored finish. In cutting, observe all the notches, perforations, etc., and mark the material accordingly.

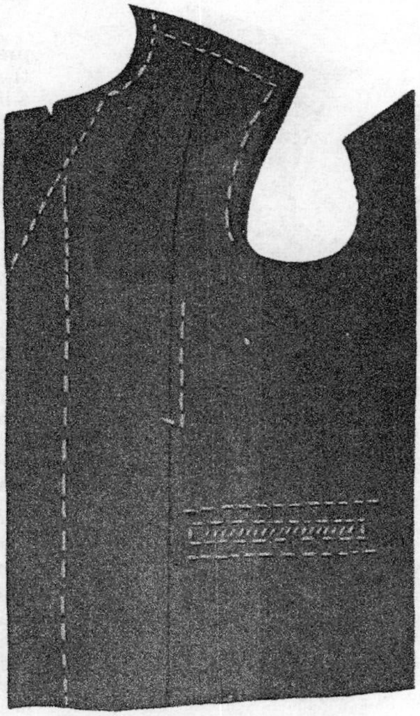

Fig. 321. Front View of Jacket, Pieced

The chalk or thread marks indicating the box plait are then brought together, and a large tuck stitched. Spread it out, bringing the sewing directly under the center line of the plait. Baste along both edges and press flat.

If preferred, the box plaits may be made separately, if the pattern does not allow for them. Turn under the side edges of the cloth three-quarters of an inch and baste. (See Fig. 322.) The plaits are then stitched to the jacket three-eighths of an inch from the edge.

A Pocket with a Lap is made in each side of the front piece, behind the box plait. For making the pocket see instructions on page 104, Chapter XX, "Pockets."

The Yoke, if one is used, is cut by the pattern and basted in position with its lower edge turned under. Stitch it flat with a row of stitching three-eighths of an inch from the edge. Cut the cloth away from under it, and press.

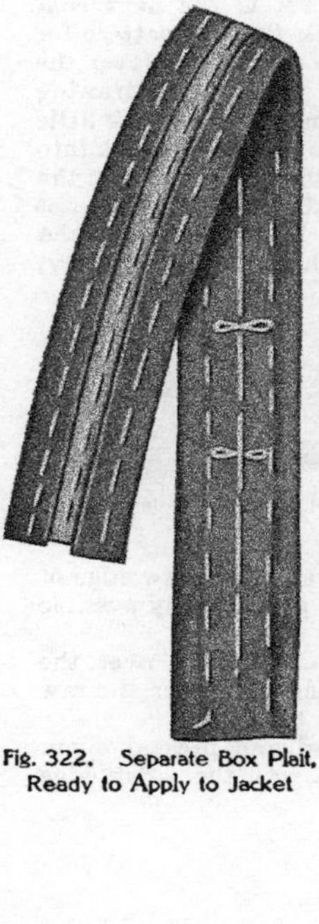

Fig. 322. Separate Box Plait, Ready to Apply to Jacket

Now face the fronts of the jacket with canvas from the shoulder, as shown in Fig. 323. The upper corners of the fronts, that are turned over to form the lapels, are made firm with padding stitches run through both cloth and canvas.

A cloth facing, a little wider than the lapels, is basted to the right sides of the fronts. Stitch a seam across the lapel corner and down the front edge. Trim away the canvas from the seam as close as possible, and turn the facing back. Baste the edge flat, and stitch it down neatly three-eighths of an inch from the edge.

The shoulder and side seams joining the fronts and the back of the jacket may now be closed. Press these seams open. Turn up the lower edge of the jacket and baste it flat.

The Collar is cut from two pieces of the cloth and one of canvas. The cloth piece for the top of the collar is a seam's width wider all around than the canvas. Baste the latter two pieces together, and trace the turning line of the collar. The crescent-shaped space thus outlined is the part that stands up in the finished collar. To give it stability and strengthen the curve, run several rows of stitching across it, parallel to the tracing. The other part of the collar is covered with "padding stitches." (Fig. 324.) Now baste the top collar piece over this foundation; turn the edges under and baste.

The collar is then basted to the jacket on the outside of the neck edge. Baste it on carefully, avoiding any possible stretching out of shape. At the points where the collar meets the lapels of the jacket, the canvas must be cut away to make a neat joining.

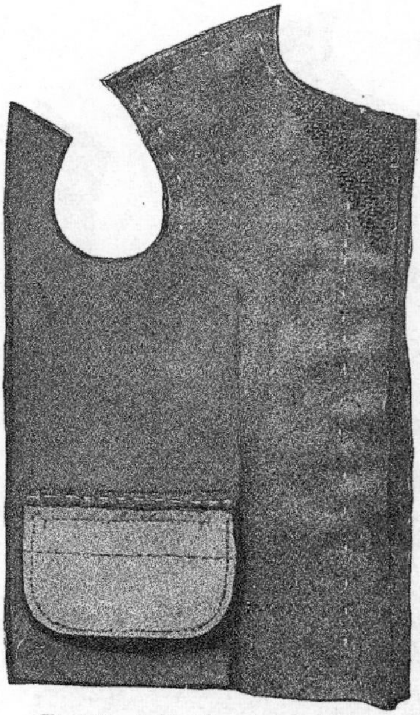

Fig. 323. Inside View of Jacket Front, Before Lining is Added

The Sleeves are cut, the seams stitched and pressed open. Turn the wrist edge up as far as the pattern allows, and baste it flat. Then run a line of stitching around it, as directed in the pattern instructions. Following the notches, baste the sleeves into position and try on the garment. If they set properly, they may then be stitched in by machine.

If cuffs are provided for, they are made separately, and slip-stitched to the sleeve over the wrist edge after the lining has been put in. (See page 54, Chapter X, "Children's Clothes.")

The Belt has an interlining of canvas, stitched in at the same time with the row of machine-stitching that finishes it three-eighths of an inch around the edge. The lining is then added by hand. Two buttonholes are made, two inches apart, at the round end of the belt, and two corresponding buttons are sewed on the straight end. An opening through which the belt is run is allowed under each box plait in the jacket.

The Buttonholes are made with eyelets as described and illustrated in Chapter II.

The Lining for the jacket is the next consideration. Cut the back by the pattern for the jacket, allowing a half-inch plait down the center, which keeps the lining from drawing the outside cloth out of shape. Baste this little plait down. Now secure the lining back into position on the inside of the jacket. Baste the raw edges at the side seams over the corresponding seams of the cloth, but do not have the bastings show through to the right side of the jacket. Do the same at the shoulder seams. At the neck edge clip the curve enough to make the lining lie smoothly; slip the raw edge under the collar and baste the latter down over it.

Each lining front is cut in one piece, with a dart-like plait allowed at the shoulder which graduates to nothing five inches below it. Baste each piece into position in the jacket. The raw edge at the side seam is turned in and hemmed down by hand, covering the raw edge of the back piece. It may be necessary to clip the edges slightly to prevent any possible drawing at the seams.

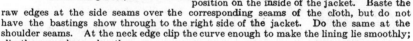

Fig. 324. Showing Padding Stitch and Machine Stitching on the Collar

The raw edges down the front are, likewise, turned in and stitched down over the cloth facing by hand. At the shoulder, the seam of the back lining laps over the raw edge of the front piece. The top collar piece is then stitched down by hand.

The sleeve lining is cut by the sleeve pattern, the seams stitched and pressed open. Slip it into the jacket sleeve with corresponding seams together. At the wrist edge turn in the lining and hem it to the cloth sleeve by hand. Hold the lining in place by running a basting thread around the sleeve about four inches from the upper edge. Lastly, turn under the upper edge of the lining, baste it down over the raw edges of the armhole and sew down by hand.

The lower edge of the jacket may now be closed in the same way; all basting threads that show are pulled out, and the jacket is given a final pressing wherever necessary.

Boys' suits should always be made of strong, durable materials of as good a quality as one can afford, for they get very hard usage, and a poor cloth will not only wear out quickly, but is also likely to stretch and lose its shape. For cold weather heavy serges and cheviots are about the best materials one can get. For the spring use lighter weight serges for every-day suits, and tweeds and homespuns for better wear. These last materials are extremely smart-looking, but they are loosely woven and are not practical for school suits. They are generally used in the light shades of gray and tan. In summer weather heavy linen crash is an excellent material for ordinary wear. The lighter linens on the order of a good-quality French linen are very nice for better suits.

CHAPTER XXIV

REMODELING

ONE ought, at the very beginning of each season, to set to work to take a critical survey of last year's wardrobe. It is the easiest way to find out exactly what new clothes are needed and exactly how far one can go with the old ones. Coats, suits and dresses that are still in sound physical condition, but which have grown out of style, should be remade. The remodeling of a pair of sleeves, the recutting of a skirt, will almost always give a new lease of life to a suit, while there are dozens of clever little ways by which one can completely obliterate the date of vintage of a gown.

Decide first what clothes are worth remaking. When the materials are badly worn it is hardly worth while going to any amount of trouble in the way of renovations. But when the material is sound and whole it is little short of criminal not to take advantage of its possibilities.

If one feels inclined to take a little trouble—and with a good dye there is practically no trouble at all—one can completely disguise a last year's suit or dress by changing it to another color.

DYEING is a very simple thing, but there are certain hard and fast rules in regard to it that must not be disregarded. In the first place you can not dye a silk or wool material with a dye intended for cotton and linen. Neither can you dye cotton and linen with a silk and wool dye. In the second place, you can't change dark colors into lighter ones. In the third place, the material must be prepared carefully for the dyeing. If there are any grease spots or stains they should be removed as thoroughly as possible. (Chapter XXV.)

Afterward the material should be washed for two reasons. The first is, that if the material is put into the dye soiled, the dirt will mingle with the dye and the result will be muddy instead of bright and clear. The second is that as much of the old dye should be taken out or "discharged," as it is called, as possible. Otherwise it will be impossible to predict how the mixture of the two dyes will turn out.

Cottons and silks can be washed in soap and boiling water, but it is not safe to use soap to any great extent on wool materials, as it softens the wool. Boil the materials about half an hour, changing the water as it becomes discolored. Keep up the washing until the water remains clear—a sure sign that all the dye has been discharged that is likely to do any harm.

It is best to dye the material while it is still wet from the washing as it absorbs the dye more readily and more evenly in that condition. Be sure to follow the directions given with the dye you use. A good reliable dye compound will be accompanied by explicit directions, which you must take care to follow. You must be especially careful in picking out a dye that will suit your material. White, of course, can be dyed any color. Pale shades can be dyed darker or changed into other slightly deeper colors. A material of one color dyed with a dye of a second color will emerge from the fray an entirely different shade from either. For instance, if you dye a yellow material with a light blue dye, you will get green; while the same light blue over light red makes purple, and over light green makes peacock. A dark blue dye over brown makes navy blue, and over yellow, bottle green. A brown over blue makes dark brown; over green makes olive brown; over red makes seal brown. There are dozens and dozens of combinations and variations of colors that one can bring out by a clever combination of dye and material. One should go back to the old safeguard of experimenting first and doing the actual business afterward.

After you've dyed your material, take it out of the dyeing fluid and hang it up until it is nearly dry. Then rinse it out in clear water to prevent its crocking. If a material has been dyed black, do not rinse until it has dried thoroughly. It will leave it a better color. If you do not dye your material, clean it carefully. Directions for removing spots, stains, etc., are given in Chapter XXV, "Care of the Clothes."

IN MAKING OVER A WAIST it is sometimes necessary to use new material; but when chemisettes, yokes and half-sleeves are in fashion, you can use net, lace, chiffon, etc. In remodeling a waist or dress, put it on a bust form and stuff out the sleeves with tissue-paper. Look it over to see where it requires alteration. Sleeves and skirts frequently need to be recut. If piecing is necessary, make the seams fall in places where they will not show or where they can be covered with trimming.

If the dress is to be entirely remodeled, rip it apart with a sharp knife or pointed scissors. Do not stretch the material, especially at the neck and armholes. Brush the seams carefully, and remove all clipped threads. If the material has changed color, use it on the reverse side if possible, even if the weave is slightly different.

After the material has been thoroughly freshened—washed, pressed or dyed—lay it out on the new pattern and see if it requires piecing. If necessary, piece the lining so that it will set comfortably. It should be easy across the bust and shoulders, and snug, but not tight, over the waist and hips. In piecing, cut the patches on the same grain of the material as the original garment. Never piece at the neck or armhole with a bias or straight piece of material. Lay the new fabric on the old, following the grain of the latter. Hem the piece down neatly, and cut the garment over by the new pattern.

Put the Lining on, and then drape the outside over it after you have cut it according to your pattern. By using fancy trimming-pieces, collars, yokes, plastrons, etc., you can almost always remodel a waist so that the piecing will never show. Lace or net for yokes, chemisettes, etc., can be dyed the color of the dress either at home or at a regular dyeing establishment. Lace can be dipped in tea to give it a rich cream color that can be made lighter or darker according to the strength of the tea.

REMODELING A SKIRT is an easy matter if the new pattern is narrower than the old skirt. In that case it is only a question of recutting; but if the pattern calls for more material than you have in the skirt itself, you will have to do some piecing. Braided bands covering the skirt seams are an excellent way of increasing the width of a skirt. Or you can raise the skirt at the waistline, refit it, and add to it at the bottom by a band or a fold. Or it may be pieced at the bottom and the line of piecing covered by wide braid, bias bands, etc.

Linen or *Piqué Skirts* can often be lengthened by bands of embroidery insertion or by bias bands of the material. These skirts are very apt to shrink around the hips. They should be ripped from their belts, raised and refitted. They will have to be lengthened.

Coats should be remodeled by an up-to-date pattern. If they require piecing, try to let it come at a seam and cover it with a stitched or braided band. Quite frequently it is easier to cut a coat suit down for one of the daughters of the house than to remodel it for the mother. But do not use a material that is old and somber for a child, without relieving it by a trimming that is bright and youthful-looking. A black-and-white pin-checked wool or a dark serge is apt to make a dull frock for a little girl, but if it is trimmed with bands of contrasting material in a suitable color it becomes childish-looking and pretty.

In making over half-worn garments into presentable and at the same time durable clothes for boys, such as suits, reefers, and overcoats, a tailored finish is the first requirement. It means neat work, even stitching and careful pressing. For the pressing you will need heavy irons, evenly heated, and a piece of unbleached muslin that can be dampened and laid over your work.

In ripping apart the old coat or suit that is to be remodeled for your little son, notice carefully all the small devices of interlining, canvas and stitching that the tailor used in making the garment. You can repeat many of them in your own work. If you use the old canvas and find that it has grown limp, you can restiffen it by dampening it thoroughly and ironing it with a heavy iron thoroughly heated. Full directions for making boys' trousers are given in Chapter XXIII, "Boys' Suits," and Chapter XX, "Pockets." Chapter XXII, on "Coats and Jackets," will give you all the necessary information you will want for finishing the jackets or overcoats.

CHAPTER XXV

CARE OF THE CLOTHES

GOOD PRESSING is a very important part of dressmaking and tailoring. Special boards and tailor's cushions may be made at home or bought from any dressmakers' supply house. (Chapter XII, page 61.)

In opening seams, dampen the seam, if the material will permit it, and press slowly, bearing down heavily on the iron. Very little dampness should be used on cashmere, as it flattens the twill and spoils the texture. Little or no dampness should be used on silk. A cloth, well wrung out of water, may be used on these materials, and their seams may be dampened slightly. Seams should be pressed over the curved edge of an ironing-board so that the seam edges will not be marked on the garment.

Velvet must not be pressed, but should be steamed so as not to injure the nap.

To steam velvet, heat an iron and place it face up between two cold irons arranged so as to hold the hot iron firmly. (Fig. 325.) Lay a damp piece of muslin over the face of the iron and draw the velvet over the muslin. The steam will have the effect of pressing the velvet without hurting the pile. Seams can be opened in this way, and this method can be used on velvet, plush, wool velvet, materials with a high nap, satin and silk.

Fig. 325. The Proper Way to Open Seams in a Velvet Coat

Velvet may be mirrored or panned by passing an iron over the surface of the velvet, ironing with the nap. After velvet has gone through this process it can be pressed as much as is necessary. If the iron can be held with the flat surface upward by a milliner's steaming-box or a tin box, the seams of perishable materials can be pressed open by running the seam over the surface of the iron.

Nearly all pressing is done on the wrong side. Suitings and heavy cloth may be pressed on the right side by steaming. Wring out a cloth as dry as possible and keep it over the place to be pressed. Have the irons hot and press firmly until the cloth is nearly dry. Turn the garment to the wrong side and press until thoroughly dry.

The shine which sometimes comes in pressing may be removed by placing a dry cloth over the shiny place. Then wring out as dry as possible a second cloth which has been thoroughly wet. Place it over the dry one, and with a hot iron pass lightly over the spot. If the material has a nap requiring raising, the place may be brushed with a stiff brush and the process of steaming repeated.

Many fabrics retain the imprint of the basting-thread under heavy pressing. For such material it is necessary to give a light pressing first, removing all basting-threads before the final pressing.

ALL CLOTHES should be taken care of as systematically as possible, as their period of usefulness depends entirely on the way they are treated. Lingerie and washable waists and dresses should be mended *before* they go to the laundry. A small hole will become a large one in washing, and not only is the work of mending doubled, but the injury to the garment is frequently irreparable.

Woolen clothes—dresses, suits, coats, skirts, etc., should be brushed regularly and watched closely for such small matters as loose buttons, frayed skirt-braids, missing hooks and eyes, and soiled chemisettes or yokes. Coats should never be left lying carelessly over chairs, and should never be hung up by the collar or armhole. They should be kept on hangers when they are not in use so that their necks and shoulders will not lose their shape.

Dresses and waists should also be kept on hangers, and if they are made of light, perishable materials they should be slipped into great bags of silkoline to keep them from the dust. The bag should be as long as the waist or dress. If one has plenty of closet room, it is much better to keep one's evening dresses hanging up in bags than to lay them in chests or drawers where they can not fail to become badly wrinkled.

Skirts should not be kept on wooden hangers, as they are likely to become stretched at the hips. Small strips of braid or ribbon should be sewed inside the waistband of each skirt—one on each side, and an equal distance apart. The skirt should be hung by these hangers on two hooks placed just far enough apart to keep the belt taut.

Winter clothes should be brushed and cleaned and then put away during the summer months with plenty of gum camphor, moth-balls or some other safe moth-preventive. Summer clothes should be put away clean and packed as carefully as possible, so that they will not need pressing when they are wanted again. Sheets of blue tissue-paper can be put between the folds of white dresses to prevent them from turning yellow.

CLEANING can frequently be done at home with very little trouble and expense.

TO CLEAN WOOLEN GOODS, the simplest method is washing in warm water and soapbark. Get ten cents' worth of soapbark and pour over it two quarts of boiling water. Let it stand until the strength is taken from the bark, strain, and pour into a tub of lukewarm water. Let the goods stand for half an hour in the suds, then rub well and rinse in another water of the same temperature to keep the goods from shrinking. Press on the wrong side before it is thoroughly dry. Experiment first with a small piece of the material to be sure that it does not change color or shrink badly.

FOR SILKS, mix six ounces of strained honey and four ounces of a pure soap with one pint of pure alcohol.

Lay each piece of silk flat on a table or marble, and with a brush cover the silk with the mixture, first on one side and then on the other. Brush the silk as little as possible and always straight up and down. Dip the silk in several tepid rinsing-waters, the last one mixed with a little honey. Do not wring the silk, but hang it up, and when half-dry iron with a cool iron on the wrong side.

A French method of cleaning black silk is to sponge the silk on both sides with spirits of wine, and then iron on the wrong side with a piece of muslin between the silk and the iron.

Ribbons may be cleansed in the same way and rolled smoothly over a bottle or round stick to dry.

VELVET is cleaned by steaming. First brush the velvet thoroughly with either a soft or stiff brush until all dust and lint are removed. It is better to use a soft brush if the velvet is not too dirty.

If a milliner's steaming-box is at hand, invert a hot iron in the box and cover the face of the iron with a good-sized piece of muslin which has been thoroughly wet. This produces steam, and the muslin must be moved along as it dries. The velvet is held with its wrong side against the muslin and brushed carefully with a soft brush until the pile of the velvet is raised. Always brush against the nap. The pile may also be raised by holding the velvet tightly over a pan of boiling water.

FOR BLACK LACES, an old-fashioned cleaning mixture is made by boiling an old black kid glove in a pint of water until half the water has evaporated. Strain, and, if necessary, add a little cold water. After brushing the lace, dip it up and down in the liquid. Then roll it over a bottle, or pin smoothly over a covered board to dry.

WHITE LACE may be washed in a suds of pure soap, then thoroughly rinsed and pinned over a covered board to dry. Some laces will stand ironing on the wrong side. Let the lace partially dry, and iron over several thicknesses of flannel.

GREASE-SPOTS on woolen or silk are best removed by naphtha, gasoline, ether or chloroform. These solvents are highly inflammable, and must, therefore, never be used near a light or flame. In applying any of them to grease-stains, place a piece of cloth or blotting-paper underneath the stain to absorb the excess liquid. Rub the spot from the outside toward the center until dry, so that the liquid will not leave a ring. Ether and chloroform are less liable to leave a ring than gasoline or naphtha.

A good mixture for removing grease-spots is made from equal parts of alcohol, benzine and ether. Powdered French chalk or fullers' earth may be used by placing the powder over the stain and holding over a heated iron. The heat will dissolve the grease, and the powder will absorb it.

MACHINE-OIL STAINS may be removed in the following manner: Moisten borax and rub it on the stain from the outside toward the center, taking care not to spread it. Pour water through the material. Washing with cold water and a pure soap will remove most stains of machine-oil.

BLOOD-STAINS may be taken out by washing with soap and tepid water. They may also be removed by covering the spot with wet laundry starch and allowing it to stand. Afterward it should be washed.

ON INK-SPOTS, if still moist, rub either salt, meal, flour or sugar, and wash in cold water. Or, lemon-juice may be put over the spot and covered with salt. Then place the article in the sun for a while, and wash. The process may be repeated, if necessary, until the ink-spot is entirely removed.

Another method for removing ink-stains is to let the material soak in javelle water, made from one-half pound of sal soda, two ounces chlorid of lime and one quart of water. After soaking a few minutes, wash in clear water.

IRON-RUST is removed by the same mediums as ink.

MILDEW is the hardest of all stains to remove, and can not always be taken out successfully. Any of the mediums used for ink and iron-rust may be tried. For silk only, dip a flannel in alcohol and rub briskly, first on one side and then on the other.

PAINT, when fresh, can be softened with vaseline and washed off with benzine. Or, it may be rubbed with equal parts of turpentine and alcohol. If a grease-spot remains, remove it with benzine. Turpentine mixed with a little ammonia is also good. Wash off with soap-suds or benzine.

* 9 7 8 1 3 3 2 5 9 8 4 9 6 *

SD - #0034 - 070723 - C0 - 229/152/8 - PB - 9781332598496 - Gloss Lamination